# The Ottoman Süryânî from 1908 to 1914

# Bibliotheca Nisibinensis

3

### Series Editor

### Aho Shemunkasho

Bibliotheca Nisibinensis is an academic publication of Fundatio Nisibinensis – a foundation for promoting Aramaic Studies. It engages with Aramaic literature and tradition in general, as well as with the socio-cultural, political, religious and linguistic aspects of the present situation of the communities, which have preserved their Aramaic inheritance.

# The Ottoman Süryânî from 1908 to 1914

Benjamin Trigona-Harany

gorgias press

2009

Gorgias Press LLC, 180 Centennial Ave., Piscataway, NJ, 08854, USA

www.gorgiaspress.com

Copyright © 2009 by Gorgias Press LLC

2009          ,

ISBN 978-1-60724-069-3                    ISSN 1946-2220

Printed in the United States of America

# TABLE OF CONTENTS

# LIST OF ILLUSTRATIONS

# PREFACE

This book is a revised and expanded version of the MA thesis in Ottoman history that I submitted to Boğaziçi Üniversitesi in 2008. It explores the Ottoman *Süryânî* community's experience of the years from the 1908 revolution and the reintroduction of constitutional rule to the Ottoman Empire until the outbreak of World War I in 1914. For many Ottoman citizens this was a period characterised by a great hope for the future, a theme which also very much dominated *Süryânî* thought.

It is my firm belief that the field of Syriac studies will benefit from the participation of Ottomanists. There has emerged a literature on the Armenian and other non-Muslim communities with an Ottoman reading of their histories, but for the *Süryânî* it has really only just begun. It is, I would argue, necessary for students of *Süryânî* history to remember that they were members of a complex Ottoman society for some 400 years and that this had a great bearing on how they saw and experienced the world around them.

At the same time, Ottomanists had little appreciation for or understanding of this small community far from the centres of power in Istanbul. The *Süryânî* were not politically or economically influential like the Ottoman Armenians, Greeks or Jews, but their history is no less interesting for it; as it turns out, the *Süryânî* were very much engaged with the Ottoman state, Ottoman society and the outside world. I contend that we Ottomanists do have something to learn from the *Süryânî* and their interactions with the state and the peoples who lived with and around them.

This work, therefore, has been written with both fields in mind. For Ottomanists, I have tried to explain the various Syriac churches, their origins and the issues which dominate Syriac studies today. For those unfamiliar with Ottoman history, I have included contextual information as well as a comparitive study of the non-

Muslim communities, including the *Süryânî*, as Ottoman subjects. It is ultimately my one hope that this work will help bridge the gap between Ottoman and Syriac studies by telling the story of the *Süryânî* journalists who documented the dramatic years between 1908 and 1914.

Benjamin Trigona-Harany
2009.10.10

# ACKNOWLEDGMENTS

I must first of all express my gratitude to Jan Beṯ-Şawoce at Södertörns Högskola in Sweden for having given me numerous copies of *Mürşid-i Âsûriyûn* and *Kevkeb Mednho* as I was embarking on my research; without his generosity then or his continued generosity over the years, neither my thesis nor this present work would have been possible.

In terms of the aid that I have been given over the course of the research and writing, many people deserve credit. I would like to express my gratitude to Yılmaz Turan in France for his constant advice. I would also like to thank İshak Tanoğlu in Elâzığ for having shown me around Harput and the *Meryem Ana Kilisesi* and for providing me valuable information about his city and its history. To these and the many others who have contributed their ideas and answered my questions, I am grateful. I would also like to show my appreciation to George Kiraz at Gorgias Press for his interest in seeing my project through to publication.

Finally, I would like to thank my professors at Boğaziçi Üniversitesi for their help and insight into my studies in Ottoman history. I owe my thesis advisor Vangelis Kechriotis a special debt for having introduced me to the Ottoman *Süryânî* and for constantly encouraging me to pursue my research.

# TRANSCRIPTION

All Ottoman Turkish will be transliterated according to normal standards. The Arabic letters *'ayn* and *hemze* are not transliterated; long vowels are indicated by a circumflex. Short vowels and all other consonants are written as pronounced in Turkish. All non-transliterated Ottoman Turkish will be rendered in the Arabic alphabet, even if it was originally written in the Syriac alphabet. In transliterations of Ottoman Turkish which contain Syriac words, I will include the original Syriac whenever necessary.

The pronunciation of Turkish letters is as follows:

| | |
|---|---|
| *c* | English *j* |
| *ç* | English *ch* |
| *g* | as in *g*arden |
| *ğ* | lenghtens a preceeding *a*, *ı*, *o* and *u* (in eastern dialects, it has a sound more akin to an Arabic غ); English *y* after *e*, *i*, *ö* and *ü* |
| *h* | English *h* |
| *ı* | similar to *e* in th*e* (capital form *I*) |
| *i* | short English *ee* (capital form *İ*) |
| *j* | as in plea*s*ure |
| *ö* | French *eu* |
| *ş* | English *sh* |
| *ü* | French *u* |

# INTRODUCTION

In December of 1908, Naûm Fâik Palak, a leading member of Diyarbakır's *Süryânî* community, addressed a letter to the *Süryânî millî meclisi* [community council] of Harput, in the Ottoman province of Mamûretü'l-Azîz.[1] The letter bore the title "if we desire progress, then we must unite" (*terakkî istersek ittihâd etmeliyiz*); in it, Naûm Fâik stated that his goal was to stimulate an awakening (*intibâh*) from the deep sleep of ignorance (*hâb-ı gaflet*) into which he believed the *Süryânî* had fallen. The euphoria surrounding the proclamation of the second Ottoman constitution some months earlier had evidently reached these outlying provinces, with the concept of progress (*terakkî*) through union (*ittihâd*) closely echoing the name of the *İttihâd ve Terakkî Cemiyeti*, the organisation that had led the revolution against the old regime. But what exactly was meant by "we"? Did it refer, in a nod to the sentiments of the day, to the Ottoman people as a whole? Or was it a call to all Assyrians, a recently conceptualised grouping composed of numerous religious denominations residing both inside and outside the Ottoman Empire? Or perhaps it was restricted to the letter's addressees, the members of the original *Süryânî* church, a community of limited size scattered across a few of the Empire's eastern provinces?

---

[1] Murat Fuat Çıkkı, *Naum Faik ve Süryani Rönesansı*, tr. Mehmet Şimşek (Istanbul: Belge Ulusarası Yayıncılık, 2004), 133-136. The letter as it appears in the book was apparently taken from a 1910 newspaper article which reprinted it in whole. The text, however, is clearly addressing the Harput delegates and is dated 19 Teşrîn-i Sânî, 1324 [2 December 1908]. Note also that in translation, the second-person singular *istersen* appears in lieu of first-person plural *istersek*; I have taken this to be a misreading as both words would have been written identically in the Arabic script.

1

This work began as an effort to provide an answer to these questions by studying the emergence of a nineteenth-century national movement in the Ottoman Empire. The *Süryânî* are one of a handful of Christian peoples grouped together through the resurrection of an ancient Assyrian identity centred on a Mesopotamian homeland. By the early years of the twentieth century, this identity had been thoroughly embraced by many – but by no means all – and had lead to the establishment of cultural and even political associations as well as the formation of a nationalist ideology which persists to the present-day.

To date, the history of pre-World War I Assyrian nationalism has been presented as consisting primarily of the activities of a small population residing in western Persia, where intellectual activity was being spurred on by missionary efforts. Such a reading, even if it is accurate, does not address a large part of the greater community conceptualised by these same nationalist writers: that of the Ottoman *Süryânî*. What acknowledgement there is of the Ottoman fraction of the equation is limited to praising a few leading figures but without any corresponding reading of their actual writings. One of the basic features which differentiates these Ottomans from their counterparts in Persia was the reliance on the Ottoman Turkish language, rather than Syriac, to propagate their ideas. The consequence of this linguistic reality is that the Assyrian nationalist scholarship is, for the most part, unable to read what its two most fêted *Süryânî*, Naûm Fâik and Âşûr Yûsuf, wrote.

While the original goal of this work was to bring a corpus of what I thought to be early Assyrian nationalist materials to light, my initial readings of these two figures quickly revealed that I would be ignoring the true nature of their writings should I follow this single line of investigation. Immediately, there appeared to be evidence that these authors at times had their sights on something greater – an Ottoman identity – and at times on something smaller – a *Süryânî* identity – completely ignoring the Assyrian one which many presupposed to be their sole focus. In short, to presume that Naûm Fâik and Âşûr Yûsuf were only, or even primarily, Assyrian in outlook would be to impose an Assyrian nationalist project upon them. In this work, therefore, I intend on using their own writings to guide the historical discussions, while striving to answer the question posed in the opening paragraph. This question remains central to understanding the *Süryânî* of the late-Ottoman world and their preceptions of the political changes which characterised the period. Naûm Fâik and Âşûr Yûsuf were very much men of this world, and their reflections provide us with some of the only sources for the study of the *Süryânî* experience of it.

These men were not mere passive observers, however. There was also a great effort being made on their part: they were on the forefront of the introduction of modernity into an Ottoman *Süryânî* community which was felt to have fallen behind the advances made by others, notably the Armenians. With respect to the failures of "union" and "progress", the focus of the present-day Assyrian nationalist literature is on the demographic decimation of the Ottoman and Persian communities during the First World War; except for in Iraq, their former strength would never again be regained. However, these sad events do not explain everything and there must be a more nuanced exploration of the aspirations of figures such as Naûm Fâik and Âşûr Yûsuf. From this we may speculate on the reasons for which these were or were not being fulfilled before 1914.

My first chapter will outline the historical context and the historiographical debates into which this work fits. Following this, there will be a historical sketch of Syriac Christianity and its adherents commencing in the fourth century and following their progress until the early twentieth century. While this will encompass more than fifteen centuries of history, the focus will be on the emergence of the distinct Syriac churches and then the Ottoman period during which time the further separation of these churches into different sects would accelerate. The theological perspective is necessary to highlight what divided the various Syriac communities and what makes any attempt to surmount these cleavages so remarkable. The historical overview will conclude with a brief survey of the early twentieth century Ottoman Empire, an introduction of Naûm Fâik, Âşûr Yûsuf and other *Süryânî* intellectuals, and some remarks on the primary sources, particularly the newspapers *Kevkeb Mednho*, *Mürşid-i Âsûriyûn* and *İntibâh*, which I have employed to develop my arguments in the later chapters.

The second chapter will contain a brief examination of the *millet* system, by which the non-Muslim communities in the Ottoman Empire were administered, and how it changed during the *Tanzîmât* (1839-1876), the reign of Abdülhamîd II (1876-1909) and the years of constitutional rule prior to the outbreak of the

First World War (1908-1914). Of primary importance are the cleavages within each *millet*, or religious community, and how these divisions manifested themselves in other areas. The comparison with other Ottoman non-Muslims serves to place the *Süryânî* in the greater Ottoman context, something which I believe to be lacking in Syriac historiography. While the Greek Orthodox and Jewish cases will be touched upon, the Armenians are of particular interest for their geographic and theological proximity to the *Süryânî*. Additionally, I will examine the *Süryânî* communities and detail their internal structures as well as their relationship to the Ottoman state.

It will be in the third, fourth and fifth chapters where I will present my analysis of primary-source readings and then offer my conclusions. I will argue that the writings of Naûm Fâik, Âşûr Yûsuf and others do not corroborate their portrayal in the secondary literature; although they both described the origins of the *Süryânî* to be Assyrian, there is no indication that, during the period in question, either man could be considered an Assyrian nationalist. Instead, I believe that they were concerned with the rights of the *Süryânî* in the Ottoman Empire and sought to emphasise the historical primacy of their church as a means of achieving these. Moreover, I will attempt to show that these men saw the Ottoman Empire as the best guarantor of the security and future of their community and consequently eschewed any notion of political sovereignty for the *Süryânî*, much less all Assyrians.

## TERMINOLOGY

Historians often struggle with terminology, which has a tendency to assume different meanings depending on the place or time. The subject of this work is no exception; indeed, it suffers acutely from these problems. Within the field of Ottoman history, Syriac Christianity is often misunderstood precisely due to this haphazardly applied and ideologically charged vocabulary. With this in mind, I have endeavoured to systematise my own usage as the first step in developing my historiographical discussion, and, perhaps more importantly, as a means to reflect the central tenets of this work through terminology. Subsequent chapters will elaborate on the rationale for my decisions and define the terms thoroughly, but it is imperative that a functional vocabulary be established at the outset.

For this particular work, the foremost question is how to designate the ethno-religious community known in Turkish as the *Süryânî*. Because this is a work on Ottoman history above all else, I have opted to replicate this usage here. *Süryânî* is moreover etymologically accurate, being a cognate of the community's self-designation and the name of their liturgical language. I have not, however, completely forsaken the English term "Jacobite", which remains familiar and unambiguous even though it does have certain serious drawbacks. As will be explained in later chapters, "Jacobite" suffers primarily from being a theologically inaccurate term and, because of this, is often considered pejorative for emphasising the "heretical" nature of the Jacobite Church. Today, the more common term for the Jacobite Church is the Syriac Orthodox Church, but this name implies some connection with the Greek Orthodox Church which does not exist – either administratively or theologically. Moreover, at the time, the Jacobite Church did not normally refer to itself as Orthodox in Ottoman Turkish or Syriac. Consequently, I will avoid this term here, though one should be aware that it does enjoy widespread usage elsewhere. On the other hand, the practical justification for using "Jacobite", despite the concerns outlined above, is that there is no viable English noun or adjective which can replace it. Furthermore, its use is in keeping with Ottoman vocabulary; the Ottoman Turkish form, *Yakûbî*, was employed – by both the state and the Jacobites themselves – to modify *Süryânî* in the same way as were the words *Katolik* [Catholic] and *Protestan* [Protestant].[2]

Furthermore, *Süryânî* and Jacobite will fulfil distinct roles in this work. *Süryânî* may be considered something of a secular or ethnic designation since, in terms of religion, a *Süryânî* may be a Catholic, a Protestant or, more commonly, a Jacobite.[3] In the late

---

[2] See Canan Seyfeli, "Osmanlı Devleti Salnamelerinde Süryaniler," in *Süryaniler ve Süryanilik*, vol. 1, ed. Ahmet Taşğın, Eyyüp Tanrıverdi and Canan Seyfeli (Istanbul: Orient Yayınları, 2005) for examples from Ottoman *sâlnâme* [yearbook]. In the newspapers used in this study, *Yakûbî* makes numerous appearances.

[3] The notion that the term *Süryânî* is secular should be treated with caution; this will be explored further below.

eighteenth century, the latter church would begin referring to itself by the denomination *Süryânî-i Kadîm* [*Süryânî* of Old].[4] This was done, starting in 1782, to differentiate the Jacobites from the *Süryânî* who had joined the Catholic Church.[5] Some Ottoman documents written during the nineteenth century used the unmodified term *Süryânî* to mean the Catholics and the full *Yakûbî Süryânî* or *Süryânî-i Kadîm* for the Jacobites, imposing yet another layer to an already complex set of terminology.[6]

Alternatives to *Süryânî* do exist, but they are problematic. "Assyrian" has become the identity of choice for some time now, and this term also maintains a sizeable following in academia and the media. In addition, "Aramaean", related to the more familiar "Aramaic", is now preferred by many, but it still lacks the widespread use that makes "Assyrian" a viable alternative. The first problem in using "Assyrian", is that it is an overarching term also used to refer to a group of communities, namely the Jacobites, Nestorians and Chaldeans, which I wish to consider separately. Secondly, and equally seriously, is that using "Assyrian"

---

[4] In all the secondary sources which I have consulted, only Justin McCarthy opts to use an adjectival Farsi *izâfet*, rather than simply write *Süryânî Kadîm*; McCarthy errs slightly, however, by writing *Süryani-yi Kadim*. See Justin McCarthy, *Muslims and Minorities: the Population of Ottoman Anatolia* (New York: New York University Press, 1983), 105. Documentary evidence – and not simply a linguistic rational – may be found in the *Süryânî-i Kadîm* church's own internal papers written in the Arabic alphabet; in these we read سريانئ قديم, with the *hemze* indicating the Farsi *izâfet*. The *hemze* also occasionally appears in the *Süryânî* periodicals, though this was definitely the exception and not the rule. In terms of Turkish grammar, *Süryânî Kadîm* only makes sense as part of a larger compound such as *Süryânî Kadîm Kilisesi*, but it has recently been adopted as a syntactic whole with the value of a noun, hence *Süryânî Kadîmler* in, for example, the title of İbrahim Özcoşar's "Osmanlı Devleti'nde Millet Sistemi ve Süryani Kadimler" in *Süryaniler ve Süryanilik*, vol. 2.

[5] Özcoşar, "Osmanlı Devleti'nde Millet Sistemi ve Süryani Kadimler," 216. I have also found reference to Catholics as being *cedîd Süryânî* or *Süryânî-i cedîd* [new *Süryânî*], in opposition to the Jacobites using the adjective *kadîm* [old]: "Hukûkumuza sâhib olalım," *Mürşid-i Âsûriyûn*, 4, no. 2 (Şubât 1912), 18.

[6] Seyfeli, "Osmanlı Devleti Salnamelerinde Süryaniler," 84.

automatically places oneself to one side of an ongoing debate concerning the historical accuracy of considering the present-day Syriac-speaking Christians as the descendants of the ancient Assyrians. This work will not argue for or against these theories *per se* despite the fact that they are fundamental to my central arguments. As such, I have consciously restricted my use of "Assyrian" and "Aramaean" to emphasise the emergence of these two terms within the *Süryânî* communities of the Ottoman Empire. This must not be seen as a rejection of either the Assyrian or the Aramaean theses, but rather a deliberate effort to emulate the contemporary vocabulary and to carefully distinguish the differences in their meanings.

The second major question is how to differentiate the *Süryânî* from the two other groups which feature in this work, the Nestorians and Chaldeans.[7] Based on the decisions above, it would be impossible to use "Assyrian" for these two communities, as is common practice today. Doing so would imply that the *Süryânî* are not in fact Assyrians, which – I reiterate – is not my intention nor the intention of Assyrian nationalists, present or past. Thus, I have continued to rely on the terms "Nestorian" and "Chaldean" for both of these Christian communities – with the same justifications and reservations that I have for "Jacobite": they are unambiguous and they were used in Ottoman times, but some considered them to be theologically pejorative or ethnically innacurate. However, even Âşûr Yûsuf and Naûm Fâik, self-described Assyrians, saw no problem in using *Nestûrî* and *Keldânî*, the two Ottoman Turkish parallels of *Yakûbî* in their own writings.

Finally, there are the two English terms which might have been employed: Syrian and Syriac.[8] In this work, these will be common terms used for the Jacobites and Nestorians and all the derivative churches. Because confessional allegiances are essentially

---

[7] Chaldeans are Nestorians who have joined the Catholic Church.

[8] Note that I have opted to use the term Syriac exclusively. In English, Syriac is often used as a noun to differentiate between Syriac Christians and the inhabitants of historical Syria or the citizens of the Syrian Arab Republic; this confusion will not present a problem here, but I believe it to be good practice.

geographic, Western Syriacs can be understood to be Jacobites and Eastern Syriacs, Nestorians and Chaldeans. *Süryânî* is never used for Eastern Syriacs. Consequently, Syrian and Syriac are not suitable translations for *Süryânî*; this is unfortunate since the words are cognates, but by convention, *Süryânî* means Western Syriac exclusively. Not all secondary sources adhere to the standards outlined above; *Süryânî*, for example, may frequently been found translated as either "Assyrian" or "Syriac".

| Ottoman Turkish | English | Location | Denomination |
|---|---|---|---|
| *Süryânî* | - | West | All |
| *Süryânî-i Kadîm* | Jacobite | West | Syriac Orthodox |
| *Yakûbî* | Jacobite | West | Syriac Orthodox |
| *Süryânî-i Cedîd* | - | West | Catholic |
| *Nestûrî* | Nestorian | East | Church of the East |
| *Keldânî* | Chaldean | East | Catholic |
| - | Syriac/Syrian | All | All |
| *Âsûrî* | Assyrian | All | All |
| *Ârâmî* | Aramaean | West | All |

Table 1 – Overview of the terminology

A final note on my use of Syriac with reference to the languages of the Eastern and Western Syriacs is in order. There has not been a classification of Syriac, ultimately derived from the Aramaic language, that has proven to be acceptable to all linguists, but the majority considers Syriac an eastern Aramaic language.[9] Its literary form – sometimes called Edessan Aramaic – survives as the liturgical language of several churches, while the modern vernaculars are variations of other Aramaic dialects. To counter these complexities, I will be using the vaguest of terms, Syriac, to refer to the multitude of mutually-unintelligible neo-Aramaic dialects spoken by Syriac Christians as well as the literary tongue. Therefore, references to Eastern Syriac and Western Syriac ought

---

[9] See, for example, Efrem Yıldız, "The Aramaic Language and its Classification," *Journal of the Assyrian Academic Society* 14, no. 1 (Spring 2000), 23-44.

not to be understood as meaning two distinct languages but rather a collection of sub-dialects spoken by the respective religious communities.[10] Likewise, there are also three slightly different scripts used to write Syriac: the classical, the Western and the Eastern. During the period in question here, the neo-Aramaic dialects of the Nestorians and Chaldeans were both written and spoken, whereas amongst *Süryânî*, the literary language was the sole written language, the vernacular tongues only ever being spoken and never being put down on paper.[11] Only recently has a written Ṭūroyo emerged.

This simplification of the Syriac also extends to my use of proper nouns. Except for the brief discussions of non-Ottoman history, I will refer to Ottoman peoples and places as they would have been known following Ottoman Turkish orthography: thus, Naûm Fâik instead of Naʿūm Fāʾiq and *Kevkeb Mednho* rather than, say, *Kūkhwa Maḏnḥā*. I will attempt to provide a proper transliteration and commonly encountered alternatives where possible, but the results will not be able to reflect accurately all the intricacies of the Syriac languages and dialects. In Chapter 1, this cursory treatment of the nomenclature will be fleshed out in somewhat more detail. Furthermore, additional information on the different Syriac language and scripts as well as the writing of Ottoman Turkish using the Syriac alphabet is to be found in Appendix A.

---

[10] Fortunately, the use of the Eastern and Western branches of Syriac almost always follows sectarian lines. The most important dialect spoken by the *Süryânî* is Ṭūroyo [Tûrânî], the language of the Ṭūr ʿAbdīn [Cebel-i Tûr] region of Mardin province. A feature which distinguishes this dialect from literary Syriac is the vowel shift of *ā* to *o/ō* despite consistencies in orthography; this bears mentioning only to avoid confusion over nouns which may either be transliterated according to the written form or be transcribed to reflect pronunciation. Another dialect, Mlaḥsō, was spoken in villages around Lice in the province of Diyarbakır. For a discussion of the dialects, see Otto Jastrow, "The Turoyo Language Today," *Journal of the Assyrian Academic Society* 1 (1986): 7-16.

[11] Consequently, these communities existed within a diglossia, the condition in which a prestigious high language (here, literary Syriac) and a low language (the spoken vernaculars) are both present simultaneously.

# 1 HISTORICAL BACKGROUND

## HISTORIOGRAPHICAL DEBATES

Syriac Christianity has suffered no dearth of scholarly attention with regards to its theology, its early church leadership, its liturgical texts and its influence on other Christian and even Islamic cultures. Today, however, when most of its members now reside in diaspora, much attention has now shifted to focus on the origins of the people and what led to their precarious presence in Iraq, Turkey and other neighbouring countries. What then of the intervening years – from the emergence of the churches to the beginning of their demise in the Middle East? The histories of this period, one which is characterised by the Ottoman Empire's dominance of the core Syriac lands, tends to concentrate on a pair of contentious issues, identity and genocide, both of which came to a head in the early twentieth century. While the remainder of the history has not exactly been ignored, the other historiographical trends have coloured it unfairly and relegated it to a secondary status.

The remainder of the Ottoman era and the role of the Syriac communities in it have received relatively cursory treatment. Recently the situation has begun to improve, with greater interest in the *Süryânî* as members of Ottoman society being taken by the Turkish-language scholarship in particular. The focus has been on the lands which are currently in the Republic of Turkey, so the same body of scholars does not appear to have, as yet, breached the Arab frontier by addressing the Iraqi Chaldeans with the same intensity. The interest has not been limited to authors who are themselves *Süryânî*; the four volume *Süryaniler ve Süryanilik*, for example, features contributions from Turkish scholars on a wide range of topics, many of which are historical in nature and with a textual analysis concentrating on Ottoman governmental documents pertaining to administrative or legal issues.[12]

## Nationalism

That the identity of Syriac Christians is a confusing one may be understood from the discussion of terminology above. There has been a great level of effort directed at cementing an ethnic identity for the adherents of the Jacobite, Nestorian and Chaldean faiths. Presently, we may identify two main competing nationalist camps, the Assyrian and the Aramaean, each promoting the validity of their respective ancestral theories.

A third, the Chaldean, is emerging as a separate identity with ethnic, rather than simply religious, connotations. The notion that Chaldeans have a unique connection with the ancient Chaldeans from Mesopotamia has gained some currency, but this is dismissed by most historians, and indeed by most Chaldeans, who identify themsevles as Assyrians.

With the exception of the Indian congregations, todays' Syriac Christians had crystallised into their basic denominational divisions – Jacobite, Melkite or Nestorian – at an early date. While losses to Islam continued, new adherents were no longer being won from other sects or local non-monotheistic religions. After the schisms in European Christianity, conversion to other denominations occurred within the rubric of the parent church: a Melkite joined the Catholic Melkite Church while a *Süryânî* joined the Catholic *Süryânî* Church. Thus, the composition of the communities did not change greatly following their first centuries of expansion. As such, theological and linguistic homogeneity was a foundation upon which a nationalist identity was developed. The ethnicity of the Syriac Christians is nonetheless a divisive topic for academic and nationalist alike.

There is large literature dealing with the ethnicity question but only a brief survey of the debate will be given here.[13] John Joseph

---

[12] *Süryaniler ve Süryanilik*, ed. Ahmet Taşğın, Eyyüp Tanrıverdi and Canan Seyfeli (Istanbul: Orient Yayınları, 2005). The collection also deals with Nestorians and Chaldeans.

and Richard N. Frye, for example, engaged in an ongoing scholarly exchange as to the origins of Assyrian nationalism. Joseph, himself a Nestorian Christian, has frequently expounded on the error of linking his co-religionists with the ancient Assyrians. His argument is based on the notion that there was probably far more incorporation of other ethnic groups, namely Jews, pre-Muslim Arabs and Zoroastrian Persians, during the expansion of the Nestorian Church than any proponent of the Mesopotamian Christians' Assyrian heritage would care to admit.[14]

The flip-side of the polemic centres on the notion that the words "Assyria" and "Syria" have the same etymological origin, using evidence taken from the time of Herodotus and in a myriad of languages spoken across the Middle East.[15] Joseph's suggestion is that "Syriac" and "Aramaean" should be considered synonyms, even if the two do not share a common etymological root.[16] In rebuttal, Frye, and others, have also endeavoured to show that the usage of the term Assyrian preceded its widespread adoption in the nineteenth century. For example, Frye notes that a Jacobite Patriarch in the twelfth century equated "Syriac" and "Assyrian", and that Carmelite missionaries in Persia during the seventeenth century used the terms interchangeably with "Jacobite".[17]

---

[13] The primary articles consulted here are: John Joseph, *The Nestorians and their Muslim Neighbors: A Study of Western Influence on their Relations* (Princeton: Princeton University Press, 1961), 13-18; Richard N. Frye, "Assyria and Syria: Synonyms," *Journal of Near Eastern Studies* 51, no. 4 (October 1992); Joseph, "Assyria and Syria: Synonyms?," *Journal of the Assyrian Academic Society* 9, no. 2 (November, 1997); Frye, "Reply to John Joseph," *Journal of the Assyrian Academic Society* 8, no. 1 (April, 1999); Odisho Malko Gewargis, "We Are Assyrians," *Journal of the Assyrian Academic Society* 16, no. 1 (April, 2002).

[14] Joseph, *The Nestorians*, 3-21.

[15] The relationship between the two words – "Syrian" and "Assyrian" – appears obvious in English, but it is much less clear in other languages, hence the persistence of the debate. The root of "Syrian" is *Suryāyā* (ܣܘܪܝܝܐ) in Syriac and *Suryān* (سريان) in Arabic, while for "Assyrian" it is *Āthūrāyā* (ܐܬܘܪܝܐ) in Syriac and either *Āshūr* (أشور) or *Āthūr* (أثور) in Arabic.

[16] Joseph, "Assyria and Syria: Synonyms?," 43.

[17] Frye, "Assyria and Syria: Synonyms," 33-34.

Since the Syriac dialects are all derived from Aramaic, the language of the Aramaean people, those who back the Aramaean thesis point this as evidence of their non-Assyrian origins. Nestorians and Chaldeans object to this position, arguing that the Assyrians merely borrowed the language from the culturally dominant Aramaeans. While the Assyrian thesis is much more widely held, many *Süryânî*, in particular those who emigrated to Western Europe in the latter part of the twentieth century, believe in the Aramaean origins of their community. The notion does, however, date as far back as the nineteenth century, and it is possible to find examples of it in Ottoman-era documents.

At the beginning of the twentieth century, the distinction between the two competing ethnic identities had yet to produce a real cleavage in the community. Indeed, in the *Süryânî* case, it appears that most simply held this self-definition based purely on religion and uncoloured – or at least unconcerned – by nationalist thought. There is, even today, the belief amongst some that neither of the ethnic epithets should be employed and that the only identity is the *Süryânî* one. Consequently, the defining factor becomes membership in the Jacobite Church, although those who belong to derivative denominations, such as the Catholics or Melkites are often claimed to be *Süryânî*.

As links with the Nestorians or Chaldeans have little or no place in this view, its supporters – often members of the religious hierarchy – are often accused of trying to divide the greater community for their own gain. The Assyrian nationalist literature is fiercely critical of those who champion this religious identity over the ethnic one and this same criticism carries over to academics: "Together with the trend of existing Western-based university scholars to stress Assyrian sectarian history and identity, the field of secular Assyrian studies is confined to Assyrians themselves scattered in secluded, and insecure, diaspora."[18] Or, in an editorial from Zinda, a staunchly Assyrian magazine, we read:

---

[18] Eden Naby, "The Assyrian Diaspora: Cultural survival in the absence of state structure," in *Central Asia and the Caucasus: Transnationalism and diaspora*, ed. Touraj Atabaki and Sanjyot Mehendale (London: Routledge, 2005), 214. Naby continues in her footnotes, first criticising

"Things have not changed much. Today, we are still suffering because of the ignorance of those who prefer the be represented by a patriarch or a bishop and claim their religious identity as superior over the other *millats*. I shudder every time I hear a Nestorian claim that as a member of the Church of the East he is more of an Assyrian than a Chaldean or a Syriac (Jacobite). He is the inheritor of the dark policies of the Moslem rulers in the Middle East ... I call these blind followers of the Nestorian, Chaldean, and Orthodox *millats* - the 'Assyrian Hizbollahs'."[19]

Many authors – Assyrian and Aramaean alike – are quick to discredit any dissenting views by privileging their own view as the only true way of reading Syriac history. It is not the object of this work to argue any of these positions. In the preceding paragraphs, I have been careful to define the greater community on the basis of Syriac as the liturgical language rather than on a belonging to a particular ethnicity, but I do not preclude the existence of any ethnic affinity. The pervasiveness of this language is the one point upon which authors agree irrespective of which side of the polemic they may lay.[20] In the present work, there could be a similar critique of my use of the term "community" as something of a surrogate for "nation", a word which is obviously being avoided. This issue may be sidestepped somewhat by resorting to Ottoman terminology, which defined the *Süryânî* based on their religious affiliations.

The question of whether the Syriac Christians of the twentieth century selected the "right" or "wrong" identity with

---

John Joseph and then writing, "[t]he more recent three-volume coffee-table set edited by Sebastian Brock, *The Hidden Pearl* (2001), represents the most flagrant catering to church institutional hierarchy to appear yet, even in the category of publications that are church-funded."

[19] Wilfred Bet-Alkhas, "*Omta*, NOT *Millat!*," *Zinda* 14, no. 5 (23 May 2008).

[20] The naming of this language is coloured by one's beliefs, however. It is frequently called "Assyrian", but this is inaccurate as it is not the Assyrian language even if it is the language spoken by Assyrians today.

respect to ethnicity is not always superseded by the more interesting question of why a particular identity was chosen. This is intriguing here, not only because "Assyrian" was not a term in common usage prior to the arrival of foreign missionaries, but also because, in theory at least, it was used in its most encompassing degree: inclusive of Eastern and Western Syriac Christians alike.

A few scholarly works have addressed the origins of the Assyrian national movement.[21] These focus, however, on the members of or converts from the Nestorian Church, especially those who lived in the flatlands lying between Lake Urmiye in western Persia and the Hakkâri mountains of the Ottoman Empire. The sudden adoption of Assyrian identity during the nineteenth century suggests outside influence, and this is usually considered to be that of the Catholic and Protestant missionaries and the intellectual activities they sponsored.

From the first arrival of Catholics, who promptly founded schools for both boys and girls, to the American-run mission schools and printing presses, a unique atmosphere had descended on Urmiye by the mid-1800s.[22] Even the Russian Orthodox would set up a large network of schools and engaged in its own publishing activities. Out of this population of perhaps 30,000 arose four separate newspapers between the mid-nineteenth century and the outbreak of the First World War. These publications, as well as the ancillary intellectual debates, contributed to a growing national sentiment into which it was hoped deep sectarian cleavages could be subsumed.[23] Despite their

---

[21] Naby, "The Assyrians of Iran: Reunification of a 'Millat,' 1906-1914," *International Journal of Middle Eastern Studies* 8, no. 2 (April, 1977); Robert William De Kelaita, "On the Road to Nineveh: A Brief History of Assyrian Nationalism," *Journal of the Assyrian Academic Society* 8, no.1 (Spring 1994) and "The Origins and Development of Assyrian National-ism" (unpublished paper); Andrea Laing-Marshall, *Modern Assyrian Identity and the Church of the East: an Exploration of their Relationship and the Rise of Assyrian Nationalism, from the World Wars to 1980* (Master's thesis, University of St. Michael's College, 2001).

[22] Joseph, *The Nestorians*, 79-80; Naby, "The Assyrians of Iran," 240.

[23] Heleen Murre-van den Berg, "The Missionaries' Assistants: The Role of Assyrians in the Development of Written Urmia Aramaic," *Jour-*

demographic superiority, those Nestorians who lived across the frontier in the Ottoman provinces of Van or Mosul did not share in this "national awakening", a point which is well emphasised in the secondary literature. But this should not imply that there was no Ottoman parallel.

What is striking about Assyrian nationalism is not that it had to contend with uniting the four different sects present in Urmiye.[24] Instead, it would come to see all of the Syriac-speaking Christians – from both the Eastern and Western churches – as belonging to a single Assyrian nation despite some fifteen hundred years of theological separation.[25] If all Syriac Christians – and all their derivative churches – were of the same Assyrian stock, then the Western Syriacs' near absence from the secondary literature is cause for concern. The incongruity of this issue is demonstrated in the opening sentence of a pioneering article by Eden Naby, in which she defines Assyrian as "Syriac-speaking Middle Easterners belonging throughout the medieval period to either of the two branches of Eastern Christianity (Jacobite and Nestorian)," coupled with the fact that all subsequent references to Assyrians and reunification pertain only to the Eastern Syriacs.[26] Nevertheless, Naby's ultimate conclusion is that the efforts of "progressive Assyrians" to overcome the inherent divisions within

---

nal of the Assyrian Academic Society 10, no. 2 (November, 1996), 11-12; Joseph, The Nestorians, 76.

[24] There was the original Nestorian Church of the East, plus the separated Catholic, (Russian) Orthodox and Protestant churches. The Western case is somewhat more complex, but for the time being we may identify three basic strains: the parent Jacobite Church and the divergent Catholic and Protestant branches.

[25] It also sometimes includes the Melkites (the Arabic-speaking Greek Orthodox) and the Maronites.

[26] Naby's title openly states that it concerns the "Assyrians of Iran", so her focus on this community is not an issue. More concerning is the fact that "Assyrian" equates "Eastern Syriac Christian" in every sentence but the first: "They were united by the same language, modern Eastern Syriac (henceforth referred to as Assyrian) ..." or "... researchers appear to have overlooked the Assyrian periodical press of the crucial period prior to World War I." Naby, "The Assyrians of Iran," 237-238.

their community failed because "world and local events conspired to doom the attempt."[27]

Robert De Kelaita has, to a degree, attempted to incorporate the *Süryânî* into his theses concerning Assyrian nationalism. His conclusion that "other than a few intellectuals and professionals, such as Ashur Yousif, adherents to it were too few" is supported by the statement that the "members of the Jacobite and Chaldean churches, unlike the Nestorians, were much more integrated, both economically and culturally, within the larger societies that surrounded them."[28] Was Assyrian nationalism so limited that it does not bear mentioning – as Naby argues – or that it can be dismissed – as De Kelaita has done? Moreover, was the ultimate failure of this movement due to integration, or was it caused by some other factors, both "world and local"? This work will address both these questions using the primary source materials to which neither De Kelaita nor Naby had access.

More generally, the Syriac case may be used as part of the larger investigation into the nature of the nation and nationalist movements. The literature is thick with scholars who emphasise the essential and primordial nature of the "Assyrian nation". As this chapter has shown, groups which were discrete territorially, linguistically, denominationally and, arguably, ethnically included themselves in the same nation with the same common Mesopotamian homeland. The commonalities – the presumption of shared origins in the early schismatic years of Christianity and the continued liturgical use of literary Syriac – sufficed to breach the differences in the minds of many. At the same time, for all their rhetoric it would seem that these early nationalists, both in the Eastern and Western cases, pursued a distinctly local agenda. This has been demonstrated by Eden Naby, for example, for the Urmiye Christians and the *Süryânî* case will be addressed in later chapters.

---

[27] Ibid., 249.
[28] De Kelaita, "The Origins and Development of Assyrian Nationalism" (unpublished paper), 19-20.

## Oppression and Genocide

The Ottomans conquered the lands inhabited by the Syriac Christians in the early sixteenth century under Sultan Selîm. By 1520, he had pushed the frontier as far east as the present Iranian-Turkish border and had captured northern Iraq, Syria, Palestine and Egypt. Ottoman control over these lands would continue without interruption until the mid-nineteenth century, when Egypt slowly began to slip away from central authority. But for the *Süryânî*-inhabited lands, this rule lasted through the First World War, and these four centuries under the Ottomans had an impact on all aspects of life. It has been, however, a feature of Syriac historiography to reduce this period into a set of simplistic conclusions:

> "Then the Turks followed, to stay for centuries – the Saljūqs, with their traditional intolerance intensified by the Crusades, were replaced by the Ottomans, who ruled, or rather misruled, loosely the remote *pashaliks* of their Asiatic empire from Istanbul …"[29]

When the same author later writes that "the modern history of the Jacobite church is very obscure compared with its ancient annals, in part owing to lack of education and national awareness", one suspects that this latter belief lies behind the perceptions in the former passage.[30]

The second major historiographical debate concentrates on the final years of this Ottoman era, mirroring the discussion concerning the fate of the Armenians.[31] While on a much smaller

---

[29] Aziz Atiya, *A History of Eastern Christianity* (London: Methuen, 1968), 210.

[30] Ibid., 212.

[31] An oft-cited first hand account is Joseph Naayem, *Shall This Nation Die?* tr. Viscount Bryce (New York: Chaldean Rescue, 1921). Secondary studies include Uğur Üngör, '*A Reign of Terror': CUP Rule in Diyarbekir Province, 1913-1923* (Master's thesis, University of Amsterdam, 2005) and Sébastien de Courtois, *The Forgotten Genocide: Eastern Christians, the Last Arameans*, tr. Vincent Aurora (Piscataway, NJ: Gorgias Press, 2004). The definitive scholarly work concerning the Syriac population is currently

scale, the scholarship argues that the genocide was not limited to the Armenians, but included the Syriac Christians living alongside them. Promoted under the name *Seyfâ* or *Seyfo* (literally "sword") by the Western Syriac community, it accuses the Ottoman authorities of a deliberate campaign of extermination against the Syriac Christian population, primarily in the provinces of Diyarbakır, Bitlis and Mamûretü'l-Azîz and in the *sancak* of Urfa. *Seyfo* is argued to have occurred in conjunction with the killings of Armenians, and there are no conflicts between the theses of the two groups. Indeed, many of their arguments are complementary since, in a number of locations, Diyarbakır and Mamûretü'l-Azîz being prime examples, the massacres were carried out jointly (or indiscriminately) against both groups at the same time.

The fate of the Nestorians of Hakkâri can not be said to be part of the same story, for the tribes there did actively participate in the revolt against the Ottoman government in parallel – if not in cooperation – with the Armenians of Van.[32] The close relationship between the Assyrian nationalist and the genocide historiography, however, has contributed to these two separate events being considered as one. The Chaldeans, who live primarily in Iraq and escaped the First World War largely unscathed, did not experience a genocide of their own. But with a shared Assyrian identity they experience victimhood vicariously through the suffering of the Nestorians and the *Süryânî* in the north.[33]

---

David Gaunt, *Massacres, Resistance, Protectors: Muslim-Christian Relations in Eastern Anatolia During World War I* (Piscataway, NJ: Gorgias Press, 2006).

[32] The sequence of events also partially transpired in western Persia – home to a sizeable Nestorian and Chaldean population – and Iraq, where the survivors ultimately found refuge under the British protectorate.

[33] Not all Chaldeans inhabited in Iraqi provinces of the Ottoman Empire, however. There were Chaldeans in Diyarbakır, Bitlis and Urfa, as well as in Persia. These Chaldeans did share the same fate as the Jacobites and Nestorians, but they were a small demographic minority in comparison. Moreover, the post-war era saw a continuation of fighting in the mandate of Iraq, where Christians fleeing both Persia and the Ottoman Empire had settled; many Chaldeans as well as Nestorian refugees lost their lives.

Unlike in the Armenian case, there has yet to emerge a concerted counter-genocide scholarship specifically focused on Syriac Christians. What exists focuses primarily on the Nestorian revolt in Hakkâri as the cause for their expulsion from that mountainous region and the Ottoman military's pursuit of them into Persia.[34] Likewise, the Great Power and missionary dimensions – ever present in Turkish historiography – is explored with respect to their role in the collapse of order and the breakdown in relations between Muslims and Christians in the Ottoman Empire.[35] An increase in the publicity of Syriac claims of genocide and in the allocation of resources to its study has awakened awareness amongst denialist groups, however.

In 2006, the discovery of a mass grave by Kurdish villagers in Mardin province led to a public dispute between a genocide scholar, David Gaunt, and the former head of the *Türk Tarih Kurumu* [Turkish Historical Society], Yusuf Halaçoğlu over its origins. Amidst charges of tampering at the site by the Turkish authorities, Gaunt and Halaçoğlu continue to disagree over even the most basic of issues, including whether the remains date back to World War I or the Roman era.[36] As has happened in the Armenian case, we should expect that there will be an increase in government-funded efforts aimed at justifying the deportation and

---

[34] Suat Akgül, *Musul sorunu ve Nasturi isyanı* (Ankara: Berikan, 2001).

[35] Salahi Sonyel, *The Assyrians of Turkey: Victims of Major Power Policy* (Ankara: Turkish Historical Society Printing House, 2001); Ali Rıza Bayzan, *Misyonerin soykırım oyunu: Ermeni-Rum/Pontus ve Süryani/Keldani gailesi'nin oluşumunda misyoner örgütlerin rolü üzerine* [The Missionaries' Genocidal Game: on the role of missionary organisations in the formation of the Armenian-Greek/Pontus and Syriac/Chaldean troubles] (Istanbul: IQ Kültür Sanat Yayıncılık, 2006). The name on the title page is slightly different from that on the cover, substituting the Nestorians for the Chaldeans.

[36] A Kurdish-oriented newspaper from Turkey was first to report the discovery, at first suggesting it contained the remains of massacred Armenians: "Ermeni Köyünde Toplu Mezar," *Özgür Gündem*, 16 Ekim 2006. The Turkish press covered the subsequent disputes between Gaunt and Halaçoğlu; as of publication these had yet to be resolved.

"incidental death" of the Syriac Christians due to their "treacherous wartime activities".

From the other perspective, the studies of the massacres of the *Süryânî* have often coloured the entire Ottoman experience, resulting in an anachronistic conclusion that it consisted of nothing but brutality and oppression. For example, we read that during the years of Ottoman rule, "Turks along with tribal Kurds commonly indulged in the same kind of mayhem and destruction [as Mongols], largely motivated by the Christian faith of the Assyrians."[37] Indeed, the history of these people was one "of daily oppression, the rape of their young women, forced conversions to Islam, individual and group murders, pillages, and ... massacres."[38] My criticism of such simplistic statements should not suggest that there were no massacres or killings during Ottoman times prior to 1914. There clearly were; most dramatic were the massacres of Nestorians in Hakkâri during the 1840s, the wide-ranging killing of Armenians across the eastern provinces in 1895 and 1896 and the massacres of Christians in Adana during 1909.

As studies of the other non-Muslim communities of the Ottoman Empire have demonstrated, however, the truth to this matter was by no means so clear cut. We know already that participation in the Ottoman state existed at various levels; non-Muslims were active in the bureaucracy and supported the project to create a cross-denominational Ottoman identity. Explaining how the Ottoman *Süryânî* did so and how they do not meet the expectations of nationalists from both sides helps to divert the historiography away from the trend of focusing on conflict throughout the Ottoman period; indeed, it is precisely when we do so that the events of the First World War become that much more tragic.

---

[37] Yoab Benjamin, "Assyrian Journalism: A 140-Year Experience," *Journal of the Assyrian Academic Society* 7, no. 2 (November, 1993), 2.

[38] Joseph Alichoran, "Assyro-Chaldeans in the 20th Century: from Genocide to Diaspora," *Journal of the Assyrian Academic Society* 8, no. 2 (November, 1994), 49.

## A HISTORY OF THE SYRIAC CHURCHES

For many, the Christian church is composed of three fundamental denominations: Orthodox, Catholic and Protestant. While together these three elements may comprise the vast majority of the Christian faithful, such a division ignores two "Eastern" strains of the religion. Understanding of these separate churches has been clouded by the bewildering array of sects, the minutiae of theological differences which distinguish them and, most seriously, highly problematic terminology. In addressing these issues, the origins of all Middle Eastern churches will require telling, but this "ancient history" should not be seen as superfluous. These communities at one time constituted roughly half of the Ottoman Empire's Christian inhabitants, and yet their exact nature and origins are rarely explained. The "Eastern Churches" include the majority of Christians living from Egypt to the Caucasus, but the scope of this chapter will be limited to those Semitic Christians who resided in the south-eastern reaches of the present-day Turkish Republic with some inevitable spilling over the borders into modern Iran, Iraq, Lebanon and the Syrian Arab Republic.

### Emergence

Within a few centuries of the life of Christ, much of the Fertile Crescent had become Christian in faith. Jerusalem was quickly overshadowed as the leading centre with the successes of evangelical activity in cities throughout the Roman Empire.[39] Today's familiar patter of sectarian divisions had yet to emerge; instead, early Christianity was a collection of independent five independent patriarchates (Alexandria, Antioch, Constantinople, Jerusalem and Rome) which had spiritual authority over the inhabitants in their geographic sphere. Although Greek served as the religion's common tongue, converts came from whatever the local population may have been. For the lands stretching from the

---

[39] Jean Corbon, "The Churches of the Middle East: Their Origins and Identity, from their Roots in the Past to their Openness to the Present," in *Christian Communities in the Arab Middle East: The Challenge of the Future*, ed. Andrea Pacini (Oxford: Clarendon, 1998), 94.

Mediterranean Sea to Mesopotamia the dominant language was Aramaic. Determining who these Aramaic-speakers were ethnically is at the heart of the present-day polemic surrounding Assyrian nationalism, a problem made more difficult since the language was in use well beyond the limits of historical Aram.

To the east of the Aramaean heartlands lay the Parthian Empire, which itself officially used Aramaic and where Christianity had also gained a sizeable following.[40] Conflict with the Roman Empire had brought Christians there through flight or as prisoners; at the time of the Parthian Empire's collapse in 225, Persia and northern Mesopotamia were home to more than twenty bishoprics, extending as far east as the Caspian Sea.[41] In the place of the Parthians, the Sassanid dynasty reinvigorated Persia and the indigenous Zoroastrian faith. The Sassanids would hold sway in the lands between the rivers Euphrates [Fırât] and Oxus [Âmû Deryâ] until their ultimate defeat at the hands of the Arab Muslim armies in the seventh century.

At first, the Romans had impeded the growth of Christianity within their empire by persecuting its adherents both at the whim of the local administration but also systematically when a threat was perceived. Only with the reign of Constantine I were measures against the Christian faith finally relaxed. This had the obvious consequence of easing the pressures on Christians, but it also resulted in a degree of centralisation in the church which, in turn, opened the way for the pseudo-theological conflicts that followed. Antioch, though distant from the political power centres of Rome and Constantinople, still remained important, with its jurisdiction extending across the Roman provinces of Syria, Cilicia, Mesopotamia and even into Arabia.[42] Moreover, Antioch retained,

---

[40] Yıldız, "The Aramaic Language," 36-37.

[41] Joseph, *Muslim-Christian Relations and Inter-Christian Rivalries in the Middle East* (Albany: State University of New York Press, 1983), 4.

[42] Ibid., 151 n. 32. Moreover, at the first ecumenical council in 325, nearly half of the delegates (150 out of 318) were from the Patriarchate of Antioch.

for the time being, its Semitic-influenced rite and liturgy distinct from those which emerged elsewhere.[43]

To resolve theological disputes and to quell heretical movements two ecumenical councils were held in the fourth century. The first of these, in 325, was convened at Nicaea [İznik] on the orders of Constantine to establish some of the fundamental tenets of the Christian faith. These Christological principles, known as the Nicene Creed, were further clarified Constantinople in 381. Moreover, the early system of having equally powerful patriarchal sees at Alexandria, Antioch and Jerusalem gave way to an order in which Constantinople – now the capital of the Eastern Roman Empire – would be supreme.[44] This ushered in the way for greater, but by no means complete, Hellenisation of Antioch as Greek began to emerge as the regional lingua franca so that the centres of Aramaic culture shifted east.[45]

A synod at Ctesiphon[46] in 410 demonstrates the march towards an autonomous church in Mesopotamia and Persia. Those present did accept the principles of the Nicene Creed even though no representatives from Mesopotamia had attended the councils of Nicaea or Constantinople.[47] A more definitive break came in 424, when bishops from the Roman Empire lost their last remaining authority over Sassanid Christians. The bishop of Ctesiphon subsequently became a Patriarch, giving birth to the Church of the

---

[43] Ibid., 9.

[44] Joseph Maïla, "The Arab Christians: From the Eastern Question to the Recent Political Situation of the Minorities," in *Christian Communities in the Arab Middle East*, 31. Rome retained a special place of honour among the five patriarchal seats due to its having been founded by St. Peter.

[45] Yıldız, "The Aramaic Language," 32-34.

[46] Ctesiphon or Taysefûn was the capital of the Sassanid empire. It sat across from Seleucia on the Tigris [Dicle], some 20 kilometres south-east of Baghdad.

[47] Laing-Marshall, *Modern Assyrian Identity and the Church of the East*, 21-22. William A. Wigram, *An Introduction to the History of the Assyrian Church or the Church of the Sassanid Persian Empire, 100-640 A.D.* (London: SPCK, 1910), 25-31.

East.[48] Thus, by the early years of the fifth century, the Aramaic-speaking Christians were divided as the subjects of two warring polities and as the congregants of the Patriarchate of Antioch, on one hand, and an effectively independent church to the east, on the other.

Not until the third ecumenical council, that of Ephesus in 431, did a split occur which would theologically distinguish the Church of the East from the rest of Christianity. At Ephesus, the Patriarch of Constantinople, Nestorius, headed a faction which underlined the distinction between the human and divine natures of Christ in opposition to the position of the Patriarch of Alexandria, who held that Christ was of a single nature.[49] While neither argument was new, the council in 431 was meant to lay the matter to rest once and for all and unify the teachings of the Church. Ultimately, the Alexandrian position won out, and Nestorius was exiled to Egypt while his supporters fled eastwards to avoid imperial persecution. The partisans of Nestorius, primarily from Antioch, took refuge in Edessa [Urfa], where they established themselves until being forced even further east in 457.[50]

In an attempt to heal the divisions of Ephesus, a fourth council was convoked, this time at Chalcedon [Kadıköy] in 451. The result was a repudiation of both the Alexandrian and Nestorian extremes in favour of a theological middle ground.[51]

---

[48] Ibid., 38-39. Wilhelm Baum and Dietmar W. Winkler, *The Church of the East: a Concise History*, tr. Miranda G. Henry (London: Routledge-Curzon, 2003), 15-21.

[49] Hence the demand by Nestorius and his followers for Mary to be called the *christotokos* (Christ-bearer) instead of *theotokos* (god-bearer) because she could only have borne Christ's human nature and not the divine.

[50] Joseph, *Muslim-Christian Relations*, 4.

[51] Strictly speaking, the term *miaphysite* and not *monophysite*, as it usually stated, should be used to describe the Alexandrian school, which never went as far as to preach the more extreme *monophysite* doctrine. Despite their lexical similarity, the translations of *monophysis* and *miaphysis* are actually somewhat different; *monophysis* refers simply to a "single nature" of Christ whereas *miaphysis* implies "a composite or unified nature" of two parts. Those who accept the position of Nestorius in which Christ has two distinct natures are termed *dyophysite*. Mebratu Kiros Gebru, *Miaphysite*

Unfortunately for the emperor, many from the Coptic and Aramaic-speaking communities in Egypt and Syria saw the new doctrine as being no better as that promoted by Nestorius and thus rebelled against the decision. Unlike the followers of Nestorius, however, this population remained largely in place, agitating against Greek rule mixing "national and anti-imperial tendencies with their religion."[52] Thus, from the Patriarchate of Alexandria arose the Coptic and Ethiopian Churches and from the Patriarchate of Antioch, the Western Syriac Church.[53] The Armenian Church, in existence since 303, was not represented at the council, but it too rejected the decisions of Chalcedon and settled on the Alexandrian position some fifty years later.[54]

If there was dissent in the Patriarchates of Alexandria and Antioch, it was not a complete one, for supporters of the imperial doctrine remained in each location. In Antioch, these became known as the Melkites[55] ("royalists") for their continued loyalty to the emperor. Their numbers included both Greek-speakers and member of the local Aramaic-speaking community, but those who rejected the Chalcedonian Creed were primarily Coptic-speakers in Egypt and Aramaic-speakers in Syria. Thus, in both locations, the patriarchal seats were subject to rival Chalcedonian and non-

---

*Christology: A Study of the Ethiopian Tewahedo Christological Tradition on the Nature of Christ* (Master's thesis, Toronto School of Theology, 2005), 1-7 and 96-103.

[52] Joseph, *Muslim-Christian Relations*, 5.

[53] Its formally name is Syriac Orthodox Church of Antioch and All the East.

[54] These three churches (counting the Coptic and Ethiopic together) are collectively known as the Oriental Orthodox Churches, but this only serves to cause confusion between it and the Eastern Orthodox Church (that of the Greeks) or the Church of the East. Here, the term Orthodox will be applied elusively to the Eastern Orthodox Church.

[55] Melkite is also spelled Malkite and (incorrectly) Melchite. The word derives from Syriac *malkāya*, "royalists", the plural of *malkā*, "king" (cf. Arabic *malik*). By convention, the term Melkite has come to refer to those Chalcedonians who later adopted Catholicism; the non-Catholic Melkites are usually known as Greek Orthodox of Antioch or Alexandria. To avoid confusion, I will specify Orthodox or Catholic, using Melkite as a general term for both communities.

Chalcedonian claims, and ultimately separate patriarchates would emerge alongside one another.[56]

The positions espoused by the Aramaic-speakers from the centres of Ctesiphon and Antioch are obviously the diametric opposites in terms of theology. And yet, we rarely read of these two communities coming into conflict with one another; the instances of intra-Christian strife are largely confined to the Roman Empire's persecution of sects which it deemed heretical. Furthermore, the Roman-Sassanid frontier lands, and especially Edessa and Nisibis [Nusaybin], became refuges for Aramaic-speaking Christians rejecting either of the councils and subsequently important theological centres. Here, the particular Aramaic dialect of Edessa with a distinctive script became the liturgical language of both churches.[57]

The Sassanid Persians seized upon the opportunity granted to them by the Nestorian following. The Church of the East had not, as of yet, taken any united stand on any side of the theological debates which were absorbing Christianity to its west. But with the backing of the Sassanid dynasts, the supporters of the Nestorian doctrine were installed into higher offices of the church hierarchy, and a 486 synod explicitly professed adherence to its tenets.[58] The rational for the decision can be explained as being as much political as theological, for the Sassanid Empire encouraged the adoption of Nestorianism amongst its Christian population, seeking to back any sect in opposition to the creed of their enemies, the Roman Empire.[59] Mistakenly then, for nearly all of its existence, the Church of the East has been labelled as the Nestorian Church, especially by those who seek to emphasise its heretical nature; as explained above, the usage has not quite fallen out of favour in

---

[56] Hence, there are both Syriac and Melkite Patriarchs in Antioch. Likewise, in Egypt, there is a Coptic Patriarch as well as a Greek Ortho-dox Patriarchate of Alexandria and All Africa.

[57] Henceforth, both the language and script of Edessa will be re-ferred to as Syriac.

[58] Baum and Winkler, *The Church of the East*, 28-30.

[59] Atiya, *A History of Eastern Christianity*, 246-256; Joseph, *Muslim-Christian Relations*, 3-7.

modern scholarship as it is used for its convenience and familiarity, though it has lost its pejorative undertones.[60]

While the Church of the East flourished in Mesopotamia and the Coptic church in Egypt, the miaphysites of Syria were suffering from the hardships imposed upon them by the Roman Empire. The efforts of Yaqūb Bar Adda'i (Latinised as Jacob Baradaeus), bishop of Edessa, in the early sixth century are credited with revitalising the anti-Chalcedonian creed amongst the Aramaic-speakers throughout the Syrian provinces. The exploits of Bar Adda'i are well documented, but his importance is perhaps best exemplified by the fact that the Western Syriac Church was henceforth known as the Jacobite Church, a misnomer which, like Nestorian, has persisted until the present-day.[61]

All of the non-Chalcedonian Churches in the Roman Empire, as well as the Church of the East initially benefited from the Arab-Muslim conquests of the seventh century. Many converted, but the relaxations on practising non-official Christianity and the privileged position which many enjoyed only strengthened the churches. The most remarkable expansion was certainly that of the Nestorian Church. Some early forays east of Persia during the fourth century gave way to a concerted missionary movement extending as far as China, Mongolia and India. The turning point only came with the devastation wrought by the Mongols on Persia, Mesopotamia and Anatolia in the fourteenth century – though the Christians suffered no worse than the Muslims. Remarkable as the expansion of the Church of the East had been, its contraction was no less sudden or impressive. By the nineteenth century only small vestiges of Nestorian Christianity remained, having been "reduced, outside India, to a regional church in Kurdistan."[62]

---

[60] It is also *theologically* incorrect to describe the Church of the East as purely Nestorian in nature. It considers Nestorius a saint and a scholar but not its founder. As such, neither the church nor its members use the Nestorian designation.

[61] Joseph, *Muslim-Christian Relations*, 6; Atiya, *A History of Eastern Christianity*, 180-184.

[62] Baum and Winkler, *The Church of the East*, 112. Even the Indian church had largely been lost to Catholicism and the Jacobites by this point.

## Missionary Activities

### *Catholic*

After the initial upheavals of the first four ecumenical councils, a period of theological stability – if not inactivity – continued until 1054, when the mutual excommunication of the Patriarchs of Constantinople and Rome created the Greek Orthodox and Roman Catholic churches respectively. The ramifications of this schism resonated in both the Syriac and Melkite communities with first the Crusades and then later missionary activity. The result was the acceptance of Catholic doctrine and the ecclesiastical supremacy of the Pope by factions within churches throughout the Middle East. These non-Latin churches, which are in communion with the Catholic Church but retain their original rites and liturgical language, are referred to by the term "Uniate".[63]

The process of schism, followed by reunification, has caused a multiplication in the number of claimants to the Patriarchal seat of Antioch. There are the Chalcedonian Melkite Church and the non-Chalcedonian Jacobite Church and each of these has in turn produced a Uniate offshoot: the Melkite Greek Catholic Church and the Syriac Catholic Church, each of which practices Catholicism according to its own rite.[64] In addition to these, the Maronite Church, which is also in full communion with Rome, traces its roots back to the Patriarchate of Antioch and indeed the church head, though resident in Lebanon, carries the title of Patriarch of Antioch to this day.

Aleppo and Mosul, by dint of significant European populations which did not exist in other cities experienced significant Jacobite conversion to Catholicism. In the mid-

---

[63] See Adrian Fortescue, *The Uniate Eastern Churches: the Byzantine Rite in Italy, Sicily, Syria and Egypt* (New York: Benziger Brothers, 1923), 1-7. These churches are also sometimes known as eastern rite churches because they are not Roman Catholics (that is, followers of the Latin rite).

[64] In Egypt, there is a parallel Coptic Catholic Church of Alexandria, while the Armenians have the Catholic Church of Cilicia. The Catholic Melkites of Egypt are headed by the Greek Catholic Patriarch of Antioch. See Ibid., 185-233.

seventeenth century, a *Süryânî* priest from Aleppo was consecrated as a Maronite bishop in the hopes of eventually having him installed as a Catholic bishop in the Jacobite Church. With French consular help, the Ottoman government had him elevated to the position of *Süryânî* Patriarch despite fierce resistance from the non-Catholics in the community. While this particular Catholic experiment was short-lived, it must be understood that until the establishment of a separate Uniate church, those with Catholic leanings – be they clergy or lay members – continued to exist within the Jacobite Church structure. When priests incorporated Catholic rituals into their liturgy, they faced opposition from parts of their congregations and even violent persecution at the behest of the non-Catholic clergy.

Despite opposition from the parent church, Catholicism enjoyed a renewed interest during the early years under Sultan Mahmûd II (reigned 1808-1839); nearly all Jacobites in Aleppo and other cities in Syria, plus bishops in Mosul and Diyarbakır, converted to Catholicism.[65] But the fate of the Uniate *Süryânî* was closely bound to that of the Catholic Armenians; when a series of anti-Catholic measures aimed primarily at the Armenians began, the Catholic *Süryânî* suffered as well. In 1817, Mahmûd II banned all missionary activity by Rome, and persecution of Catholics by the parent churches was encouraged, leading Catholic Armenians were executed and converts were forced from the capital.

Catholic fortunes changed, however, when the Ottomans suffered military defeat in the 1820s and the European powers forced it to relent on its anti-Catholic policies. Evidently emboldened by these favourable conditions, the Catholic *Süryânî* leadership emerged from hiding amongst the Maronites in Lebanon and set up residence first in Aleppo and then in Mardin itself – the stronghold of the Jacobite Church. An 1838 imperial decree that converts to Catholicism could choose any of the Eastern rites – but not the Latin one – aided the Syriac Catholics. By this time Catholicism was well-entrenched in certain *Süryânî* regions. Mardin had a strong Catholic community by mid-century,

---

[65] Charles Frazee, *Catholics and Sultans: the Church and the Ottoman Empire, 1453-1923* (London: Cambridge University Press, 1983), 293.

although most of the rural areas surrounding it remained vigorously attached to the Jacobite Church. In Iraq, where there were also Jacobites living alongside the more populous Eastern Syriacs, the majority had converted to Catholicism. Confrontations over the use of church properties even escalated into open conflict which was only resolved with the intervention of Ottoman authorities.[66]

Also in Iraq, a Catholic counterpart to the Nestorian Church had first emerged during the fifteenth century and eventually outstripped the parent church in terms of the number of faithful. Disputes over succession to the patriarchal seat of the Church of the East were exacerbated the tendency of the contenders to pledge allegiance to Rome in an attempt to gain legitimacy for their claim.[67] Traditionally, succession had been hereditary, a nephew of the previous patriarch being selected for the duty, but the first split in Nestorian Church came as an objection to this system.[68] In the eighteenth, and even into the nineteenth century, multiple patriarchs existed from three main lines: Mosul (sometimes Uniate), Hakkâri (never Uniate) and Diyarbakır (always Uniate).[69] In 1692, there were two separate patriarchs accepted by Rome, while at one

---

[66] Joseph, *Muslim-Christian Relations*, 49-55.

[67] See Joseph, *The Nestorians*, 29-33; Atiya, *A History of Eastern Christianity*, 276-279; Baum and Winkler, *The Church of the East*, 116-123. Each is flawed, containing inconsistencies within its own pages and in comparison with the others. More succinct is Frazee, *Catholics and Sultans*, 209-213, and especially Murre-van Den Berg, "The Patriarchs of the Church of the East from the Fifteenth to Eighteenth Centuries," *Hugoye: Journal of Syriac Studies* 2, no. 2 (July 1999).

[68] The tradition of hereditary succession made this Nestorian patriarchate the only one not subject to approval of the Ottoman government. Joseph, *The Nestorians*, 35.

[69] Instead of Mosul, we often read Alqosh (Alkuş), the patriarchs' actual place of residence. The first line was also occasionally resident in Cizre. The second, Hakkâri, line began in 1553 and had at times also been seated at Diyarbakır and Siirt. While in the Ottoman *sancak* of Hakkâri, it was located in the village of Koçanes, which is today known as Konak Köyü. Koçanes was not far from Çölemerik, which is the present-day city of Hakkâri. The third, Diyarbakır, line was established in 1681 and died out in 1828.

point in 1771, all three lines had professed a Catholic belief.[70] Moreover, in the nineteenth century, there were rival claims to the seat in Mosul, one of which was from a Uniate, giving a total of four different claimants to the leadership of the Eastern Syriac community. By about 1840, the confessional affiliation and rights to succession had settled, with the Diyarbakır line dying out, Mosul becoming the home of the Catholic Patriarch and Hakkâri remaining as the seat of the Nestorian Church of the East.

### Protestant

The second period of interest by missionaries began, perhaps not surprisingly, during the period of anti-Catholic sentiment during the reign of Mahmûd II. On the eastern and western fronts, Protestant missionaries primarily from the United States, and to a lesser extent Britain, converged on the Christian towns and villages of the eastern Ottoman Empire. Encouraged by the open conflict with the Catholics, the Protestants established themselves in areas such as Midyat and Hakkâri, where anti-Catholic opposition was strongest.[71]

In dealing with the Protestant threat, the Jacobite hierarchy also used the only avenue open to it: threatening the congregation. This took the form of physical violence at times, but the main method was disproportionate taxation since no officially recognised religious community existed to protect converts to Protestantism. Those in charge of assigning the taxes of community members would simply increase the share owed by the Protestants, whose failure to pay would subsequently result in arrest and imprisonment. Once pressure had been put on the state to grant Protestants the same privileges accorded to other denominations, Jacobites in certain areas turned the tables on their church by threatening to convert to Protestantism in order to avoid taxation.[72] Ultimately, missionary efforts would not be directed primarily at

---

[70] Frazee, *Catholics and Sultans*, 211. The Vatican did not always accept such professions. For this reason, the Hakkâri patriarchs were never actually Uniate even if they occasionally claimed to be.

[71] Joseph, *Muslim-Christian Relations*, 56-57.

[72] Ibid., 76.

the *Süryání*; the Armenians, with their massive numbers, offered a far greater reward, and it was to them that the missionaries turned their attention.[73]

The Nestorian Church and its Uniate offshoot have been mentioned above along with the confusion over succession and allegiance to Rome. In the nineteenth century, the two patriarchates stabilised with the Nestorian patriarch in Hakkâri, and the Chaldean patriarch, after 1828, resident in Mosul. European concepts of these churches changed with an 1820 British "rediscovery" around ancient Nineveh (modern Mosul) of the "Assyrians, who still conversed in a language similar to that spoken by Jesus and the Apostles."[74] Unfortunately, for the Protestant missionaries, most of their Ottoman forays came to naught; the largest expedition aimed at Ottoman Nestorians in Hakkâri ended in abrupt failure during the 1840s, with thousands of Christians massacred by Kurdish tribesmen.[75] The consequence was the missionaries' withdrawal from Hakkâri and the maintenance of an exclusively Nestorian stronghold there.

The greatest battleground for converts were the plains around Urmiye on the Persian side of the border. The Catholic missionaries did not have quite the head-start as compared to the regions to the south, and consequently, the Protestants recognised the opportunity this afforded. Also peculiar to Urmiye was the participation of Russian Orthodox missions, which had begun to play a role as the Russian Empire envisaged expansion into the area. By the early twentieth century, the Orthodox were claiming to have the largest congregation in Urmiye, with as much as two thirds of the total Syriac population.[76] Nevertheless, the Nestorian, Catholic and Protestant communities remained significant in size, though the latter was split by a persistent rivalry between missionaries from different countries.

---

[73] Ibid., 56-66.

[74] Atiya, *A History of Eastern Christianity*, 280. This was the first designation of the Eastern Syriacs as "Assyrians" in English.

[75] See Joseph, *The Nestorians*, 51-67.

[76] Naby, "The Assyrians of Iran," 240-245; Baum and Winkler, *The Church of the East*, 133-134.

The fragmentation of the larger Syriac-speaking community due to conversion was not accompanied by a corresponding alliance between the Catholic or Protestant branches of the Eastern and Western Syriac Churches. By preserving their rites, the fundamental similarities between, say, all *Süryânî* were not lost. A major side-effect of missionary activity was that by the twentieth century, the notion of an Assyrian past had became well-established amongst the Nestorians and Chaldeans, although it had yet to become quite so prevalent amongst the *Süryânî*.

## Population Distribution

The main centres of the *Süryânî* lay to the northeast of Syria, in the lands of upper Mesopotamia, and especially in the hilly terrain of what is known as Ṭūr ʿAbdīn in Syriac and Cebel-i Tûr in Ottoman Turkish.[77] Centred on Midyat, Cebel-i Tûr is roughly bordered by the towns of Mardin to the west, Hasankeyf to the north, Cizre to the east and Nusaybin to the south. It was in the villages of the region that the Syriac language survived as a vernacular and that the Christians outnumbered the Muslims. Moreover, it was home to a number of important monasteries and, between the twelfth and twentieth centuries, to the residence of the Jacobite patriarch in Mardin.[78]

Other important urban centres in the late nineteenth and early twentieth centuries may be inferred from the locations of the Jacobite metropolitans and bishops: Jerusalem; Mosul; Akra (a *kazâ* in the *vilâyet* of Mosul near the *Mar Mattî* monastery); Diyarbakır;

---

[77] It has been noted that the name Cebel-i Tûr constitutes a tautology as both the Arabic *cebel* and the Syriac *ṭūr* mean "mountain". In issues of *Mürşid-i Âsûriyûn*, this redundancy is occasionally extended even further with the addition of the Turkish equivalent, giving Cebel-i Tûr Dağ: "Mürşid'den suâline cevâblar," *Mürşid-i Âsûriyûn*, 4, no. 10 (Kânûn-ı Evvel 1912), 150.

[78] Joseph, *Muslim-Christian Relations*, 18-20. Prior to coming to Mardin in 1171, the Patriarch had been resident in Diyarbakır and Malatya. While in Mardin, the actual seat was at the *Deyrü'z-Zaferân* monastery, a few kilometres outside of the city proper.

*Deyrü'z-Zaferân*; Damascus, Homs[79] and Hama; Harput and Malatya; Adana; Cizre [Cezîretü'l-Ömer] and Şırnak; Nusaybin; Siverek (a *kazâ* in the *vilâyet* of Diyarbakır); Midyat; Beşiri and Garzan [Kurtalan] (both in the *sancak* of Siirt); and Bitlis, Siirt and Şirvan (all in the *vilâyet* of Bitlis).[80]

The Catholic *Süryânî* were also widely distributed across Ottoman territories. In the late eighteenth century, there were bishops of: Mardin and Nusaybin; Mosul; Baghdad; Bucak and Hısn-ı Mansûr [Adıyaman]; Beirut and Tripoli; and Damascus.[81] By 1869, the patriarchal seat had moved from Aleppo to Mardin, where it would remain until after the First World War. Clearly, in both cases, the ecclesiastical structure did not mirror Ottoman administrative divisions with dioceses lying across or being divided by provincial borders.[82]

Just as the Kurdish territories fell across the Ottoman-Persian border, so did those of the Nestorians and Chaldeans. The primary region of Eastern Syriac settlement was from Lakes Van and Urmiye in the north down to Hakkâri and Mosul in the south. The Hakkâri region, much like Cebel-i Tûr of the *Süryânî*, was small,

---

[79] Homs [Humus] in Syria would be the patriarchal seat of the Jacobite Church from 1933 until 1959, when it moved to its present location, Damascus.

[80] The information has been taken from the fifty-third Ottoman state *sâlnâme* published in 1315 [1897/1898]: Seyfeli, "Osmanlı Develet Salnamelerinde Süryaniler," 75-78. The hierarchy of Ottoman administrative divisions was: *vilâyet* [province]; *sancak* [county]; *kazâ* or *livâ* [district]; and *nâhiye* [township]. These were governed by a *vâli*, *mutasarrıf*, *kaymakam* (originally *kâim-i makam*) and *müdîr* respectively. In most cases, the administrative seat of a *vilâyet* was located in a *sancak* with the same name. Hence, in the *vilâyet* of Diyarbakır, there was a *sancak* of Diyarbakır as well as a *sancak* of Ergani and a *sancak* of Mardin.

[81] This information comes from the 1305 [1889/1890] *sâlnâme*: Seyfeli, "Osmanlı Develet Salnamelerinde Süryaniler," 91-92. There were also patriarchal representatives in Egypt, Diyarbakır, Adana, Urfa, Siverek, Cizre, Deyrü'z-Zûr and Midyat.

[82] Some of these religious centres may have been "phantom bishoprics that owed their survival only to the few solid monasteries maintained and preserved by a handful of monks", however. See de Courtois, *The Forgotten Genocide*, 3.

mountainous and relatively densely populated by Christians – although it too was shared with sedentary and nomadic Kurdish tribes. As noted above, Hakkâri and Iraq were Nestorian and Chaldean respectively, whereas Urmiye was the main area of confessional heterogeneity. Outside of the provinces of Baghdad, Basra and Mosul, other populations of Ottoman Chaldeans could be found clustered around several bishoprics: Diyarbakır and Meyyâfârkîn [Silvan]; Mardin and Nusaybin; Siirt; Cizre; and İmâdiye.[83] Smaller populations were found in cities such as Damascus, Beirut, Aleppo, Urfa and Adana. Few Nestorian communities were present outside of Hakkâri or a short distance away in the vicinity of Mosul, although there are records of their presence in the provinces of Diyarbakır and Bitlis.[84]

Population estimates for the Syriac communities are problematic. Ottoman census data is confused with respect to terminology; the 1330 [1914] census, for example, had categories for *Süryânî*, *Süryânî-i Kadîm* and *Yakûbî* making it very difficult to differentiate between Jacobite and Catholic *Süryânî*. The combined figures for these three groups suggests that there was a population of some 66,000 in the Ottoman Empire.[85] All Protestants were grouped together irrespective of previous religious affiliation, so separating the *Süryânî* Protestants from Armenians and Greek Protestants is not possible. Unofficial estimates of the *Süryânî* population give higher figures, although these just as often suffer from the same problem of inaccuracy as the official.[86] The *Süryânî* newspaper *İntibâh* printed population figures that estimated that there were some 70,000 *Süryânî Yakûbî*, although the editor believed that "there is no doubt this would be two or three times greater"

---

[83] Taken from the 1298 [1880/1881] *sâlnâme*. Seyfeli, "Osmanlı Devlet Salnamelerinde Süryaniler," 101-102. İmâdiye was administratively part of the *sancak* of Hakkâri although today it lies in Iraq.

[84] Joseph, *The Nestorians*, 23 and Oswald Parry, *Six Months in a Syrian Monastery* (London: Horace Cox, 1895), 41.

[85] Kemal Karpat, *Ottoman Population 1830-1914: Demographic and Social Characteristics* (Madison: University of Wisconsin Press, 1985), 170-189.

[86] Vital Cuinet, for example, listed both Uniate and non-Uniate Chaldeans in his tables: McCarthy, *Muslims and Minorities*, 105-106.

once the Jacobites in India were counted.[87] There is somewhat more consensus with respect to the Nestorian numbers in Hakkâri, most of which fall into the range of 50,000 to 75,000 and for those of Urmiye, roughly 35,000.[88] The number of Chaldeans is difficult to determine with one source giving 100,000 Chaldeans, "mostly in Iraq".[89] Ottoman census figures from 1914 have over 10,000 Chaldeans living in the provinces of Bitlis and Diyarbakır, but elsewhere they are incomplete.

## THE OTTOMAN EMPIRE: 1908 TO 1914

### Revolution and Counter-Revolution

By the turn of the twentieth century, many in the Ottoman Empire had grown weary of the reign of Sultan Abdülhamîd II for his authoritarianism and other perceived failures in running the state. Opposition was headed by the Young Turks, a group composed primarily of students and military officers who would establish the *İttihâd ve Terakkî Cemiyeti* [the Committee of Union and Progress] out of earlier organisations after congresses in 1902 and 1906. While the CUP would be at the forefront of activities, they worked with other parties who likewise were in opposition to Abdülhamîd. The confrontation between the two sides precipitated a bloodless *coup d'état* in 1908 and the restoration of constitution rule, some 30 years after the first Ottoman constitution had been annulled by Abdülhamîd himself.

The post-1908 period saw a parliament elected and major checks on the Sultan's power put into place. The Young Turks were, however, forced to weather a fierce backlash against policies

---

[87] The same figures gave a total of 1,690,000 Armenians and 80,000 Nestorians. "Hıristiyân terakkîsi," *İntibâh*, 3, no. 12 (Teşrîn-i Evvel 1912), 4-5.

[88] Ibid., 102-103; Karpat, *Ottoman Population*, 192; Naby, "The Assyrians of Iran," 238. One estimate for Urmiye has some 44,000: Arian Ishaya, "Ethnicity, Class, and Politics: Assyrians in the History of Azerbayjan, 1800-1918," *Journal of the Assyrian Academic Society* 4, no. 2 (November, 1990), 4. There were also small Eastern Syriac communities in Georgia and in Russia proper.

[89] Baum and Winkler, *The Church of the East*, 136.

which had angered the religious establishment and other deprivileged groups. The CUP quickly put down the revolt when it broke out on 13 April 1909 [31 Mart 1325] by using its close ties to the military units in the Balkan provinces, notably the Macedonian *Hareket Ordusu*. Abdülhamîd's exact role in this 1909 counter-revolution has been the source of scholarly debate; nevertheless, the CUP took the opportunity to rid themselves of the figurehead for their own opponents, and within a few weeks Abdülhamîd was deposed and sent into exile in Salonika. The new Sultan, Mehmed Reşâd, assumed the throne but would wield little influence, with the political parties being the focal point of power struggles.

As alluded to above, the period with which this work is concerned – 1908 to 1914 – has been overshadowed in Syriac historiography by the events of the subsequent years. But this interval was one of great hope in the Empire, and it would have been difficult to predict the misfortune that was to come.[90] The new era brought about a sudden outburst of intellectual and political activity that had previously been impossible. At the beginning of 1908, there were 120 Ottoman newspapers and journals; in the first months after the revolution, this number rose to some 730.[91] The dramatic increase in the number of periodicals in the Ottoman Empire was due as much to the loosening of restrictions on publishing as to the hopes for the future. Naûm Fâik was open in expressing that the spirit of the revolution was behind the establishment of his newspaper, *Kevkeb Mednho*, a year later in 1909:

> "The liberty and equality which the constitution has granted to all the various Ottoman peoples and nations have become the means for us to enjoy the glorious blessing of fraternity and for the advancement of our

---

[90] The infrastructure to conduct the deportations and massacres during the war years were, in fact, secretly established before the actual outbreak of hostilities: Taner Akçam, *A Shameful Act: The Armenian Genocide and the Question of Turkish Responsibility*, translated by Paul Bessemer (New York: Metropolitan Books, 2006).

[91] Orhan Koloğlu, *Osmanlı'dan Günümüze Türkiye'de Basın* (Istanbul: İletişim Yayınları, 1992), 54.

schools, the opening of printing presses, the printing of newspapers and periodicals using the Syriac language and education allowing the *Süryânî* to understand their own history as well as the present wretched state of our community ..."[92]

The revolution having been completed and constitutional rule having been restored, elation and hope in the Ottoman Empire slowly gave way as the reality of the problems facing the new government became apparent. Support for the revolution of the Young Turks had come from many quarters, but the common celebration of the return to constitutional rule and the end of Abdülhamîd's despotism belies serious rifts between their representatives and the CUP. Moreover, the internal cleavages which divided each community themselves preclude any outright statement of a community's overarching stand in favour of a single position. Where there was discord, there were also alliances between factions which had in common nothing except a single enemy. The vested interests which existed for each course of action were largely concrete prior to 1908, though jostling did continue up until the outbreak of World War I, when the old systems disappeared completely.

The new era of politics ushered in by the 1908 revolution also brought contests for power in the lead up to the elections for the new parliament later in the same year. A collection of opponents of the CUP from several different ideological positions coalesced into a handful of small parties. By 1911 most of these united in their distrust of the CUP to form the *Hürriyet ve İtilâf Fırkası* [Party of Freedom and Understanding].[93] Since the parliament was not under the control of the CUP, tensions existed between the secretive committee, the rest of the government and non-CUP officers in the military. The tide even turned enough that powerful

---

[92] Çıkkı, *Naum Faik ve Süryani Rönesansı*, 133-134.

[93] It is also often known by its French name, the *Entente libérale*. As will be discussed on page 105 below, a Chaldean Christian, Dâvud Yûsufânî, held a leading position in the party.

CUP members were being sent into provincial exile by their rivals.[94] The political manoeuvrings would only be settled in 1913, with a CUP orchestrated coup.

After 1908, there were also both successful negotiation for and open protests against the proportion of representation to be accorded to the non-Muslim communities. The ancestry of these activities lies in earlier times but can be best observed in the conferences which were held immediately prior to 1908. The earlier of the two, convened in Paris in 1902, highlights the cleavages endemic to the Young Turk movement itself, but also saw the active participation of non-Turkish delegates representing the national interests of their communities. Figures such as İsmâîl Kemâl Bey illustrate how the allegiances of these Ottoman politicians may appear confused. Part of the Albanian contingent, he was a pro-British and pro-Greek supporter of Albanian independence from Ottoman rule. And yet, İsmâîl Kemâl Bey was in Paris sitting alongside the Young Turks ostensibly part of a movement to save the Empire. This fact ought not to be understood as exemplifying an ideological bond but rather in light of there being a common enemy, Abdülhamîd, whose overthrow would require the cooperation of all.

This Albanian example was no exception. Other non-Turkish groups – Muslim and non-Muslim – were actively engaged in the Young Turk activities, irrespective of the fact that their stated objectives were frequently irreconcilable with CUP aims. Participation by the opponents of Abdülhamîd was by no means absolute, however; some non-Muslim groups worked closely with the CUP while others maintained a distance from the Young Turks, instead preferring to align themselves with opposition parties. Nevertheless, the era saw the involvement of many non-Muslim groups and organisations in mainstream Ottoman politics.

## Ottomanism

The CUP was well aware of the benefit of having non-Muslim groups participate in their movement and as a consequence they

---

[94] Jan Erik Zürcher, *Turkey: A Modern History*, new edition (London: I. B. Taurus, 2004), 99-103.

revitalised the notion of a common identity for all Ottoman citizens irrespective of religious or ethnic affiliation. The expression of hope that the non-Muslims vested in the CUP and the constitution of 1908 clearly had in them overtones of Ottomanism, a concept which dated back to the previous century. Such sentiments were not necessarily tied to a party affiliation but were often popular outbursts of emotion, as one account shows:

> "The squares, roads and streets of the two cities [Harput and Mamûretü'l-Azîz] are crowded with both locals and the inhabitants of villages near and far! Turk, Armenian, Kurd and *Süryânî* all together, hand in hand ... embracing, kissing ... flags in hand! Long live freedom! Long live justice! Long live equality! The cries echo high into the air ..."

> "Despotism has given way to constitutional rule ... Oppression will cease. Justice will prevail over all. Peace will reign far and wide. All – irrespective of race or religion – will be friend and brother. Jails will empty. The courts will close ..."[95]

The themes of freedom (*hürriyet*), justice (*adâlet*), equality (*müsâvât*) and fraternity (*uhuvvet*) are commonly encountered in the writings from 1908, but the concept of an overarching Ottoman identity grounded in these principles pre-dated the declaration of the second constitution. Imperial edicts in 1839 and 1856 had also promised equality to all in the eyes of the state, and the 1876 constitution further promised that all subjects would be Ottomans irrespective of their faith. But while Ottoman patriotism was espoused by some intellectuals around this time, Islam, or being Muslim, was still an integral component of being an Ottoman. This trend was reinforced during the time of Abdülhamîd, pan-Islamic ideals reigned supreme in the government.

Legislated equality was opposed by some Muslims who saw it as an erosion of their own superior status under Ottoman law, but

---

[95] İshak Sunguroğlu, *Harput Yollarında*, vol. 4, (Istanbul: Yeni Matbaa, 1958), 327-332.

it also had its opponents amongst the non-Muslim segments of society who stood to loose through the abolition of certain privileges that they enjoyed under the old system. Ottomanism meant a measure of secularisation of the administrative apparatus and this obviously did not appeal to those with vested interests in the religious hierarchy. More specifically, non-Muslims did not savour the prospect of being drafted into the Ottoman military, and the resistance to the implementation of such measures in the mid-nineteenth century had resulted in the effective return of the old poll tax (*cizye*) that was levied on non-Muslims but this time under a new name, the *bedel-i askerî*, a military exemption fee payable by Christians and Jews.

Some non-Muslims, however, were willing to abandon the status quo despite the hardships it might bring: *Yeprad*, an Armenian publication also from Harput, reported that the local religious leadership had lent its support to the idea of Armenian recruits in the armed forces in a public lecture.[96] Non-Muslims who believed in Ottomanism, argued for general service in principle and on the grounds it was a practical means of strengthening the bonds between the different peoples of the Empire.[97] Even the *Dashnaktsutiun* and the *Hnchakian*, the Armenian revolutionary parties usually associated with armed opposition to the Ottoman state, were supportive of military service for all as a basis for the equal treatment of all Ottoman citizens.[98]

Likewise, there was extensive Greek, Jewish, Bulgarian and Vlach participation in political activities supportive of the Ottoman

---

[96] Ohannes Kılıçdağı, *The Bourgeois Transformation and Ottomanism among Anatolian Armenians after the 1908 Revolution* (Master's thesis, Boğaziçi University, 2005), 75-77. Kılıçdağı likewise recounts a similar theme in the Armenian press of Sivas.

[97] Rober Koptaş, *Armenian Political Thinking in the Second Constitutional Period: the Case of Krikor Zohrab* (Master's thesis, Boğaziçi University, 2005), 119-121.

[98] Ibid., 118.

state.[99] There was, of course, also much opposition to the Ottoman Empire in the form of national movements, just as a Turkish nationalism was developing that would ultimate come to see the region's non-Muslim inhabitants as enemies of the Turkish nation. But, for a period, the dominant trend in Ottoman public life was to emphasise the equality of all the elements that constituted the Empire. The benefit of hindsight provides contemporary observers with the knowledge that Christians were eradicated from the territories that would constitute the Turkish Republic. But, as others have pointed out, the Young Turks – whatever their true feelings – were at least paying lip service to Ottomanism during the pre-World War I period.[100]

## International Crises and Ottoman Christians

The international community saw the political upheavals beginning in 1908 as an opportunity to strike against the Ottoman Empire. In short order the government lost its remaining *de jure* authority over Bosnia, which had been occupied by the Austro-Hungarian Empire since 1876. Meanwhile, the semi-autonomous Ottoman province of Bulgaria, which had already incorporated Eastern Rumelia (Rûmeli-i Şarkî) in 1885, established a fully independent kingdom, and the island of Crete unified with Greece. The new government was realistic: force was simply not an option, so retaliation was restricted to measures such as a boycott of Austro-Hungarian goods, part orchestrated and part spontaneous. This caused hardships for Armenian and Greek importers and shopkeepers, especially in the occasional cases where non-Muslim merchants were specifically targeted.[101]

---

[99] See Karpat, "The Memoirs of N. Batzaria: The Young Turks and Nationalism," *International Journal of Middle East Studies*, 6, no. 3 (July, 1975), 279-280.

[100] This is argued in M Şükrü Hanioğlu, *The Young Turks in Opposition* (New York: Oxford University Press, 1995).

[101] Zürcher, *Turkey: A Modern History*, 103-104. Greeks in particular were subjected to a such a campaign in a few specific locations, but in general the boycott was directed at Austro-Hungarian goods and not individuals: Hervé Georgelin, "Boycottage des non-musulmans à Smyrne et

Nevertheless, with a single exception, non-Muslims did not suffer violent reprisals during the events of 1908 and 1909. The one instance occurred in the southern province of Adana, where several thousand Armenians and other Christians were massacred during the course of the counter-revolution, but this localised backlash did not deter non-Muslim expectations from the constitutional era.[102] Once it had restored order, the CUP government took action against Muslims suspected of involvement in the slaughter and the trials would result over a hundred of those convicted being executed, including the provincial governor.[103]

The CUP had only a short respite before they were thrown back into another situation in which they had little opportunity to oppose international pressure for them to relinquish territories. In 1911, Italy manufactured an excuse to declare war on the Ottoman Empire over the *vilâyet* of Trâblus-ı Garb [Libyan Tripoli], which was essentially cut off from the rest of the Empire by the presence of the British in Egypt. After a year of fighting, the Ottomans accepted the loss of their last remaining African province as well as the Dodecanese Islands to the Italians since a second, more serious, conflict had begun in the Balkans.

A joint attack in late 1912 by Montenegro, Serbia, Bulgaria and Greece quickly overwhelmed the Ottoman Empire and precipitated the *Bâb-ı Âlî* coup by an inner circle of the CUP that felt challenged by rival forces in the government as well as by its

---

dans le vilayet d'Aydın d'après les archives diplomatiques," *Revue du Monde Arménien Moderne et Contemporain* no. 4 (1998).

[102] Aykut Kansu quotes the findings of a parliamentary commission: 17,000 Armenians killed: *Politics in Post-Revolutionary Turkey, 1908-1913* (Leiden: Brill, 2000), 122-125. Adana was also home to a sizeable Syriac Christian population and one source claims that of the victims some 850 were *Süryânî* and 422 were *Keldânî*: Gaunt, *Massacres, Resistance, Protectors*, 44-45. When *Kevkeb Mednho* noted the high level of orphaned children and widowed Christian women in the *vilâyet* of Adana, there were also *Süryânî*: "Urfa'da konferans," *Kevkeb Mednho*, 1, no. 16 (11 Şubât 1911), 8.

[103] Zürcher, *Turkey: A Modern History*, 99. *Mürşid-i Âsûriyûn* reported on the government's involvement in repairing damaged [*muhterik*] churches in Adana: "Ceridelerden," *Mürşid-i Âsûriyûn*, 4, no. 3 (Mart 1912), 45-47.

lack of control over the parliament. Under the new government headed by Enver and Talât Paşa, the First Balkan War ended with the loss of all of the Ottoman Empire's European possessions except Istanbul and the Dardanelles. During a second war which immediately followed the first, the Ottoman border was pushed back west and Edirne was recptured; despite this victory, this string of conflicts humiliated the state, its leadership and its Muslim population.[104]

In accordance with the new terms of military service dictated by Ottomanism, non-Muslims served on the Balkan fronts; moreover, the populace participated in the voluntary contribution of funds towards the purchase of arms – notably warships.[105] That being said, the Balkan – and to a lesser extent the Italian – Wars marked the end of Ottomanism as a practical ideology in the mind of the CUP. The country was inundated by Muslim refugees fleeing from reprisals in the provinces incorporated into the independent Balkan states, and sentiments had turned away from the notion of a multi-ethnic empire and more towards Turkism or pan-Islamism as the unifying ideology, although little was done openly to put such an ideology into practice until 1915.[106]

It is into this context that this work fits. Largely characterised by hopes and not fears, it was a time during which much appears to contradict both what is encountered in much Syriac historiography and during which much does contradict what would happen immediately afterwards. However, to understand the *Süryânî* intellectuals of the early-twentieth century, the promise of Ottomanism and constitutionalism must not be forgotten.

---

[104] Zürcher, *Turkey: A Modern History*, 103-109.

[105] Kılıçdağı, *The Bourgeois Transformation and Ottomanism among Anatolian Armenians*, 68-69.

[106] Zürcher, *Turkey: A Modern History*, 128-130. This is also covered in great detail by Akçam, *A Shameful Act*.

## SOURCES FOR THE STUDY

### Syriac Journalism

An attempt to draw out perceptions of any belief from the past is determined by the sources which historians have at their disposal. With respect to distributed publications, this limitation is not exclusively a matter of what the researcher has at his or her disposal – even if this is the first obstacle to surmount – but also encompasses the questions of how widely the sources in question were read and how well they represented contemporary ideas.

For this work, the subject will primarily be two early twentieth-century Ottoman newspapers, *Mürşid-i Âsûriyûn* [Guide of the Assyrians] (Harput, 1909-1914) and *Kevkeb Mednho* [Star of the East] (Diyarbakır, 1910-1912), and one from the *Süryânî* immigrant community in the United States, *İntibâh* [Awakening] (College Point, New York, 1909-1915).[107] While these are the most renowned examples of Ottoman *Süryânî* journalism, they are not unique; prior to the entry of the Ottoman Empire into World War I, several other newspapers were also published by *Süryânî* intellectuals: *Kevkbo d-Suryoye* [Star of the *Süryânî*] (Harput, 1910); *Safro d-Nuhro* [Light of the Dawn] (Harput?, 1910?); *Hayât* [Life] (Harput, 1910); *Şifuro* [Trumpet] (Diyarbakır, 1911-1914); *Savto d-Oromoye* [Voice of the Aramaeans] (the United States, 1913-?); and *el-Hikmet* [Wisdom] (Mardin, 1913-1914).[108] All of these had actually been preceded by a quarterly from India, *Simeth Haye* [Treasure of Life], which was published by *kas* Mattî in the Syriac language, but this was thought to have already folded by 1910.[109]

---

[107] There exists considerable discrepancies in the naming of these journals. Identification is made particularly difficult when Syriac transliteration systems are employed for what are in fact Ottoman Turkish names and *vice versa*.

[108] For an overview of these and other periodicals see Benjamin Trigona-Harany, "A Bibliography of *Süryânî* Periodicals in Ottoman Turkish," *Hugoye: Journal of Syriac Studies* 12, no. 2 (Summer, 2009).

[109] The only contemporary reference to *Simeth Haye* that I have found comes from an article by Naûm Fâik: "Mürşid-i Âsûriyûn cerîdesi," *Kevkeb Mednho*, 1, no. 18 (11 Mart 1910), 7-8.

Remarkably, none of these rich materials has yet to be subject to a thorough study. My own research has uncovered a number of references to their existence, but only one author has relied upon any of the constituent materials. The work in question, a semi-biographic account of Naûm Fâik's accomplishments from the 1930s, draws on articles from *Kevkeb Mednho* but only to a very limited extent.[110] The section on printing from a recent series on the *Süryânî* of the Ottoman Empire and the Turkish Republic contains one short study of, again, *Kevkeb Mednho*; while the journal's background is richly described, we learn nothing new of the actual contents.[111] Considering the fact that Naûm Fâik is one of the most venerated of all Ottoman *Süryânî* intellectuals, it is particularly surprising that his early works have gone unread by the present-day Assyrian scholarship which regards him so highly.

The lack of attention from Ottoman scholarship is less surprising: none of the papers appears to be found in any of the public collections in Turkey, nor do catalogues of Ottoman periodicals list them.[112] This work, therefore, is in part an attempt to encourage the use of these sources which provide us with some of the only written accounts by the *Süryânî* laity in the Ottoman Empire. Part of the reason that neither Ottoman nor Syriac scholars have undertaken a proper study of *İntibâh*, *Kevkeb Mednho* or *Mürşid-i Âsûriyûn* is that these publications fall into a linguistic no man's land into which neither group is prepared to enter. The predominant language of the newspapers is Ottoman Turkish, a tongue foreign to most scholars of Syriac studies or Assyrian nationalist movements. At the same time, the alphabet in which

---

[110] The work in question was originally published in 1936 and written primarily in Arabic and Syriac; a Turkish translation appeared in 2004: Çıkkı, *Naum Faik ve Süryani Rönesansı*.

[111] Mehmet Şimşek, "Şark Yıldızı Gazetesi," in *Süryaniler ve Süryanilik*, vol. 4.

[112] Hasan Duman, *Başlangıcından Harf Devrimine Kadar Osmanlı-Türk Süreli Yayınlar ve Gazeteler Bibliyografyası ve Toplu Kataloğu, 1828-1928* (Ankara: Enformasyon ve Dokümantasyon Hizmetleri Vakfı, 2000). One of the few authors on Ottoman journalism to have recognised the existence of *Kevkeb Mednho* and *Şifuro* was Cavit Orhan Tütengil in *Diyarbakır Basın Tarihi Üzerine Notlar* (İstanbul: İstanbul Matbaası, 1954), 21-22.

Ottoman Turkish was written is not the Arabic script familiar to Ottoman scholars, but rather the Syriac, a script used uniquely by the *Süryânî* community.[113]

## *Mürşid-i Âsûriyûn*

The first of the newspapers, *Mürşid-i Âsûriyûn*, was launched in 1909[114] by Âşûr Yûsuf, a instructor of writing at the Euphrates College, an American missionary school in Harput.[115] Although Harput's non-Muslim population was predominantly Armenian, there was a small *Süryânî* presence there as well. The settlement itself had been an Ottoman administrative centre until this function was reassigned to the town of Mezre, renamed Mamûretü'l-Azîz, in the 1860s.[116] The two were essentially twin cities with Harput built around a hilltop castle some five kilometres from Mezre on the plains below. Five of Harput's twenty-two

---

[113] There was a long tradition of writing Arabic using Syriac characters, a system called *Gerşûnî*. For a treatment, see Appendix A.

[114] The exact month in which *Mürşid-i Âsûriyûn* began appearing is uncertain, but it was probably in the month of April or May of 1908, a conclusion based on a report in *İntibâh* from January 1910 which mentioned "the announcement of the publication of the newspaper *Mürşidü'l-Âsûriyûn* by professor Âşûr Yûsuf efendi from seven or eight months ago" (*muallim Âşûr Yûsuf efendi tarafından yedi sekiz mah mukadem neşrine mübâşeret edilen "Mürşidü'l-Âsûriyûn" gazetesi*): "Mürşidü'l-Âsûriyûn gazetesi," *İntibâh*, 1, no. 1 (Teşrîn-i Sânî 1909), 4. This is the only instance that I have found to the Arabic *Mürşidü'l-Âsûriyûn* rather than the Farsi *Mürşid-i Âsûriyûn*.

[115] A few basic details concerning *Mürşid-i Âsûriyûn* are available in: De Kelaita, "On the Road to Nineveh," 13-14 and "The Origins and Development of Assyrian Nationalism," 19-20; Abdulmesih BarAbrahem, "The Question of Assyrian Journalism Revisited," *Journal of the Assyrian Academic Society* 9, no. 1 (April, 1995), 5; Gabriele Yonan, *Journalismus bei den Assyrern: Ein Überblick von seinem Anfängen bis zur Gegenwart* (Berlin: Zentralverband der Assyrischen Vereinigungen, 1985) ['Asurlar'da Gazetecilik: Başlangıcından günümüze kadar bir bakış," translation and serialisation by Erol Sever], *Hujâdâ* 12, no. 7/8 (Juli-Agusti 1989), 39]. None of these authors have, however, read Âşûr Yûsuf's writings.

[116] After the establishment of the Republic of Turkey, Mamûretü'l-Azîz was shortened to first El-Azîz and then Elâzığ.

neighbourhoods were primarily inhabited by non-Muslims; the *Süryânî* were concentrated in the smallest of these, the *Süryânî mahallesi*, with some 60 households.[117] Excluding Catholic and Protestant converts, the Harput *Süryânî* were apparently served by a total of three churches, one of which, the *Meryem Ana Kilisesi* (also known as the *Kızıl Kilise* or *Yakûbî Kilisesi*), was first constructed in 179 AD according to an inscription and Ottoman documents.[118]

Image 1 – Harput *Süryânî-i Kadîm* quarter in 1902

The Euphrates College had been established by the American Board in 1878 as Armenia College, later changing its name in 1888 due to objections from the government.[119] The student body at the Euphrates College was overwhelmingly Armenian, but it is known

---

[117] Sunguroğlu, *Harput Yollarında*, vol. 1, 239-242.

[118] The other two churches were the *Süryânî Kilisesi* and the *Mar Şemûn Kilisesi*. Sunguroğlu, *Harput Yollarında*, vol. 1, 348-356. Only the *Meryem Ana* remains today in Harput.

[119] Frank Andrews Stone, "The Heritage of Euphrates (Armenia) College," in *Armenian Tsopk/Kharpert*, ed. Richard G. Hovannisian (Mazda: Costa Mesa, California, 2002).

that there were Syriac Christians who attended the college as well.[120] Late in 1909, the year of *Mürşid-i Âsûriyûn*'s founding, the Armenian-language *Yeprad* was also established by an Armenian professor at the same school.[121] These two joined the government-run *Mamûretü'l-Azîz*, which had already been appearing for a quarter of a century by 1909, as the sum of local journalistic production. Both *Mürşid-i Âsûriyûn* and *Yeprad* survived until the outbreak of the First World War, when Âşûr Yûsuf and his Armenian colleague were later imprisoned and ultimately executed along with most other teachers from the Euphrates College.[122]

What I call *Mürşid-i Âsûriyûn* appears as *Asurilerin Mürşidi* in Turkish and anything from *Murşëd Oţuryun* to *Mhadyana d-Atur* in transliterated Syriac. On the masthead of the publication itself, we read exactly ܐܫܘܪܝܘܢ ܡܪܫܕ [mrşd āşūryūn], where the latter word is the Arabic plural for *Âsûrî* [Assyrian] and the former is the Arabic *mürşid* [guide]. The reading that Âşûr Yûsuf intended was *Mürşid-i Âsûriyûn*, with the two words joined by the unwritten Farsi *izâfet*, as was common in Ottoman Turkish.

---

[120] Sunguroğlu, *Harput Yollarında*, vol. 2, 90 and see note 488 on page 176 below.

[121] Kılıçdağı, *The Bourgeois Transformation and Ottomanism among Anatolian Armenians*, 4-5. There is a picture of Âşûr Yûsuf on page 108 (miscaptioned as Aşod Yusuf). He is also pictured in Stone, "The Heritage of Euphrates (Armenia) College," 223.

[122] Âşûr Yûsuf's death was recorded in an eyewitness account given by a relative from Harput: Naayem, *Shall This Nation Die?*, 215. A similar reference appears in David Perley, "The Jacobites," in Yusuf Malek, *The British Betrayal of the Assyrians* (Chicago: Assyrian National Federation, 1934). On the killing of instructors at Euphrates College, see Tracy Atkinson, *The German, the Turk and the Devil Made a Triple Alliance: Harpoot Diaries, 1908-1917* (Princeton: Gomidas Institute, 2000), although no mention of Âşûr Yûsuf is made.

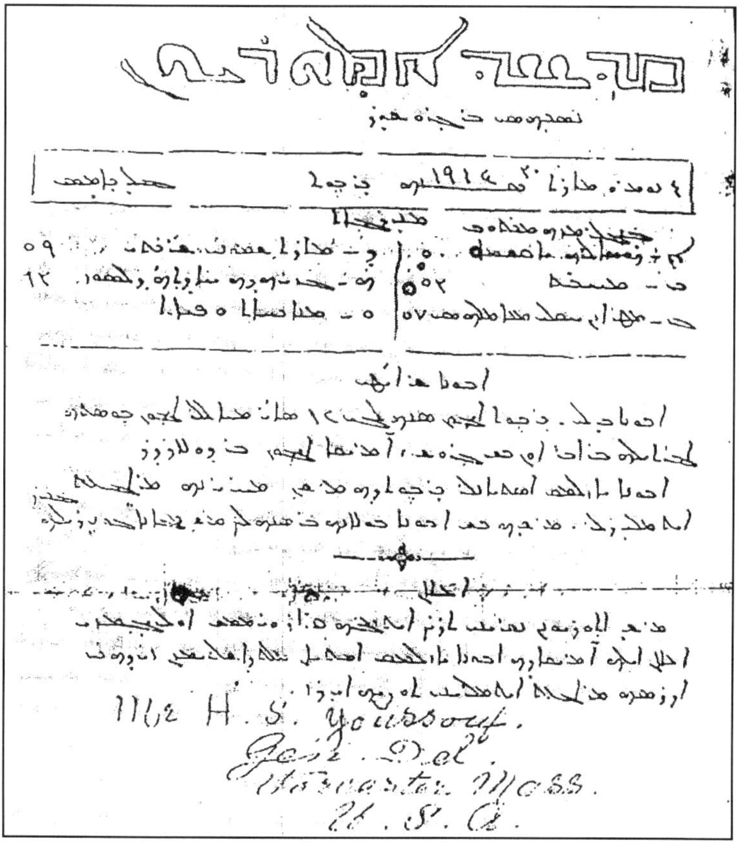

Image 2 – *Mürşid-i Âsûriyûn*

Unfortunately, only a little information is available about the origins of the newspaper and its founder. Âşûr Yûsuf we know to have been born on 20 May, 1858 in Harput and was educated at the Central Turkey College in Antep, another American mission school, although he was unable to complete his education for lack of money. By the late 1880s, Âşûr Yûsuf was a teacher at an American school in Izmir. He is also said to have taught at a number of other schools in the Ottoman Empire, including the Central Turkey College itself and institutions in Amasya, Malatya and Antakya, but it is not clear what affiliation these other schools had.[123] Âşûr Yûsuf was married in 1895 to Arşaluys Oğgasyan, an Armenian with whom he would have six children.[124] We may note that in Harput, as in Izmir and probably everywhere else, he was working for Protestant institutions, but Âşûr Yûsuf was himself almost certainly a Jacobite.[125]

Oral tradition in Elâzığ holds that Âşûr Yûsuf was aided in the publication of *Mürşid-i Âsûriyûn* by Yakûb Denho [Tanoğlu], a teacher and *şemmâs* in the *Süryânî-i Kadîm* church in Harput.[126] In support of this one can point to the tendency for editorialising articles to employ the third-person plural rather than the singular; there is, unfortunately, no direct mention of Yakûb Denho or of any other assistant in *Mürşid-i Âsûriyûn*. In fact, the only references to Yakûb that I have found in *Mürşid-i Âsûriyûn* are in the budgets for the *Süryânî* community in Harput; there, *muallim* [teacher] Yakûb Efendi is listed as having received a wage of 854 *gurûş* in 1910 and 100 *gurûş* in 1911.[127] Additionally, in 1914 an exchange of letters between Yakûb Denho and Naûm Fâik was printed in *İntibâh*, but again there is no mention of his having any affiliation with *Mürşid-i Âsûriyûn*.[128]

---

[123] Aleks Sodo, "Ասուր Ա. Եուսուֆ," in Assyrian Five Association, *Ասորոց Ախոյզգական Թախկիրան* (Boston: Assyrian Star Press, 1919), 3-6; Perley, "Notes on the Article"; Yonan, "Asurlar'da Gazetecilik," *Hujâdâ* 12, no. 7/8 (Juli-Agusti 1989), 39; and "Süyânîlerin talîm ve terbiyesi için başkalar yardım eder mi?," *Mürşid-i Âsûriyûn*, 5, no. 8 (Temmûz 1913), 118.

[124] Alis Nazaryan, *Արիւնոտ ձայնը* (Beirut: Mshak, 1962), 9. I would like to express my gratitude to Ohannes Kılıçdağı for translating these details from Armenian.

[125] From reading *Mürşid-i Âsûriyûn* alone one would conclude that Âşûr Yûsuf was a Jacobite; he would, for example, speak of Patriarch Abdullah as *patrikimiz* [our patriarch]. However, a letter from his wife to *Assyrian Progress*, a periodical based in the United States, did imply that he was Protestant: *Assyrian Progress*, 3, no. 9 (September 1934), 4.

[126] This information was related to me by Yakûb's grandson, İshak Tanoğlu.

[127] "Harpût millet meclisinin senevî hesâbları," *Mürşid-i Âsûriyûn*, 5, no. 1 (Kânûn-ı Sânî 1913), 10-13.

[128] See "Açık mektûb," *İntibâh*, 5, no. 3 (Şubât 1914), 3, and "Harpût'ta Yakûb T. Denho efendiye," *İntibâh*, 5, no. 7 (Hazîrân 1914), 5-6.

*Mürşid-i Âsûriyûn*, which described itself as "a scientific, literary, economic and political newspaper (*fennî, edebî, iktisâdî, siyâsî ga-
zetedir*)", was generally published once a month, with the first page
comprised of the masthead and a table of contents followed by
fifteen pages of single-column text.[129] In practice, the newspaper
seems to have appeared somewhat less regularly. In 1911, for
instance, the April issue was not published due to lack of paper and
ink.[130] Then in 1912, there were two issues in November (numbers
seven and eight) and no less than four issues in December
(numbers nine through twelve). In 1913, however, the distribution
was even, except for the month of March, when two issues were
published. Although *Mürşid-i Âsûriyûn* appeared in Ottoman
Turkish using the Western Syriac alphabet, Âşûr Yûsuf did on one
occasion print an Arabic-language letter from one of his readers
and at least two Syriac-language poems.[131] But despite being a
*Süryânî*, Âşûr Yûsuf did not know the Syriac language in either its
literary or colloquial form; this he admitted in his preface to the
two aforementioned poems.[132]

In two issues from 1911, Âşûr Yûsuf made mention of *yağlı
kâğıd* being necessary for the printing of *Mürşid-i Âsûriyûn*.[133] From
this and the appearance of the printed characters we may deduce
that the newspaper was the product of either lithography or

---

[129] An exception is the first issue of the third volume, which contained twenty and not sixteen pages.

[130] "Gâh yağlı kâğıdımız gâh mürekkebimiz hitâmpezîr olduğundan
Nîsân nüshasını neşr edemedik. Onu noksânını başka bir sûrette ikmâl
edeceğimizi beyân ederiz.": [untitled article], *Mürşid-i Âsûriyûn*, 3, no. 4
(Hazîrân 1911), 19.

[131] "Arabiyü'l-ibâre bir müdâfaa," *Mürşid-i Âsûriyûn*, 3, no. 10 (Teşrîn-i
Sânî 1911), 164-165; *Mürşid-i Âsûriyûn*, 3, no. 1 (Kânûn-ı Sânî 1911), 4-7
and *Mürşid-i Âsûriyûn*, 3, no. 2 (Şubât 1911), 28-29.

[132] "Biz her ne kadar Süryânîce bilmez isek de Süryânîce bilen ehl-i
merâklar okumakla onları takdîr edeceklerdir." Since Âşûr Yûsuf did not
provide a translation of the letter – something he often did for English
and Armenian texts – there is no evidence that he knew Arabic either.

[133] The lack of this paper was cited as the reason for the late delivery
of the issue: "Havâdis-i mahalliye," *Mürşid-i Âsûriyûn*, 3, no. 2 (Şubât
1911), 36. The paper was also mentioned in the quote from footnote 138 .

mimeography, robust processes whereby handwritten text can be reproduced in large quantities. While this may seem a less advanced technique than moveable type, for complex scripts such as that used by the *Süryânî*, lithography or mimeography could under certain circumstances be a preferable means of printing.[134] Âşûr Yûsuf did ask his readers, "would it be reasonable for the *Süryânî* to procure cast type for the printing of newspapers at a press?", so it is clear that the limitations were financial and not technical.[135] Towards the end of 1913 there was a further announcement in *Mürşid-i Âsûriyûn* that an order had in fact been placed and that should the type arrive in time, it would be in use for printing in the issues of the coming year.[136]

---

[134] Such printing techniques was particularly widespread in Persia and the Indian subcontinent, where the *nestalîk* calligraphic style for the Arabic script was prevalent. At the same time, Syriac-language newspapers in Persia used moveable type due to the fact that the script used for writing Eastern Syriac would have been easier to cast in metal than for either the more cursive script favoured by the *Süryânî* or the complex ligatures of *nestalîk* calligraphy. See Juan R. I. Cole, "Printing and Urban Islam in the Mediterranean World, 1890-1920," in *Modernity and Culture: from the Mediterranean to the Indian Ocean*, ed. L. Fawaz and C. A. Baily (New York: Columbia University Press, 2002), 349 and Edward Granville Browne, *The Press and Poetry of Modern Persia: partly based on the manuscript work of Mírzá Muḥammad 'Alí Khán "Tarbiyat" of Tabríz* (Cambridge: University Press, 1914), 7-9 and 42. Even today, there is still at least one hand-written daily newspaper being published in India, although the *Musalman* from Chennai [Madras] is now reproduced using offset printing techniques rather than lithography or mimeography: Scott Carney, "A Handwritten Daily Paper in India Faces the Digital Future," *Wired* (July 7, 2007).

[135] Responses to the question "Süryânî milleti için matbaa hurûfâtı getirip matbaa vâsıtasıyla cerîde neşr etmek kâr-ı akl mıdır?" are printed in "Mürşid-i Âsûriyûn'un suâline cevâb," *Mürşid-i Âsûriyûn*, 5, no. 3 (Mart 1913), 41. Earlier he printed a quote of "751 frank veyâhûd 37 ½ fransız lirası", which was more than double the amount he had thus far collected for this purpose: "Matbaa hurûfâtına dâir malûmât," *Mürşid-i Âsûriyûn*, 3, no. 4 (Hazîrân 1911), 16-17.

[136] "İhtâr," *Mürşid-i Âsûriyûn*, 5, no. 12 (Teşrîn-i Sânî 1913), 196.

The price of a single copy of *Mürşid-i Âsûriyûn* in 1912 and 1913 was one *gurûş*.[137] Rates for a one year subscription were more favourable, being set at ten *gurûş* for readers in Harput or fifteen *gurûş* for those in other parts of the Ottoman Empire, postal charges included. Foreign subscribers were asked to pay one dollar or five francs. As of late 1911, Âşûr Yûsuf also had what may be described as an agent in the United States; subscription requests from American *Süryânî* were to be directed to one Hanna S. Youssouf in Worcester, Massachusetts (see Image 2 above).[138]

However, Âşûr Yûsuf repeatedly warned of the near impossibility of remaining solvent. Towards the end of his newspaper's fourth year of publication, a notice appeared stating, "we have suffered so that the *millet* [community] would profit". Over the two previous years, issues had been sent free of charge to *Süryânî* in both the Ottoman Empire and the United States, and not even the cost of postage had been forthcoming from these subscribers despite the newspaper's repeated appeals. At this point, Âşûr Yûsuf was considering the closure of *Mürşid-i Âsûriyûn* for a lack of money although in the year's remaining issues, he made it clear that he had decided not to discontinue his efforts after all.[139]

The parallel establishment of *Yeprad* and *Mürşid-i Âsûriyûn* suggests that there was either a common catalyst or perhaps even cooperation between the two publishers. It should be noted that since *Yeprad* used moveable type for printing, there is no reason to believe that there was any sharing of equipment.[140] Âşûr Yûsuf frequently included articles written by Armenians, but I have not

---

[137] At the time, a hundred *gurûş* equalled one Ottoman lira, which in turn was worth slightly less than £1 sterling.

[138] The name and address were written in the Latin alphabet. Note that Âşûr Yûsuf's spelling "Youssouf" supports my preference for the Ottoman-styled "Yûsuf" rather than "Yusef" or "Yusif", as are frequently encountered in other works.

[139] "Mühim bir ilân," *Mürşid-i Âsûriyûn*, 4, no. 7 (Teşrîn-i Sânî 1912), 110.

[140] When Âşûr Yûsuf did purchase metal type, the announcement stated that the order was for letters (*matbaa hurûfâtına sipâriş verilmiştir*). This suggests that he already had access to a printing press, although it is impossible to demonstrate that it would have been the one as used by *Yeprad*.

been able to uncover an article, or even an author, appearing in both newspapers. Moreover, I have seen only one passing reference to *Yeprad* in the pages of *Mürşid-i Âsûriyûn*, something which is surprising in light of the fact that the borrowings from other newspapers were so common.[141] Consequently, I would look outside the Euphrates College and to the 1908 revolution as having been the true motivation for the establishment of both *Yeprad* and *Mürşid-i Âsûriyûn*.

Remarkably, Âşûr Yûsuf drew on the press of not only the Ottoman Empire, but also the United States and even India, to provide material or articles for his newspaper. Ottoman publications which he used included the mainstream *İkdâm* and *İctihâd*,[142] a publication from an uncertain source, *Tan*,[143] and the *Süryânî* newspaper *Şifuro*. *İntibâh*, which was published out of the United States, was another common source, as were English-language American newspapers, notably those from Worcester, Massachusetts, the *Worcester Telegram* and the *Worcester Evening Gazette*.[144] *Râhnümâ* [Guide], from which several articles were

---

[141] *Yeprad* is mentioned in "Hukûkumuza sâhib olalım," *Mürşid-i Âsûriyûn*, 4, no. 2 (Şubât 1912), 18.

[142] Abdullah Cevdet, a Kurdish intellectual from Arapkir in the province of Mamûretü'l-Azîz, began *İctihâd* in Geneva in 1904, later publishing it in Cairo and then in Istanbul until his death in 1932. Abdullah Cevdet, sometimes accused of being an atheist, was perhaps the first to suggest the usage of the Latin alphabet for the Ottoman Turkish language (Âşûr Yûsuf's own interest in such matters will be discussed starting on page 187): Hanioğlu, "Garbcılar: Their Attitudes toward Religion and Their Impact on the Official Ideology of the Turkish Republic," *Studia Islamica* no. 86 (1997), 143.

[143] Although Âşûr Yûsuf always wrote *Tan*, no newspaper by that name is recorded as having existed at the time: Duman, *Başlangıcından Harf Devrimine Kadar Osmanlı-Türk Süreli Yayınlar ve Gazeteler Bibliografyası ve Toplu Katalogu*. The similarly-named *Tanîn* was one of the leading contemporary Ottoman newspapers, but it is difficult to imagine Âşûr Yûsuf repeatedly making such an orthographic error.

[144] "Doktor Yûsuf Türk ve Balkan muhârebesinde îfâ-yı hidmet ettikten sonra vatana avdeti," *Mürşid-i Âsûriyûn*, 5, no. 10 (Eylûl 1913), 159 and "Doktor İbrâhîm Yûsuf Türk ve Balkan muhârebesinde sekiz buçuk ay

reprinted, was an Armenian Protestant newspaper printed in Turkish using the Armenian alphabet.[145] From the press at the Central Turkey College in Antep, where Âşûr Yûsuf himself had studied, came *Yeni Ömr* [New Life], another Armenian publication with apparent Protestant affiliations.[146] Other sources included *Avedaper* [Messenger] and *Puzantiyon* [Byzantium], both Armenian newspapers published in Istanbul.[147] At least one article was also taken from an English-language newspaper named *Armenia* based in Marseilles.[148] Finally, *Western Star* was the source for events in India. Since 1863, the newspaper had been published out of Cochin [Kochi], the seat of one of the two princely states of Kerala, where India's Syriac Christians were concentrated.[149]

---

îfâ-yı hidmet ettikten sonra yine Amerika'ya avdeti," *Mürşid-i Âsûriyûn*, 5, no. 12 (Teşrîn-i Sânî 1913), 194-195.

[145] Conflicting information as to the editor – Lütfî Leonyan or R. Hovanes Krikorian (a former professor at the Central Turkey College) – and the place of publication (Antep or Istanbul) may be found in the following: Joseph K. Greene, *Leavening the Levant* (Boston: Pilgrim Press, 1916), 141; Hasmik A. Stepanyan, *Ermeni harfli Türkçe kitaplar ve süreli yayınlar bibliyografyası (1727 – 1968)* (Istanbul: Turkuaz Yayınları, 2005), 597; Duman, *Başlangıcından Harf Devrimine Kadar Osmanlı-Türk Süreli Yayınlar ve Gazeteler Bibliografyası ve Toplu Katalogu*.

[146] Every article that Âşûr Yûsuf took from *Yeni Ömr* pertained to missionaries and their work around the world. Stepanyan, *Ermeni harfli Türkçe kitaplar ve süreli yayınlar bibliyografyası*, 593-594.

[147] "Ceridelerden," *Mürşid-i Âsûriyûn*, 3, no. 8 (Eylûl 1911), 146.

[148] *Mürşid-i Âsûriyûn*, 4, no. 8 (Teşrîn-i Sânî 1912), 121. The ideas espoused by the newspaper *Armenia* were vital to the creation of the influential *Armenakan* and *Hnchakian* parties: Louise Nalbandian, *The Armenian Revolutionary Movement: the Development of Armenian Political Parties through the Nineteenth Century* (Berkeley: University of California Press, 1963): 94-106.

[149] *Mürşid-i Âsûriyûn*, 4, no. 11 (Kânûn-ı Evvel 1912), 170. Some very basic information on *Western Star* is available in Robin Jeffrey, "The Three Stages of Print: testing ideas of 'Public Sphere,' 'Print-Capitalism' and 'Public Action' in Kerala, India," in *Asia Examined: Proceedings of the 15th Biennial Conference of the ASAA, 2004, Canberra, Australia*, ed. Robert Cribb. (Canberra: Asian Studies Association of Australia, 2004). *Western Star* also appears as a source in *İntibâh*.

## Kevkeb Mednho

*Kevkeb Mednho* was published once every other Saturday in the city of Diyarbakır by Naûm Fâik, a teacher at the local *Süryânî* school and deacon in the Jacobite church.[150] In his biography of Naûm Fâik, Fuat Çıkkı states that there were 26 issues of *Kevkeb Mednho* in the first year and 17 in the second.[151] The same source gives 27 April 1910 as the date of the first issue and 27 April 1912 as the last, but in actuality, the first issue appeared on 16 July 1910. The date of the final instance of *Kevkeb Mednho* can only be calculated based on the information provided by Çıkkı that there were 17 issues in the second year. Projecting forward from the final copy in my possession, number 14, *Kevkeb Mednho* ceased publication on 27 July 1912.

In Turkish-language sources, *Kevkeb Mednho* is sometimes called *Kevkeb Şark* or *Şark Yıldızı*, while in other languages it may be *Kukhwa Madnha*, *Kukhwa d-Madinha* or something similar. Note that Naûm Fâik never wrote the name with the relative particle *d-*, instead preferring the classical Syriac construct. He used two Ottoman Turkish translations for the Syriac name of his paper: the Turkish *Şark Yıldızı* and the Arabic *Kevkebü'ş-Şark*.[152] Using the Arabic alphabet, he wrote كوكب مدنحا [Kevkeb Mednhâ].[153] In selecting *Kevkeb Mednho*, I have tried to imagine how Naûm Fâik's Ottoman Turkish-speaking readership would have interpreted the name of his newspaper, especially considering the placement of vowel points on the masthead of *Kevkeb Mednho* and in Âşûr Yûsuf's writing. My use of this more Ottoman Turkish form may be questionable, but I have opted to do so as part of a conscious

---

[150] The masthead contains the phrase "presently published once every fifteen days (*muvakkaten on beş günde bir defa neşr olunur*)", but it was clearly issued once every fourteen days. The same statement is observable on other Ottoman publications, such as the first Kurdish-language newspaper, *Kürdistân*.

[151] Çıkkı, *Naum Faik ve Süryani Rönesansı*, 56.

[152] These may be seen in "Tebrîk," *Kevkeb Mednho*, 1, no. 16 (11 Şubât 1911), 7 and "Tebrîk," *Kevkeb Mednho*, 1, no. 19 (25 Mart 1911), 7 respectively.

[153] "Dicle cerîde-i ferîdesi," *Kevkeb Mednho*, 1, no. 19 (25 Mart 1911), 8.

effort to situate *Kevkeb Mednho* as well as *Mürşid-i Âsûriyûn* in their proper Ottoman context.

The layout of *Kevkeb Mednho* followed a standard format over its two year existence. It was printed on eight 25×36 centimetre pages, each of which contained two columns of text.[154] Like *Mürşid-i Âsûriyûn*, the Diyarbakır paper was reproduced using lithography or mimeography and appeared entirely in the Western Syriac script.[155] It differed, however, in that it was a trilingual publication; a clear majority of text was, again, in Ottoman Turkish, but it also contained a significant number of Arabic-language articles and a smaller number in literary Syriac, again using the Western Syriac alphabet. The breakdown between the three languages varied from issue to issue, but the distribution remained consistent. There was less borrowing from or commentary on articles from other newspapers in *Kevkeb Mednho* than in *Mürşid-i Âsûriyûn*, although Naûm Fâik does appear to have been a reader of Âşûr Yûsuf's publication as well as the other *Süryânî* periodicals.[156]

The masthead did change somewhat over time but the basic layout remained constant. *Kevkeb Mednho* was priced slightly higher than *Mürşid-i Âsûriyûn*. In early 1911, a one year subscription cost 17 *guruş*; with postage, the price was 20 *guruş* for those in the Ottoman Empire and 25 for foreign subscribers. There was an increase towards the end of the year, with the rates being 20 *guruş* for Diyarbakır, 25 *guruş* for elsewhere in the Ottoman Empire and $1.50 for the United States.

---

[154] The dimensions are recorded in Tütengil, *Diyarbakır Basın Tarihi*, 21. The first two issues appeared with only four pages due to a shortage of quality paper in Diyarbakır: *Kevkeb Mednho*, 1 no. 2 (31 Temmûz 1910), 1. By the third issue, Naûm Fâik had rectified this problem.

[155] On one occasion, an article was printed using the Arabic alphabet: "Dicle Cerîde-i Ferîdesi," *Kevkeb Mednho*, 1, no. 19 (25 Mart 1911), 8. This, a letter to the local newspaper *Dicle*, was meant for general, not merely *Süryânî*, consumption.

[156] See, for example, "Mutrân İlyâs efendinin Mârdîn'e azîmeti," *Kevkeb Mednho*, 1, no. 22 (6 Mayıs 1911), 20.

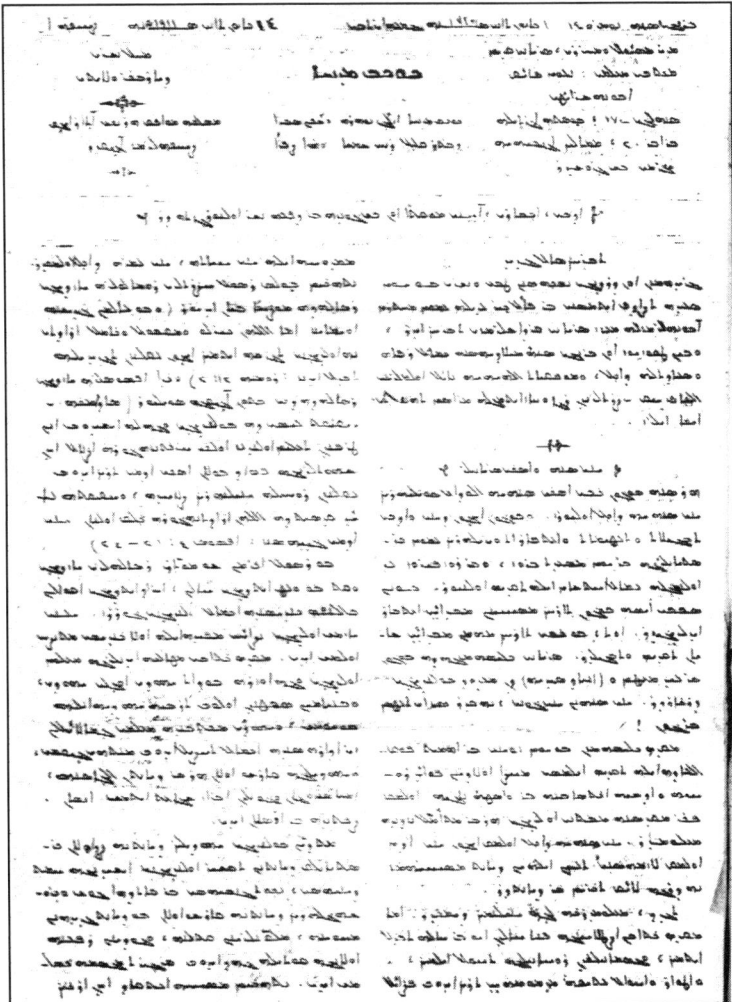

Image 3 – *Kevkeb Mednho*

On Naûm Fâik's life and activities outside the publishing of *Kevkeb Mednho*, much information is given in Çıkkı's work. Born in 1868 to İlyâs and Seyyide, Naûm İlyâs Palak – later nicknamed *fâik* [the excellent] – received a primary and secondary education in his native Diyarbakır, learning Syriac, Arabic, Ottoman Turkish and Farsi. At the age of twenty, he began teaching, first in Diyarbakır and then in a village in the *kazâ* of Garzan in the *vilâyet* of Bitlis.

Over the next decade he taught in *Süryânî* schools in a number of locations (Urfa, Hısn-ı Mansûr and Homs) and spent time at monasteries in Beirut and Jerusalem. Returning to Diyarbakır in 1904, Naûm Fâik took up teaching once again and began running the printing press for the metropolitanate and the community council.[157] His works there continued until 1912, when he made the decision to emigrate, and so Naûm settled with his family in Paterson, New Jersey, the home of most Diyarbakır *Süryânî* in the United States. Unless otherwise noted, my discussions and understanding of Naûm Fâik will concern only the period prior to his leaving the Ottoman Empire.[158]

Naûm Fâik is celebrated for more than his journalism, however; he was instrumental in setting up the *İntibâh Cemiyeti* [Society of the Awakening], a *Süryânî* charitable organisation with branches around the Ottoman Empire and in the United States.[159] Additionally, he authored or translated some thirty-four books on numerous subjects, but especially those related to the *Süryânî*, their history and their language.[160] Naûm Fâik passed away in 1930, and is still eulogised today for his intellectual activities and for being one of the most ardent proponents of Assyrian nationalism, despite the fact that very little of his work is available today.

---

[157] Çıkk, *Naum Faik ve Süryani Rönesansı*, 21-28.

[158] In addition, my reading of Naûm Fâik is almost entirely limited to the Ottoman Turkish-language articles from the issues of *Kevkeb Mednho* in my possession. The occasional exceptions – either translations from other languages or articles appearing in *İntibâh* – will be mentioned.

[159] *İntibâh* will be discussed in detail below on page 163. It must be noted that there was also a Naûm Palak in the United States who was active in the *Süryânî* community. His letters and articles about his activities often appeared in *İntibâh* and, like Naûm Fâik, he was involved in the *İntibâh Cemiyeti*, though in this case, the Paterson branch. I have made every effort to distinguish between the two, but I believe that the two have sometimes been confused in other sources.

[160] A complete list of his works maybe found in Çıkk, *Naum Faik ve Süryani Rönesansı*, 74-97.

## Şifuro, el-Hikmet and the Harput Periodicals

Naûm Fâik receives most of the credit for the publication of *Kevkeb Mednho*, but there should also be recognition of the efforts of Beşâr Hilmî [Edîb Beşâr Borucu] both in supporting the newspaper during its short existence and for maintaining the presence of Syriac journalism in Diyarbakır after 1912 with a publication of his own, *Şifuro*.[161] The first issue of *Kevkeb Mednho*, for example, indicated that Beşâr Hilmî had covered all the expenses for the establishment of the newspaper, and according to one source, he also published one issue of *Kevkeb Mednho* following Naûm Fâik's emigration from Diyarbakır in September of 1912.[162] This latter claim, however, is difficult to reconcile with the fact that *Şifuro* was already appearing by that time.

Beşâr Hilmî's publishing of *Şifuro*, was – in terms of duration at least – more successful than *Kevkeb Mednho*. Secondary sources invariably state that Beşâr Hilmî established his publication in 1912 as a continuation of the abandoned *Kevkeb Mednho*, following closely the format of the older newspaper, with the same dimensions, layout and frequency of publication. However, the first issue of *Şifuro* dates to 14 Mayıs 1327 [27 May 1911], and indeed, Naûm Fâik printed in *Kevkeb Mednho* an article – which also appeared on 14 May 1911 – concerning the first issue of *Şifuro*.[163]

---

[161] Çıkkı, *Naum Faik ve Süryani Rönesansı*, 59. Çıkkı (in translation) gives his name as Edip Beşar Burucu Efendi whereas Başar Hilmi Boreji is given in Yonan, "Asurlar'da Gazetecilik," *Hujâdâ* 12, no. 7/8 (Juli-Agusti 1989), 38 and Bişar Hilmi Borucu in Gabriyel Akyüz, *Tüm Yönleriyle Süryaniler* (Mardin: Kırklar Kilisesi, 2005), 299. According to one secondary source, there was a *Süryânî* Burucu family in Diyarbakır following the establishment of the Turkish Republic: Şimşek, *Süryaniler ve Diyarbakır*, 2nd ed. (Istanbul: Chiviyazıları, 2003), 132-135. But considering the name of Beşâr Hilmî's own newspaper, *Şifuro* [Trumpet], it seems possible that he was known as *borucu* [trumpeter].

[162] Yonan, "Asurlar'da Gazetecilik," *Hujâdâ* 12, no. 7/8 (Juli-Agusti 1989), 38.

[163] Tütengil again printed the dimensions and layout of *Şifuro*, and they are identical to *Kevkeb Mednho*, although the former had four rather than eight pages per issue: *Diyarbakır Basın Tarihi*, 21-22. Amongst those who have given this incorrect date for the start of *Şifuro* are: Akyüz, *Tüm*

Image 4 – *Şifuro*

*Yönleriyle Süryaniler*, 229-300; BarAbrahem, "The Question of Assyrian Journalism Revisited," 5; Benjamin, "Assyrian Journalism," 9; and Yonan, "Asurlar'da Gazetecilik," *Hujådå* 12, no. 7/8 (Juli-Agusti 1989), 38.

Despite the fact it began appearing in 1911, issues of *Şifuro* from 1913 continue to indicate that the publication was still in its first year of operation, something which possibly indicates that Beşâr Hilmî did in fact work on *Kevkeb Mednho* for some period in 1912. In any case, Beşâr Hilmî would continue to issue his own newspaper until was killed on the outskirts of Diyarbakır in 1914.[164]

Interestingly, although *Şifuro* was written entirely in Ottoman Turkish, half of the text was in "plain Turkish" (*sâde Türkçe*), meaning that it was written in the Arabic alphabet, while for the other half, the Syriac alphabet was employed. Later issues may have been entirely in the Syriac script, but there is not enough evidence to state this with certainty. With respect to the press, Naûm Fâik explicitly stated that Beşâr Hilmî was employing a mimeograph machine for printing, presumably the same that was used for *Kevkeb Mednho*. The announced prices were 15 *guruş* for domestic and 20 *guruş* for international subscriptions.[165]

Mardin-based *el-Hikmet* was a short-lived publication containing articles written in Arabic; rarely, texts in Syriac or Ottoman Turkish, with the latter being in the Arabic alphabet, also appeared in the journal. Unlike the other *Süryânî* periodicals, *el-Hikmet* had close ties to the Jacobite religious hierarchy, being printed at the *Deyrü'z-Zaferân* monastery, the seat of the Patriarch. The first issue appeared in August of 1913, but as with *Şifuro* and *Mürşid-i Âsûriyûn*, publication ceased at about the time of the outbreak of hostilities, the last issue appearing in July of the following year.[166]

---

[164] Şimşek, *Süryaniler ve Diyarbakır*, 202-203; Akyüz, *Tüm Yönleriyle Süryaniler*, 299.

[165] "Şifuro yani Boru cerîdesi," *Kevkeb Mednho*, 1, no. 24 (3 Hazîrân 1911), 28. Âşûr Yûsuf mentions the first issuance of *Şifuro* as well, though only incidentally: "Âsâr-ı atîka zuhûru," *Mürşid-i Âsûriyûn*, 3, no. 4 (Hazîrân 1911), 11.

[166] Âşûr Yûsuf's announcement of *el-Hikmet*'s establishment indicated that the language and alphabet were exclusively Arabic: "Ve diğeri (el-Hikmet) nâmla Arabiyü'l-ibâre Arabî hurûfâtıyla müellefi Mîhâîl Hikmet Çıkkı Efendi Mârdîn'de Deyrü-z'Zaferân matbaasından sâha-ı vücûda gelmekte ve memûl ederiz ki muhteviyâtıyla Arab Süryânîlerine pek çok

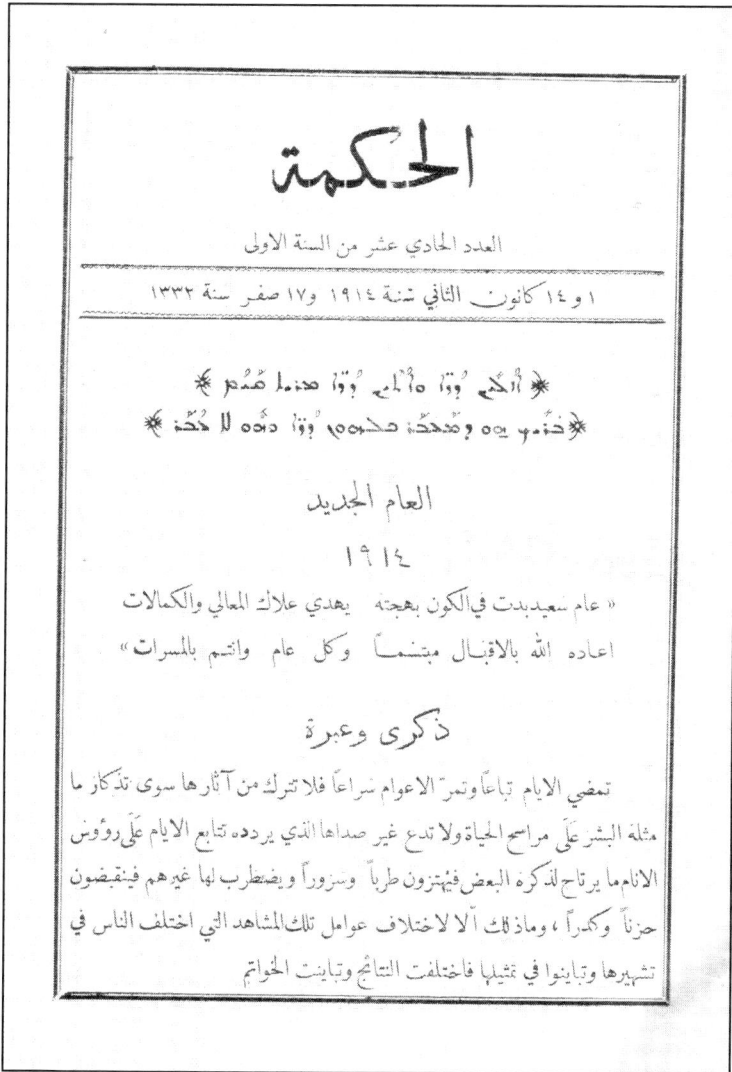

Image 5 – *el-Hikmet*

fâideli olacaktır." See "Süryânîler için iki yeni cerîde dahâ," *Mürşid-i Âsûri-yûn*, 5 no. 9 (Ağustos 1913), 148.

The paper had a readership throughout the Ottoman Empire as well as subscribers in the United States, Canada and Argentina.[167] Following the war, *el-Hikmet* was revived in Jerusalem once more with the support of the Patriarchate, with issues appearing between the years 1927 and 1931. Finally, in 1952, the Turkish-language *Öz Hikmet* began circulation, again in Mardin, until it was closed by a court decision in 1955.[168]

The three remaining *Süryânî* publications in the Ottoman Empire, *Kevkbo d-Suryoye*, *Hayât* and *Safro d-Nuhro*, were all short-lived and based in Harput. *Kevkbo d-Suryoye* was published by the *mutrân* of Harput, Abdünnûr, in Ottoman Turkish, Arabic and Syriac, while a local *keşîş*, Pavlûs, issued the Ottoman Turkish-language *Hayât*.[169]

The only known copy of *Hayât* to have survived mentioned the final publication, *Safro d-Nuhro*, which probably also appeared out of Harput.[170] The author of the article mentioned that "the nephew of *mehâneci* [tavern keeper] Donabed" had contributed to *Safro d-Nuhro*. The Donabed family is from Harput, though by this time, there were also members living in Massachusetts. In any case, as reported by *Mürşid-i Âsûriyûn*, neither *Kevkbo d-Suryoye* nor *Hayât* managed to survive until the end of 1910.[171]

---

[167] See the back cover of *el-Hikmet*, 1, no. 3 (11 Eylûl 1913).

[168] Taşğın, "Sezginin ve Bilgeliğin Sembolü: Öz Hikmet Dergisi," in *Süryaniler ve Süryanilik*, vol. 4, 51-56.

[169] See "İctimâ-ı umûmî müntahabları," *Kevkeb Mednho*, 1, no. 5 (10 Eylûl 1910), 2 and "Hayât," *Kevkeb Mednho*, 1, no. 9 (5 Teşrîn-i Sânî 1910), 8. A list of the contents of *Kevkbo d-Suryoye* from its first issue were published by Cebbûr Boyacı: "Kevkbo d-Suryoye, yani Kevkebü'l-Süryân cerîdesi," *İntibâh*, 1, no. 8 (Hazîrân 1910), 7.

[170] See *Hayât*, 1, no. 4 (21 Eylûl 1910), 2.

[171] In a summary of the important events of 1910, Âşûr Yûsuf wrote that "(Kevkbo d-Suryoye [ܟܘܟܒܐ ܕܣܘܪ̈ܝܐ] ve Hayât) nâm iki cerîdenin doğ-ması ile ölmesi bir oldu. Ama (Kevkeb Mednho [ܟܘܟܒ ܡܕܢܚܐ]) muktedir bir el ile devâm olunup milletimize hidmet etmekdedir.": "Geriye doğru bir atf-ı nikâh," *Mürşid-i Âsûriyûn*, 3, no. 1 (Kânûn-ı Sânî 1911), 3.

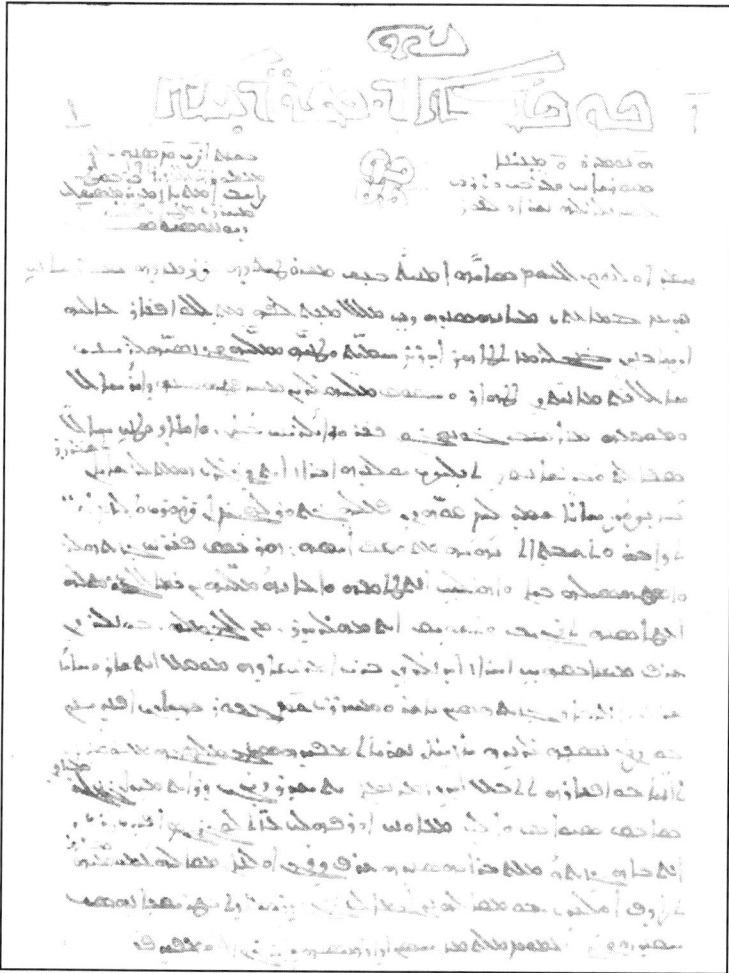

Image 6 – *Kevkbo d-Suryoye*

### İntibâh and Savto d-Oromoye

Two further publications deserve mention here despite the fact that they were not published in the Ottoman Empire itself. Following his emigration to the United States at the turn of the century,

Cebbûr Boyacı, another native of Diyarbakır, established *İntibâh* [Awakening] in 1909.[172] This monthly publication, based in College Point, New York, appeared trilingually in Ottoman Turkish, Syriac and Arabic and it had a similar level of influence as the two other newspapers which are the primary focus of this study. In fact, based on the subscriber lists, there is reason to believe that *İntibâh* was the most widely-read of the *Süryânî* periodicals. In the Ottoman Empire, Cebbûr Boyacı had arranged for individuals in Diyarbakır, Harput, İstanbul and Baghdad to act as his agents in the collection of subscription dues.[173]

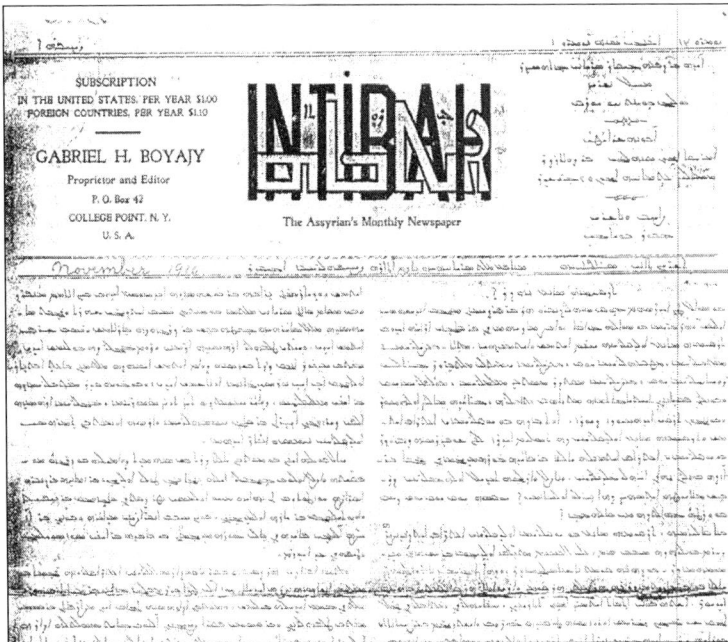

Image 7 – *İntibâh*

As mentioned above, a number of *İntibâh* articles were republished in *Mürşid-i Âsûriyûn* to much praise, and the editor also

---

[172] In English he gives his first name as Gabriel.
[173] "Türkiye'de vekîllerimiz," *İntibâh*, 4, no. 1 (Teşrîn-i Sânî 1912), 8.

provided responses to Âşûr Yûsuf's frequent appeals for ideas on reform in the *Süryânî* community at large. *İntibâh* differed from the publications based in the Ottoman Empire differed in that it contained much more of what could be termed current events. *İntibâh* closed in 1915, after beginning to appear irregularly during late 1914. Naûm Fâik would more or less open the same publication but under the name *Bethnahrin* [Mesopotamia], publishing it biweekly from 1916 until 1926, excluding a short stretch in 1921 and 1922 during which he worked on another newspaper, *Huyodo* [Unity].[174]

The *Süryânî* cultural and educational organisation known as the *İntibâh Cemiyeti* does not appear to have had any direct links to the newspaper of the same name although they shared, along with *Mürşid-i Âsûriyûn* and *Kevkeb Mednho*, much in common with respect to their goals. On the other hand, *Savto d-Oromoye* [Voice of the Aramaeans], run by Diyarbakır native Senharîb Bâlî [Balley], is known to have been a publication of the *İntibâh Cemiyeti* in the United States. An article in the August 1913 issue of *Mürşid-i Âsûriyûn* announced the establishment *Savto d-Oromoye* (and *el-Hikmet*), stating that its language of publication would again be Ottoman Turkish with Syriac letters.[175] That Âşûr Yûsuf printed a lengthy response to an article that had appeared in *Savto d-Oromoye*

---

[174] Çıkkı, *Naum Faik ve Süryani Rönesansı*, 68 and Akyüz, *Tüm Yönleriyle Süryaniler*, 296 and 305.

[175] Akyüz, *Tüm Yönleriyle Süryaniler*, 300 and "Süryânîler için iki yeni cerîde dahâ," *Mürşid-i Âsûriyûn*, 5 no. 9 (Ağustos 1913), 148. Âşûr Yûsuf also referred to *Savto d-Oromoye* by its Ottoman Turkish form, *Ârâmîlerin Sadâsı*. Secondary-source references to this newspaper – that of Akyüz excepted – incorrectly ascribe to it the name "Voice of the Assyrians", but with Âşûr Yûsuf giving both the Syriac original (ܐܪܡܝܐ، ܩܠܐ) and the Ottoman Turkish translation, there can be little doubt that the reading here is the correct one. *İntibâh* also recorded the same names in Syriac and Ottoman Turkish. For examples of "Voice of the Assyrians", see *Ünlü Asurlardan (Kildanilerden, Süryanilerden) Seçmeler II*, ed. Kuroš Hërmëz Nazlu (Södertälje, Sweden: Nsibin Yayınevi, 1996), 63-65 and Benjamin, "Assyrian Journalism," 27.

suggests that he was a subscriber.[176] In late 1913, Cebbûr Boyacı levelled an accusation of being an Armenian mouthpiece at *Savto d-Oromoye*, saying that the publication's board of directors had asked Sabrî *hoca*, an Armenian immigrant from Diyarbakır, to serve as editor. Cebbûr Boyacı was further incensed that the *İntibâh Cemiyeti* was planning to pay $1.50 per article for Sabrî *hoca*'s services.[177]

Other periodicals affiliated with *Süryânî* in the United States prior to World War II included *The New Assyria*, *Bethnahrin*, *Huyodo*, *The Aramean*, *Babil* and *Assyrian Progress*. Of these, *The New Assyria*, *Bethnahrin*, *Huyodo* and *Babil* were wholly or partially written in Ottoman Turkish; *The Aramean* and *Assyrian Progress* were written in Arabic and English respectively, while *Babil* was predominantly in Armenian, with a smaller number of Ottoman and English articles. These fall outside the scope of this work though I have consulted them on occasion for the background information they provide.

### Importance of the Press

Most signed articles in *Kevkeb Mednho* are directly attributable to Naûm Fâik by name or as *muharrir* but the newspaper's practice of accepting submissions means that there are frequently articles contributed by *Süryânî* from locations outside Diyarbakır. The statement "our pages are open to all works in accordance with our goals" appeared on the front page of each issue and indicates that *Kevkeb Mednho* intended to serve as something of a forum for Ottoman *Süryânî* to express what was important to them.[178] In *İntibâh*, Cebbûr Boyacı or *muharrir* is most frequently encountered, although in late issues, Naûm Fâik's name began to appear directly as the author of some articles.

Similarly, many of the articles in *Mürşid-i Âsûriyûn* are signed by Âşûr Yûsuf himself. Alternatively, many bear the signature

---

[176] "Yine Hindistân meselesi," *Mürşid-i Âsûriyûn*, 5 no. 13 (Kânûn-ı Evvel 1913), 206-211.

[177] "Ârâmîlerin Sadâsı, Ermenî borusundan çıkıyor," *İntibâh*, 5, no. 1 (Teşrîn-i Sânî 1913), 8.

[178] Whether the target audience were the *Süryânî-i Kadîm*, all *Süryânî* or all Syriac Christians is a complicated question which will be addressed at length below.

*mürşid* [guide], *muharrir* [editor] or *muharrir-i mürşid* [editor of *Mürşid*], all of which were almost certainly *noms de plume* of Âşûr Yûsuf himself, although they could possibly refer to his purported assistant, Yakûb Denho. For the purposes of my study, I have treated all of these as the works of Âşûr Yûsuf exclusively as there is no evidence to the contrary. A significant number were also contributed by *Süryânî* from around the Ottoman Empire or from the United States; in such cases the author's name was given in full or as initials, or alternatively the article was ascribed simply to *muhabir* [reporter]. Naûm Fâik himself is said to have contributed to *Mürşid-i Âsûriyûn*, but no such attribution exists in the issues which I have examined.[179]

We are also faced with the question of consumption, something which is notoriously difficult to gauge. The distribution of readership may be estimated for the *Süryânî* press thanks to the articles and letters written by readers. Even more fortuitously, in *Kevkeb Mednho* and *İntibâh*, subscribers arranged according to city or region of residence were periodically listed on the journals' final page. This does not amount to circulation figures, but I have established the existence of subscribers in numerous locations, including Istanbul, Adana, Urfa, Mosul, Jerusalem, Homs, Hama, Baghdad, Aleppo, Damascus, Beirut and Zahle, besides the core areas of *Süryânî* settlement. There were even subscribers in places such as Samsun, Salonika and Kosovo, where *Süryânî* would probably be found only as government officials. Outside the Ottoman Empire, there were readers from as far away as Egypt, Tbilisi, the United States, Canada, Argentina and India.[180] For *Mürşid-i Âsûriyûn*, we actually have a figure for the number of subscribers in 1910; according to an article in *Kevkeb Mednho* it was no more than 70 or 80 individuals, something Naûm Fâik

---

[179] Çıkkı, *Naum Faik ve Süryani Rönesansı*, 54.

[180] Subscribers in Canada appear to have been restricted to Montreal, while those in the United States were in primarily in New Jersey, Massachusetts, Rhode Island and New York, with single instances from Maryland, Illinois and California.

considered to be frustratingly small for what was the first Ottoman *Süryânî* periodical.[181]

Reviewing the names of letter writers and lists of subscribers, we first note that there were many religious figures, from the rank of *mutrân* [metropolitan] down to *keşîş* [priest] and *şemmâs* [deacon], among them.[182] The *Süryânî-i Kadîm* Patriarch even wrote a letter to *İntibâh* from India in 1910, so even if he was not a subscriber, he nevertheless felt the influence of the press to be sufficiently high that he should explain his activities to the *Süryânî* public through it.[183] There is a good chance that every *mutrân* received copies of *Mürşid-i Âsûriyûn* or *Kevkeb Mednho* although I do not have evidence for each figure. But we do know that lower ranking clergymen in places such as Vîrânşehir, Bitlis, Siirt, Adana, Meyyâfârkîn and Venk (near Malatya) were subscribers. Several monasteries or schools were also recipients: *Deyrü'z-Zaferân*, *Mar Markos* (Jerusalem), the school teacher Nâsîf in Hama and the *Süryânî* schools of Urfa and Adana. Moreover, in some instances, subscribers were explicitly described as the congregation as a whole, for example in the villages of Keferdiz, Ağvan (between Harput and Malatya) and Gerger (near Hısn-ı Mansûr), or as a local organisation, such as the members of the *İntibâh Cemiyeti* in Siirt.[184] It is therefore clear then that one subscription did not necessarily equate one reader; Âşûr Yûsuf himself alluded to this fact when he said that besides reading the newspaper, his subscribers were "to encourage others to read [it]."[185]

Therefore, in both cases we can establish that there was an active and geographically dispersed readership who, through their

---

[181] "Mürşid-i Âsûriyûn cerîdesi," *Kevkeb Mednho*, 1, no. 18 (11 Mart 1910), 7-8.

[182] For a full explanation of church hierarchy see page 79 below.

[183] "Patrikimizden mektûb," *İntibâh*, 2, no. 2 (Kânûn-ı Evvel 1909), 4.

[184] See "Hediyeler," *Mürşid-i Âsûriyûn*, 5, no. 6 (Mayıs 1913), 88-90, "İntibâh hediyesi," *İntibâh*, 2, no. 3 (Kânûn-ı Sânî 1911), 8 and "Abone vusûlü," *Kevkeb Mednho*, 2, no. 5 (7 Teşrîn-i Evvel 1911), 8.

[185] "Mühim bir ilân," *Mürşid-i Âsûriyûn*, 4, no. 7 (Teşrîn-i Sânî 1912), 111: "Biz memûl eder ettik ki millettaşlarımız kendi milletlerine mahsûs cerîdelere mâlik olmalarını bermûcib-i bereket addedip çokları onu kırâat ettikten başka sâirleri de okumağa teşvîk edeceklerdir."

letters and contributions, shared many of the same concerns and beliefs as Âşûr Yûsuf and Naûm Fâik. But at the same time, we must recognise that the majority of *Süryânî* – probably the vast majority – were illiterate rural dwellers without access to the education available to those in centres such as Diyarbakır, Harput, Urfa or Mardin.[186] The oral transmission of newspaper content would have gome some ways to bridging this gap. For this reason, the fact that subscriptions were often held in the hands of public figures or jointly by the community members is an important point to make.

However, many *Süryânî* would have been incapable of understanding *Kevkeb Mednho* or *İntibâh*, and especially *Mürşid-i Âsûriyûn*, even if it was read to them simply because they could not speak the language of publication. In many locations, knowledge of Ottoman Turkish might have been limited to those who needed the language for dealing with the authorities or for business purposes.[187] Furthermore, it should also be noted that *Kevkeb Mednho* saw itself first of all as a literary journal and that accordingly, the Ottoman Turkish employed by Naûm Fâik was considerably more sophisticated than the spoken vernacular or even that found in the pages of *Mürşid-i Âsûriyûn* and *İntibâh*.[188]

---

[186] That being said, Ottoman government sources recorded 49 *ihtidâiye* (primary), 5 *rüşdiye* (middle) and 1 *idâdiye* (high) schools belonging to the *Süryânî* in 1897, so educational opportunities were by no means limited to the large centres. Özcoşar, "Süryani Kiliselerinde Eğitim," in *Süryaniler ve Süryanilik*, vol. 1, 201. These numbers may be compared with the some 150 *Süryânî* villages said to exist in the Cebel-i Tûr region alone: Perley, "The Jacobites," 107.

[187] de Courtois, *The Forgotten Genocide*, 17-18 and 64. Unfortunately, there are no references offered as substantiation for his claim that only people in such positions could understand Ottoman Turkish.

[188] Naûm Fâik evidently saw little need to follow the practice of the government-run provincial press in using a more "popular tongue (*lisân-ı umûmî*)" understandable by all: İsmail Eren, "La presse turque en Yougoslavie (1866-1986)," in *Presse turque et presse de Turquie*, ed. N. Clayer, A. Popovic and T. Zarcone (Istanbul: Isis Press, 1992), 279. As we will see, Âşûr Yûsuf actively subscribed to this belief.

Elsewhere, many *Süryânî* are known to have been native speakers of Kurdish.[189] In Mardin, Arabic was the dominant language, so much so that it replaced Syriac not only amongst the general populace but even at the monastery of *Deyrü'z-Zaferân*, where the Patriarchate was centred.[190] *Kevkeb Mednho*, and to a lesser extent *İntibâh*, did cater to the Arabophone *Süryânî*, but those in Cebel-i Tûr would have been disadvantaged by the fact that the Syriac used by Naûm Fâik was the literary tongue, a language unintelligible to speakers of the local Ṭūroyo dialect.

Finally, a claim also exists that all Christians spoke Armenian exclusively in Diyarbakır, Urfa and wherever else there was a high Armenian population.[191] An early twentieth-century observer remarked that in Harput – and indeed the *vilâyet* of Mamûretü'l-Azîz as a whole – there were only a handful of Syriac speakers and that the local *Süryânî* preferred to use Turkish for their outside affairs and Armenian amongst themselves.[192] Likewise in the province of Bitlis, Armenian was the native language of the Syriac Christians, who even used it in church services.[193] We may also add to this the supposition that Armenian was the language

---

[189] In 1888, Naûm Fâik taught in a village where all the *Süryânî* were Kurdish-speaking: Çıkkı, *Naum Faik ve Süryani Rönesansı*, 22. A recent example of such a situation in Cebel-i Tûr may be found in Ramazan Aras, *Migration and Memory: Assyrian Identity in Mardin Kerboran/Dargeçit* (Master's thesis, Boğaziçi University, 2005). Gabriyel Akyüz suggests that some articles in *Kevkeb Mednho* were written in Kurdish: *Tüm Yönleriyle Süryaniler*, 296. Âşûr Yûsuf at one point requested his readers to write articles in Kurdish so that more Kurdish-speakers could benefit: "... Kürd Süryânîlerine cerîdelerimizden bir hisse çıkarmak için Kürdceye âşînâ olanlardan arasıra Kürdce bendler dahi yazıp veyâ yazdırıp neşr etmelerini refiklerimizden ricâ ederim." See "Süryânî lisânının kesb-i hayâtı," *Mürşid-i Âsûriyûn*, 5, no. 13 (Kânûn-ı Evvel 1913), 206.

[190] "Süryânî lisânının kesb-i hayâtı," *Mürşid-i Âsûriyûn*, 5, no. 13 (Kânûn-ı Evvel 1913), 202.

[191] de Courtois, *The Forgotten Genocide*, 17 and 64. Some anecdotal evidence is given by the author to back up his claim but no source is referenced.

[192] Sunguroğlu, *Harput Yollarında*, vol. 1, 258.

[193] Mesrob Krikorian, *Armenians in the Service of the Ottoman Empire* (London: Routledge & Kegan Paul, 1977), 117 n.2.

which Âşûr Yûsuf, whose wife was Armenian, spoke at home, something supported by the fact that two of his children published books in Armenian.[194] Likewise, the Armenian-language newspaper for *Süryânî*, *Babil*, was published in Boston in 1920 and 1921 by a group which also published pamphlets in the same language.[195] There was even a Syriac-language bible printed in the Armenian alphabet.[196]

In terms of written languages, Ottoman Turkish and Arabic were the most practical options for reaching the widest possible audience. Syriac remained an ideological choice, the ideal to which Naûm Fâik and others wished to adhere; it was acknowledged, however, that using Syriac was ultimately not a suitable means of communicating with the larger community since it would be "without meaning and without benefit" in the words of Âşûr Yûsuf.[197]

Ottoman Turkish would only fall by the wayside as the preferred medium of communication with the end of World War I, after which time few *Süryânî* remained in the Turkish Republic, the majority now residing in English or Arabic-speaking regions. The adoption of the Latin alphabet in the late 1920s and then the Turkish language "reforms" of the 1930s would spell the end of Ottoman Turkish as a living tongue, although the Beirut-based *Süryânî* biweekly *Leşono d-Umto* continued to appear in Ottoman Turkish even as this process was occurring inside Turkey.

---

[194] The two books are Alis Nazaryan's *Արիւնոտ Ժայռող* and Rasîn Âşûr Yûsuf's unpublished, handwritten account of his father's life.

[195] See the aforementioned *Աառւող Անգռւզակաքան Ռահվիրան*.

[196] "Süryânîyü'l-hurûf Ermenîce bir İncil meselesi," *İntibâh*, 5, no. 7 (Hazîrân 1914), 2.

[197] "Lakin şunu da ilâve etmeliyiz ki şu eserler Türkî ve Arabî lisânlar ile mahlût olmalı yoksa Türk Süryânîleri için manâsız ve fâidesiz olacaktır.": "1913 senesi takvîmi," *Mürşid-i Âsûriyûn*, 5, no. 8 (Temmûz 1913), 130.

# 2 THE OTTOMAN *MİLLET* SYSTEM

The Ottoman *millet* system was a means for the Ottoman government to administer its non-Muslim population using the religious authorities as the mediators between the state and people. Each Ottoman non-Muslim perforce belonged to either the Armenian, Greek Orthodox or Jewish *millet*, with Catholic, Protestant and other communities only later being recognised as distinct. Thus, an Ottoman Bulgarian in the mid-nineteenth century belonged to the Orthodox *millet* by virtue of his religion and remained so irrespective of where he chose to reside within the Empire. He paid taxes to Orthodox (usually Greek) clergymen, who then passed the funds on to the state, and was subject to Orthodox rules, regulations and, should the need arise, legal action.

Much of the literature concerning Syriac Christians continually treats the *millet* system as if it was an practice common to all Middle Eastern states, unchanging over time. We read, for example, that in Persia, the *millet* system "was established ... during Sassanid rule in the third century A.D."[198] While it clearly drew on the Islamic principle of the *dhimmī* (Turkish *zimmî*) – the "people of the book" – the *millet* system was an administrative practice unique to the Ottoman Empire.[199]

However, it is now acknowledged that even in the Ottoman administration the word *millet* did not always have the meaning which was ascribed to it in the nineteenth century. During the reorganising and recentralising of the *Tanzîmât* (1839-1876), the *millet* system became what is familiar from the secondary literature.

---

[198] Ishaya, "Ethnicity, Class, and Politics," 4-5.

[199] The fact that the word *millet*, although borrowed into Ottoman Turkish from Arabic, may well have its origins in Syriac – albeit with a different meaning – may help to explain the attraction to the term: Frederick Denny, "Some Religio-Communal Terms and Concepts in the Qur'ān," *Numen* 24, fasc. 1 (April, 1977), 34-35.

Prior to this time, the inconsistencies in nomenclature (*cemâat*, *tâife*, *diyânet* were amongst the terms used) "strongly suggests that there was no overall administrative system, structure, or set of institutions for dealing with non-Muslims."[200]

In the first chapter there have been several references to the Armenians and other non-Muslims of the Ottoman Empire, but in this chapter, the other communities will constitute the focus to formulate a context for a discussion of the *Süryânî*. In the Armenian case, the foremost rationale is that the very same comparison appears overtly in the pages of *Mürşid-i Âsûriyûn*, there used as a means of measuring the successes and failures of the *Süryânî* community's own attempts to reform and advance themselves. But even without such a motivation, the desire to address the *Süryânî* as Ottomans necessitates a look at the formation and parallel activities found in the other non-Muslim communities. The Armenians, Greeks and Jews each experienced the upheavals of the nineteenth century in their own way, producing different movements, different internal conflicts and different reactions to the political restructurings that accompanied the revolution of 1908 and the return to constitutional rule.

One difference between the Armenian and Greek cases on the one hand and the *Süryânî* case on the other is that in the former, there was a clear geographic distinction between the urban intellectual centres and the rural areas in which the bulk of the population lived. But with the *Süryânî*, these were essentially collapsed into one single location: Diyarbakır and Harput, the centres of Syriac intellectual activity, were in the immediate vicinity of Mardin and the most heavily *Süryânî* region, Cebel-i Tûr.[201]

---

[200] Benjamin Braude, "Foundation Myths of the *Millet* System," in *Christians and Jews in the Ottoman Empire: the Functioning of a Plural Society*, ed. Benjamin Braude and Bernard Lewis (New York: Holmes & Meier Publishers, 1982), 74.

[201] Of the six pre-war *Süryânî* newspapers (excluding the short-lived *Safro d-Nuhro*, *Hayât* and *Kevkbo d-Suryoye*), four were published in Diyarbakır or by natives of the city residing in the United States. Âşûr Yûsuf also extolled the virtues of the Harput *Süryânî* for their leadership in providing charitable donations and for the many of their number who appear

As a result, the intellectuals – Naûm Fâik and Âşûr Yûsuf included – had an intimate knowledge of the more rural areas, and consequently, they targeted to an extent both an urban and a rural audience in their newspapers. The same can not be said for the most of the Armenian and Greeks resident in the capital, whose reforms often disadvantaged those in the provinces despite the fact that intellectual activity was by no means limited to Istanbul or the other large coastal cities. Of course, in the United States, the *Süryânî* did posses a diaspora of their own.[202] These recent emigrants contributed to the intellectual debate of the Ottoman Empire-based press as well as producing their own publications starting at roughly the same time as those of Naûm Fâik and Âşûr Yûsuf. Notably silent, however, were those *Süryânî* in the capital, the centre of virtually every other Ottoman community's intellectual activity.[203]

Geography was only one division present in the non-Muslim communities, however. The *Tanzîmât*, during which the state underwent numerous transformations, resulted in sweeping redistributions of power and the codification of laws pertaining to the internal administration of the communities. To an extent, the state precipitated some of these changes, but the main thrust came from within as part of a struggle between elements seeking to either assert or retain their authority. Even when the divisive matters were political, conflict manifested itself in a number of different ways, with many of the most fierce struggles occurring over issues such as education or language. The nineteenth-century

---

on the list of subscribers to the newspaper *İntibâh*: "Abone bedeli," *Mürşid-i Âsûriyûn*, 5, no. 6 (Mayıs 1913), 90.

[202] Unlike their Armenian counterparts in India, the Malankara Syriac communities do not appear to have played a contributory role in the development of the Ottoman congregations. Conversely, their religious brethren in India weighed heavily on the minds of the *Süryânî* with a local schism and Patriarch Abdullah's subsequent four-year sojourn in the Subcontinent attempting to minimise the damage. *Mürşid-i Âsûriyûn* and *Kevkeb Mednho* followed these events particularly closely, as will be discussed below on page 156.

[203] This includes even those without a traditionally large presence in the city, such as the Bulgarians and the Kurds.

also saw the state recognise the religious split and allowed the establishment of separate Catholic and Protestant institutions. But as the number of converts was small in comparison to membership in the original churches, the main non-Muslim activity remained within the context of the old communities.

Religion may have been the defining characteristic upon which the very existence of the *millet* was based, but in the nineteenth century it found its primacy seriously challenged. Even before the *Tanzîmât*, however, the laity had had a role in administration whereby primates – the local wealthy and privileged – were entrusted with providing certain services to the state.[204] A council of these elders (*ihtiyâr heyeti*) had local responsibilities and helped mediate between the community and the state. At the time, however, the powers of the lay members did not infringe on those of the religious authorities, who were responsible for fundamental matters such as the registration of births, deaths and marriages. In addition, what educational opportunities existed were usually purveyed by the clergy. Besides this civic role, ecclesiastical courts provided a judicial system for matters religious and secular alike, although the local primates would have often been available to mediate disputes before they reached such a stage.

Ultimately, however, both parties would be challenged under the *Tanzîmât* reforms when the traditional structures were altered, and new rising groups began demanding their own share of power. With the *Tanzîmât*, in theory, old practices were to be eliminated, but in reality the primates often managed to retain some of their authority within the new order despite the reforms. One means for doing so was by using their traditional influence to secure positions on the local councils which were being established during the *Tanzîmât*. Likewise, the clergy were by no means stripped of their position; if anything, the *millet* system was reinforced during the *Tanzîmât* and the *milletbaşı* continued to be the Patriarch, or the Chief Rabbi in the Jewish case, but now with powers backed by law

---

[204] These local leaders were known as *primkur*, *voyvoda*, *çorbacı* or *kocabaşı* depending on their location within the Empire; I have not encountered any such terminology being applied to a *Süryânî*.

and not merely tradition.[205] And yet, the clergy and old lay elites did face a determined opposition from new elements, who sought to obtain some of the newly available powers for themselves.[206]

During the course of the *Tanzîmât* and the reign of Abdülhamîd the cleavages in the communities would manifest themselves in a number of areas, most notably the administration of schools and the use of vernacular rather than classical languages for education and publishing. And while the traditional *millet* leaders often found themselves on the opposite side of newly empowered lay groups, the conflicts should not be construed as simply being fuelled by tension between secular and religious ideologies. During the second constitutional period, these same divisions would often continue to dictate the relationship between various groups and the CUP and would produce political alliances in mainstream Ottoman politics. At the same time, recent scholarship has investigated non-Muslim interest in Ottomanism replacing the earlier view of it being nothing more than a ploy by the Young Turks to gain temporary support from Christian and Jewish Ottoman citizens.

## THE ARMENIAN *MILLET*

Even in the pre-*Tanzîmât* era, there had been a tradition of lay involvement in local Armenian affairs, whether it be in electing local priests or forming mixed councils with religious leaders.[207] The Armenian community as a whole, however, had come to be dominated by a group of powerful individuals in the capital who carried the title of *amira* and who had obtained their wealth and position through state service or as moneylenders (*sarrâf*). Both

---

[205] Sia Anagnostopoulou, "Tanzimat ve Rum Milletinin Kurumsal Çerçevesi: Patrikhane, Cemaat Kurumları, Eğitim," in *19. Yüzyıl İstanbul'unda Gayrimüslimler*, ed. Pinelopi Stathis, tr. Foti Benlisoy and Stefo Benlisoy (Istanbul: Tarih Vakfı Yurt Yayınları, 1999), 9-10.

[206] The "new element" could consist of individuals from a number of different backgrounds, often grouped together under the mantle of "the middle class".

[207] Vartan Artinian, *The Armenian Constitutional System in the Ottoman Empire, 1839-1863: A Study of its Historical Development* (Istanbul, undated), 19.

secular matters and the patriarchal elections were effectively under the control of this wealthy elite. They were also critically important within the *millet* in that they bankrolled construction of buildings such as hospitals, schools and churches, as well as mediating between the state and the community. But by the middle of the nineteenth century, the dominance of this group was successfully challenged on two separate fronts.

In the late eighteenth and early nineteenth centuries, we can also see the emergence of a second powerful group of Armenians in the guilds (*esnâf*). Due to their wealth and organisation, the *esnâf* of Istanbul began to participate in community affairs by providing financial help to the Patriarchate or mediating between the *millet* and state. More importantly, however, the *esnâf* began to finance schools in the capital, and control over the educational system would consistently be a point of contention between the competing factions during the *Tanzîmât* era. Naturally, we can speak of the *amira* as being more resistant to change and for this reason they have been labelled as intransigent in contrast to the *esnâf*, who clearly were not happy with the *status quo*.

The abolition of tax-farming by the *Gülhâne Hatt-ı Hümâyûnu* of 1839, otherwise known as the *Tanzîmât Fermanı*, meant that the perceived need for the *sarrâf* was suddenly eliminated and while the replacement system of direct taxation only lasted for two years before the old was reinstated, the *esnâf* used the interval to push for a greater role in the community. The financially troubled *amira* were not completely without recourse during these difficult times; they still had some influence in the state through their old contacts and their position further improved once the old taxation system was reintroduced in the 1840s. It became clear the *esnâf* alone were not capable of bankrolling the *millet*, and with the *amira* once again financially stable, they resumed playing an important, if somewhat curtailed, role in the affairs of the community.[208]

A second challenge came from the newly educated Armenians returning from the universities of Paris and other cities in Europe. These educated youths were socially mixed, being from *amira*, *esnâf* and even poor families. Ideologically, they were heavily influenced

---

[208] Artinian, *The Armenian Constitutional System*, 53-58.

by mid-nineteenth century French thought, heavily infused with positivist, scientific ideas and notions of democratic rule. Converts to both Catholicism and Protestantism, even though they were outside the Armenian *millet* proper, participated in the formulation of a programme to redress the conditions of the Ottoman Armenians. The first aspect would be a reformation of governance, although their activities were aimed at the *millet* and not the Empire as a whole.[209]

In 1849, Armenian students in Paris founded the *Ararat Society*, a non-sectarian, non-political organisation dedicated to lifting the people out of its "miserable condition". In their proclamation, they stated that only they, "the elite of [the] nation", were in a position to undertake the measures necessary to reverse the ignorance that was causing these maladies. The intellectuals with the support of the Porte introduced a system which provided for the separation of secular and religious affairs and the creation of two independent councils for their administration. Although the system did not completely abolish crossovers between the two spheres, the provision is still interesting as it ran contrary to the history of clerical involvement in the secular and lay interference in the religious. This was, moreover, a step towards the ultimate goal of legislating the sharing of power between the various interested groups, something the intellectuals embarked upon with the proclamation of the 1856 *Hatt-ı Hümâyûn*, the *Islâhât Fermânı*, which called for *millet* reorganisation.[210]

In 1863, after *amira* influence had a first proposal thrown out, a statute drafted by prominent intellectuals was adopted by the Armenian *millet* and approved by the Ottoman government. Using their good relations with the Porte and their alliance with the *esnâf* – demonstrating the shift in power away from the *amira* – the

---

[209] Aylin Beşiryan, *Hopes of Secularization in the Ottoman Empire: The Armenian National Constitution and the Armenian Newspaper,* Masis*, 1856-1863* (Master's thesis, Boğaziçi University, 2007), 44-63. There were also Armenian intellectuals educated in Russian institutions and active in the Caucasus.

[210] Artinian, *The Armenian Constitutional System*, 64-80.

intellectuals were able to push for the written formalisation of the rules for governing the Armenian *millet*.

Often referred to as a "national constitution", the *Nizâmnâme-i Millet-i Ermeniyân* dictated the powers to be wielded by the Patriarch and established a "national council" which would incorporate representatives from the *amira*, the *esnâf* and the church hierarchy.[211] Moreover, the members sitting on the councils would be elected by the community, although the system did not enfranchise women or the poor (Catholics and Protestants were also naturally excluded) and most representatives would come from Istanbul and not the provinces. Nevertheless, it would be liberal in comparison to those drafted by the Greek and Jewish communities.[212] Authority over religious issues – such as the appointment of clerics and religious education – remained in the hands of the patriarchate, but other important powers, including the administration of schools, hospitals, the budget and justice – ended up in the hands of the civilian councils.[213] Lest the contentious nature of the changes not be entirely clear, the dispute over the powers granted by the *nizâmnâme* were enough to cause rioting and bloodshed in churches.[214]

Passions were no less inflamed over the controversial question of reforming the Armenian language. Among the young Armenian intelligentsia arose the notion that the classical language (*Krapar*) had become obsolete and needed to be replaced by a literary

---

[211] *Nizâmnâme-i Millet-i Ermeniyân* [Regulation of the *Millet* of the Armenians] was the title used by Armenians. It has been noted that the Ottoman authorities termed it the *Ermenî Patrikliği Nizâmâtı* [Armenian Patriarchal Regulations] and this reflects the Ottoman view of the *millet* as a religious community, whereas the Armenian authors of the document evidently envisioned that it would be bringing secularism: Artinian, *The Armenian Constitutional System*, 103-104 and Beşiryan, *Hopes of Secularization in the Ottoman Empire*, 199-201.

[212] Artinian, *The Armenian Constitutional System*, 104; Koptaş, *Armenian Political Thinking*, 24-28. Only 40 of 140 deputies came from outside Istanbul.

[213] Gülnihâl Bozkurt, *Gayrimüslim Osmanlı Vatandaşlarının Hukukî Durumu (1839-1914)* (Ankara: Türk Tarih Kurumu, 1989), 181-182.

[214] Artinian, *The Armenian Constitutional System*, 87.

language based on the vernacular. This was fiercely opposed by the religious establishment and their conservative political allies. One of the major architects of the Armenian and Ottoman constitutions, Krikor Odian, was also behind the drive for the establishment of this new tongue and only narrowly avoided being excommunicated for his beliefs. The Armenian press was also involved in the issue of language reform; the leading journal, *Masis*, extolled the virtues of the vernacular and published replacement words for terms borrowed into Armenian from other languages.[215] During the nineteenth century, language became a battleground for the old guard and those calling for reform and progress.

The reforms being advocated in the political and intellectual centres were not directed at alleviating the problems of the bulk of the Armenian population, that is to say, those living in the provinces. Although not the first political organisations, the *Hnchakian* and *Dashnaktsutiun* emerged out of disenchantment with the slow progress of reforms and became the two most influential Armenian parties of the nineteenth and early twentieth centuries. They advocated Socialist ideas as a means to rescue the Armenian population from their suffering, something which naturally found opposition amongst the wealthy *amira* and the Patriarchate. Moreover, the *Hnchakian* overtly called for an independent Armenian state composed of territories under both Ottoman and Russian rule. Founded in Geneva in 1887, the *Hnchakian* became popular amongst intellectual circles of Istanbul but also in the provinces and Russia. The *Dashnaktsutiun*, on the other hand, was established in Tbilisi three years after the *Hnchakian* to coordinate the efforts of like-minded revolutionary groups.

Although the two groups had nearly identical beliefs, *Hnchakian* and *Dashnaktsutiun* remained two separate entities differentiated by their respective commitment to socialist and

---

[215] Ibid, 63-64 and 71-72; Beşiryan, *Hopes of Secularization in the Ottoman Empire*, 60-70; Johann Strauss, "Diglossie dans le domaine ottoman: évolution et péripéties d'une situation linguistique," *Revue des mondes musulmans et de la Méditerranée* no. 75-76 (1996).

nationalist principles.[216] Armenians played a part in the movements opposing Abdülhamîd leading up to the revolution of 1908. The *Dashnaktsutiun*, for example, participated at the 1902 Young Turk congress in Paris, receiving reluctant support from the majority faction for their demands.[217] At the second congress of opposition parties, the *Dashnaktsutiun* agreed on a joint statement guaranteeing the integrity of the Ottoman Empire.

The divide in the Armenian community remained evident in the political activities which followed the Young Turk revolution in 1908 and the proclamation of the second Ottoman constitution. Support for the new regime was nearly universal among individual Armenians as well as the revolutionary parties, who publicly declared their support. The first obvious impact of the revolution was the legalisation of the *Hnchakian* and *Dashnaktsutiun*, their subsequent involvement in mainstream Ottoman politics and the abandonment of armed struggle to achieve their objectives.[218] The *Dashnaktsutiun* in particular continued their close relationship with the CUP, winning four seats in the first parliament. Although it renounced independence as its goal, the *Dashnaktsutiun* continued to campaign for the relief of the Armenian peasantry, who struggled under the adverse conditions of the eastern Ottoman Empire. Towards this end, they achieved modest success in having the government resolve property disputes with the local Kurdish populations although instability and violence continued throughout the pre-war period.

The agreements between the CUP and the *Dashnaktsutiun* caused some unease in certain parts of the Armenian community, however. The *Hnchakian* first of all objected to its rival's successes at the expense of its own, and secondly its mistrust of the CUP increased after the Adana massacres in 1909. As a consequence, the *Hnchakian* would seek an alliance with the opposition *Hürriyet ve İtilâf Fırkası* for the 1912 elections. In fact, by this time, even the

---

[216] Nalbandian, *The Armenian Revolutionary Movement*, 115-131 and 151-178; Koptaş, *Armenian Political Thinking*, 37-52.

[217] Hanioğlu, *The Young Turks in Opposition*, 197-198.

[218] Koptaş, *Armenian Political Thinking*, 53-57. There were also the much smaller *Ramgavar* and Reformed *Hnchakian* parties.

relationship between the *Dashnaktsutiun* and the CUP was breaking down; the 19 seats promised to the Armenians never materialised, with only ten being won in 1912 – down from 11 in 1908. Nevertheless, the CUP government maintained close contacts with the Armenian party right up to the start of the First World War. The motivation behind the alliance of the *Hnchakian* with the *Hürriyet ve İtilâf Fırkası* was essentially the same as that of their rivals with the CUP: a means of gaining a say in politics.[219] In any case, both opposition parties would be sidelined by the *Bâb-ı Âli* coup and they could bring little united pressure to bear on the ruling CUP government.

The revolutionary parties were not, however, the only Armenian presence in Ottoman politics. The *amira*-supported Patriarchate also opposed the CUP and its agenda which would see the removal of even more *millet* privileges. From the perspective of the commercial elites and the *amira*, an independent Armenia and even agitation by revolutionaries would only serve to harm their commercial interests. Immediately following the revolution of 1908 elections, the Patriarchate attempted to assert control over the *Dashnaktsutiun* but antagonism between the Patriarchate and the CUP prevented the former from succeeding.[220] Otherwise, certain Armenian intellectuals participated in politics independent of any organised group, the prime example being Krikor Zohrab, lawyer, editor of the journal *Masis* and twice deputy for Istanbul in the Ottoman parliament.[221]

Never a member of the CUP or the *Dashnaktsutiun*, Zohrab supported and encouraged both to cooperate in accordance to his Ottomanist ideals using his "supra-party" position to mediate between the different communities. Personally, he saw himself as both an Ottoman and an Armenian, a dual identity which posed no

---

[219] Ibid., 77-72.

[220] Feroz Ahmad, "Unionist Relations with the Greek, Armenian, and Jewish Communities of the Ottoman Empire, 1908-1914," in *Christians and Jews in the Ottoman Empire*, 418-420. Kansu, *The Revolution of 1908 in Turkey* (Leiden: Brill, 1997), 167-170.

[221] An excellent analysis of Zohrab's thought is Koptaş, *Armenian Political Thinking*, 73-136.

problems in his formulation. For example, he made impassioned appeals for the drafting of Christians into the Ottoman armed forces in parliament on the basis that it was a necessary step in the formation of an Ottoman identity. Indeed, it is difficult to find a more ardent supporter of Ottomanism than Krikor Zohrab. Even if he saw Ottomanism as a means to rescue the Armenians from their precarious situation in the provinces, it is evident that he also very much believed in the Ottoman ideal.[222]

## THE ORTHODOX *MILLET*

The *Millet-i Rûm* bore the Ottoman Turkish name for the Greek subjects of the Empire, but in reality it also comprised vast numbers of non-Greeks professing the Orthodox faith.[223] The Greek predominance was not just in name, however, with Greek as the liturgical language and the upper echelons of the religious hierarchy being their domain to the exclusion of others. This state of affairs naturally bred resentment amongst the non-Greek Orthodox; the Bulgarian struggle for both ecclesiastical and national independence would be a rallying point for the Ottoman Greeks and for the Greek state.[224] And yet this forced unity did not free the Greek community from extremely divisive debates in the nineteenth and early twentieth centuries.

Traditionally the Orthodox community had been dominated by a group of wealthy families with ties to a number of important positions in the Ottoman Empire. Known as the Phanariots for the Fener district of Istanbul in which they inhabited, they were frequently employed as translators or in other sensitive government positions. For example, the two Danubian principalities, Moldavia and Wallachia, were headed by a Phanariot appointed by the Ottoman sultan. With strong ties to the state, the Phanariots were

---

[222] Ibid., 135-136.

[223] In the late Ottoman period, Orthodox groups included Bulgarians, Arabs, Albanians, Serbs, Romanians and Georgians.

[224] The *Süryânî* used the fact that the Bulgarians were eventually granted their own *millet* as a rationale for the creations of one for the *Süryânî-i Kadîm*: İbrahim Özcoşar, *Bir Yüzyıl Bir Sancak Bir Cemaat: 19. Yüzyılda Mardin Süryanileri* (Ankara: Beyan, 2008), 65.

able to exert considerable control over the Orthodox Church through the manipulation of Patriarchal elections.

In 1821, however, the Greek uprising spread to the Peloponnese from the Danubian Principalities, ultimately culminating in the establishment of an independent Greek kingdom. Reprisals against the numerous remaining Greek subjects followed as the state lost confidence in the loyalty of the community as a whole. For the Phanariots, this meant that the posts they had relied upon for their primacy within the Orthodox community were subsequently largely barred to them. Some of the old guard did in fact re-emerge in the second half of the nineteenth century, joined by new families who had risen through profitable commercial ventures. This wealthy group sought to protect their economic standing in the Ottoman economy, while at the same time vying for position within the *millet*.

As we have already seen, the *Tanzîmât* statesmen attempted to legislate the authority – and the limits on it – held by the members of the *millet* in the hopes of asserting greater central control over the non-Muslim communities. Thus, the state sought to relieve the lucrative privilege of collecting taxes from the hands of the Orthodox priests and instead issue them salaries, something which they would oppose fiercely.[225] The Patriarchs who opposed the implementation of secularising measures were therefore doing so not necessarily due to their extreme piety; indeed, they counted amongst their supporters the richest Greeks with ties to the Ottoman state.

Indeed, the Patriarch had the dual role of heading the Ottoman administrative unit which was the *millet-i Rûm* while at the same time serving as the spiritual leader of all Orthodox Christians, irrespective of citizenship – although he was recognised in this role mainly by Greek speakers. The second of these duties was placed in an especially precarious position in light of the promises of the *Tanzîmât*. Since religious leaders had the exclusive authority over spiritual matters, struggles over power transformed into a question

---

[225] Bozkurt, *Gayrimüslim Osmanlı Vatandaşlarının Hukukî Durumu*, 171 and Anagnostopoulou, "Tanzimat ve Rum Milletinin Kurumsal Çerçevesi," 11.

of what constituted the spiritual and what was merely lay in nature.[226] Despite disputes – there were serious disagreements especially over how Patriarchs would be elected – the high clergy and the notables had a similar vision for the administration of the *millet*. Importantly, these groups were also responsible for the Greek domination of the *millet* as a whole, and hence were acting within the framework of the Ottoman Empire, to which they remained largely loyal.

The Ottoman Greek intelligentsia were active in the publishing and dissemination of Greek letters with a "national revival" undertone; they also formed part of the process of educating the Ottoman Orthodox in the Greek language. With Orthodox speakers of Turkish, Albanian and Slavic languages as well as various Greek dialects, the schooling in a single language was a priority. The intelligentsia was joined by the emerging middle class and the middling clergy. None of these groups had the same vested interests in the preservation of the old order that their superiors did, and as such were open to change and the potential benefits that it would bring them.[227] But they did seek to assert themselves and gain control over educational institutions and other community affairs at the expense of the old elites and the religious establishment.

An expression of these sentiments was in the *Society of Constantinople*, an organisation originally formed with the task of combating illiteracy and other social ills as well as resisting outside threats, such as missionary activities. In the early twentieth century, it became increasingly active in political affairs. Although it shared certain interests with the Greek state, especially hostility towards the Bulgarians, the two never worked together.[228] Indeed, the

---

[226] Anagnostopoulou, "Tanzimat ve Rum Milletinin Kurumsal Çerçevesi," 11.

[227] Thanos Veremis, "The Hellenic Kingdom and the Ottoman Greeks: The Experiment of the 'Society of Constantinople'," in *Ottoman Greeks in the Age of Nationalism*, ed. Dimitri Gondicas and Charles Issawi (Princeton: Darwin Press, 1999), 183-186.

[228] Ibid., 183-184 and Vangelis Kechriotis, "Greek-Orthodox, Ottoman Greeks or just Greeks? Theories of Coexistence in the

leadership of the *Society of Constantinople* rejected Hellenic irredentism in favour of creating a new empire – not a nation state – in which the Greeks would be the leading element.[229] Reflecting divisions between the elites and the middle class, many Ottoman Greeks continued to support the expansion of the Greek state, although even the latter sought a rapprochement with the Ottoman Empire.

On the other hand, Iōakeim III, twice Greek Orthodox Patriarch (1878-1884 and 1901-1912), presents another face of the rejection of Hellenic irredentism and supporter of the autonomy of the church from the Greek state. At the same time, Iōakeim was wary of the CUP and received coolly the 1908 revolution, seeing the development as a threat to its privileges.[230] It seemed a return to the secularism of the *Tanzîmât*, and as Patriarch, Iōakeim believed in the unity of the church above the Greek nation. But Iōakeim's position divided the community – and even the church, although there was compromise during his second term once relations between Greece and the Ottoman Empire bettered. He also opposed some lay figures with vested interests while many of the lower ranking clergymen openly defied their Patriarch by working with Greek authorities to promote nationalism.[231]

The influence wielded by the *Society of Constantinople* is observable in the fact that 16 of 24 Greek deputies in the Ottoman parliament were members. In any case, all of the Greek deputies tended to vote in a bloc on all matters affecting the community as a whole. A consequence of its influence was that the Patriarch was forced into working with the *Society*, despite the latter's support from the middle class. For the 1912 elections, the *Society* cooperated with the *Hürriyet ve İtilâf Fırkası* having a similar motivation as the

---

Aftermath of the Young Turk Revolution," *Études balkaniques*, 1 (2005), 54.

[229] In English-language scholarship, the Greek Kingdom is signified by the adjective "Hellenic" while the Ottoman Greeks are simply "Greek".

[230] Ahmad, "Unionist Relations with the Greek, Armenian, and Jewish Communities of the Ottoman Empire," 407.

[231] Veremis, "The Hellenic Kingdom and the Ottoman Greeks," 184-187.

*Hnchakian*: a say in Ottoman politics.[232] Whatever their beliefs, however, the members of the *Soceity* were not converts to Ottomanism in the model of Krikor Zohrab. And the disillusionment that set in after 1912 – the number of deputies dropped from 23 to 15 – hastened their abandonment of their support for a multi-ethnic empire.

But this should not imply that no Ottomanist Greeks existed. Several parliamentarians were members of the CUP or at least collaborated with it. Emmanouēl Emmanouēlidēs, a prominent Greek from Izmir, was an outspoken supporter of the CUP during the period from 1908 until 1912. With his entry into the parliament during a by-election in 1911, Emmanouēlidēs, the Ottoman patriot, argued for non-Muslim participation in the armed forces, defended the constitution and, ultimately, was, in time, denounced as a traitor by the supporters of the Hellenic state.[233] However, with the death of Iōakeim and the closure of the second sitting of the parliament, support for the CUP and belief in the Ottomanism would wane and the Greek *millet* would find itself again subject to the irredentism of the Greek state.

## THE JEWISH *MILLET*

The smallest of the traditional Ottoman denominations, the Jewish *millet* experienced slightly different pre-*Tanẓîmât* division than the Armenians and the Orthodox. The strength of the Jewish laity in conducting important functions such as tax collection meant that election to the position of *hahambaşı* (of which there were several in the Ottoman Empire) was often dictated on secular rather than religious grounds. Because of the lack of a strict hierarchical order in which any one rabbi held primacy over his peers and the fact that Ottoman Jewry was split into Sephardic, Ashkenazi, Mizrahi and other groupings, affiliation with one's neighbourhood was

---

[232] Catherine Boura, "The Greek Millet in Turkish Politics: Greeks in the Ottoman Parliament (1908-1918)," in *Ottoman Greeks in the Age of Nationalism*, 196-197.

[233] Kechriotis, "On the Margins of National Historiography: the Greek *İttihatçı* Emmanouil Emmanouilidis: Opportunists or Ottoman patriot?" (forthcoming paper).

more important than affiliation with the Jewish community as a whole. This, coupled with the influence of local primates, meant that whenever efforts were made to establish the Istanbul *hahambaşı* as the head of the Jewish *millet*, opposition was fierce.

A year after the establishment of a Catholic *millet* in 1834, the first moves were made to elect a Chief Rabbi who would wield real powers. The newly granted authority was based on the provision of services for the state, including tax collection. And while the loss of revenues by certain lay members was resented, real conflict centred on matters such as the administration of community schools. The cleavage was not simply between the lay and religious members of the community, but rather those supporting and those opposing the *status quo*. Indeed, the conservative side – composed of those who stood to lose from change – was able to organise the dismissal of a Chief Rabbi who they felt was particularly unresponsive to their demands. As with their Armenian counterparts, the moneylenders (*sarrâf*) lost much of their livelihood, while the guilds saw their influence expand. Part of the rebalance in power, however, was due to geographic considerations, with old Jewish neighbourhoods losing their former importance to newer, more centrally located ones.

Trouble in the 1860s was sufficiently disruptive that the state was forced to intervene to resolve disputes over education and the community budget. Following in the footsteps of the Armenians and Greeks and in the hopes of resolving the reoccurring disputes, a set of organic laws (known as the *Hahambaşı Nizâmnâmesi*) was enacted in 1865 in order to rebalance the powers within the *millet* and reinforce state authority over the community as a unit. Input from the laity was authorised through the creation of councils dominated by non-religious members. Unfortunately for the state, this did not resolve the conflicts within the *millet*. In the capital, the division between the progressives and conservatives continued, while in the provinces, the local congregations maintained their independence from the authority of their titular head, the Chief Rabbi.[234]

---

[234] The preceding information concerning the Jewish *millet* has been taken from Ilan Karmi, *The Jewish Community of Istanbul in the Nineteenth*

Reform did not merely surround the administration of the community, however, with some of the most intractable disputes occurring within the domain of education. Cleavages arose between the laity and the clergy over the curriculum of schools as early as the eighteenth century when there was an increased emphasis on secular subjects. But even within the laity, control – if not the content – of education provoked bitter disputes which necessitating government intervention. These reflected the deep splits in the community. Two of the main promoters of a secular education for Istanbul's Jewry were the influential Camondo family as well as the France-based *Alliance israélite universelle*, the efforts of which were opposed by many in the religious establishment.[235]

Despite these divisions, when it came to the Young Turks and the 1908 constitution, the Ottoman Jewish community was the most united in its support. This hinged on the fact that, unlike the Armenians and the Greeks, the Ottoman Jewry had no national aspirations of their own. Zionism had a large following in Europe, but found little support in the Ottoman Empire; in any case, Zionists were not, publicly at least, advocating an independent state carved out of Ottoman territory.[236] In fact, Jewish communities, which had a significant presence in the Balkans, stood to lose through the successes of Bulgarian and especially Greek nationalism.

It is, therefore, not surprising that there were several prominent Jewish members of the Young Turks, the CUP and even the Turkish nationalist movement. The first post-Abdülhamîd *hahambaşı*, Nahum Haim, for example, had been an acquaintance of many Young Turks in Paris and was sympathetic to their movement. Through this cooperation, Jews served in several roles in the administration and benefited economically when Armenians and Greeks fell out of favour with the authorities.[237] Three

---

*Century: Social, Legal and Administrative Transformations* (Istanbul: Isis Press, 1996), 27-46 and 105-115.

[235] Karmi, *The Jewish Community of Istanbul*, 57-71.

[236] Ahmad, "Unionist Relations with the Greek, Armenian, and Jewish Communities of the Ottoman Empire," 426. Also see page 116 below.

[237] Ibid., 427-428 and Karmi, *The Jewish Community of Istanbul*, 122.

Sephardic Jews were elected as deputies in both the 1908 and 1912 parliaments, one each in Istanbul, Salonika and Izmir while one Mizrahi Jew represented Baghdad.[238]

## THE *SÜRYÂNÎ MİLLET*

### Administration

As with the other communities, the religious authorities acted as mediators between the state and the populace, making the churches an extension of the Ottoman administration. At the head of the Jacobite hierarchy was the titular Patriarch of Antioch, who always took the name İgnâtiyûs [Ignatius] upon election.[239] The Patriarch was followed in order of precedence by the ranks of bishop (*episkopos*), priest (*keşîş*) and deacon (*şemmâs*).

At the top level of ecclesiastical administration came the archbishops or metropolitans (*mutrân*), of which there were eight in the late Ottoman period.[240] Traditionally, the patriarch appointed one of these as the *mafryânâ*, a title unique to the Jacobite Church indicating a *primus inter pares* from amongst the metropolitans. By the end of the nineteenth century, however, this had ceased to be a functioning position. Below the metropolitans came the bishops (*episkopos*), of which the more important were known as *serepiskopos* [head bishop]. Priests who had lost their wives could forego remarriage and rise to the rank of *üskuf*, but they had no

---

[238] Kansu, *The Revolution of 1908 in Turkey*, 252-264 and 293.

[239] Only the given name will be used here, so Mar İgnâtiyûs Abdullah, who was Jacobite patriarch from 1906 until 1915, will always be referred to simply as Abdullah.

[240] Fortescue lists the metropolitan seats as Jerusalem, Mosul, the monastery of Mar Mattî near Mosul, Mardin, Urfa and Harput, while two more had no fixed see: *The Lesser Eastern Churches* (London: The Catholic Truth Society, 1913), 339-340 as well as Atiya, *A History of Eastern Christianity*, 221. Today, the archbishoprics in the Republic of Turkey number four: the monasteries of *Deyrü'z-Zaferân* and *Mar Gabriyel* (both in the province of Mardin); Istanbul; and Adıyaman.

opportunity to advance any further and remained lower in the hierarchy than the metropolitans and other bishops.[241]

The local clergymen (*keşîş* or *kas*) generally served in the town of their origins. A *keşîş*, who unlike a bishop was able to marry, earned his living through secular means such as farming, although some could collect funds for providing services such as baptisms and marriages or presiding over funerals.[242] In a particularly important diocese in which the position came with both religious and civil responsibilities, the priest could be known as a *horepiskopos*, but this appears to have been something less dependent on the religious than the lay activities.

Below the *keşîş* were the *şemmâs*, who performed a number of functions during church services, although the particulars are not of great importance. There are no more than a handful of passing references to *Süryânî* with the rank of *şemmâs* in the primary sources I have consulted. Members of the priestly class were, however, exempt from Ottoman taxes and obligations such as the military service for non-Muslims which was introduced in 1909. Consequently, even the position of *şemmâs*, which offered no direct supplementary income, was a desirable one.[243]

---

[241] The word *üskuf* derived from the Greek word for bishop, *episkopos*; in light of the mitre worn by high-ranking Orthodox clergymen, the same word was also adopted to refer to the flat headgear of the Janissaries.

[242] Atiya, *A History of Eastern Christianity*, 219-222. Article 40 of the *Süryânî Nizâmnâmesi* provided for the right to collect fees based on tradition: quoted in Şimşek, *Süryaniler ve Diyarbakır*, 309.

[243] "Şemmâslar askerlikten muâfur," *Mürşid-i Âsûriyûn*, 5, no. 6 (Mayıs 1913), 95. The question of military service outweighed religious considerations for some Christians. In 1911, reports of massive conversion to the Nestorian Church came from the provinces of Mosul and Bitlis. In the former, the converts were erstwhile Chaldeans, who sought to escape their obligations by becoming Nestorians and immediately entering the ranks of the clergy. Meanwhile, according to reports from Bitlis, some 500 to 1000 persons were converting to Nestorianism every day causing the local *vâli* to appeal to the government for instructions. In this instance, the newspaper noted that the governor's telegraph had not specified whether the converts were Armenians or Kurds: "Cerîdelerden," *Mürşid-i Âsûriyûn*, 3, no. 8 (Eylûl 1911), 146.

A final position of note was that of *patrik vekîli* [patriarchal representative], religious figures who were specifically assigned the duties of mediating between the community and state. The most important of these was the one resident in Istanbul, usually a *mutrân* or *episkopos*, and the primary contact between the *millet* and the central government.[244] Other patriarchal representatives could be found in other cities where either there was no *mutrân* or where a more formalised channel between the community and the state would be desirable. Hence Diyarbakır, the capital of the *vilâyet* in which both Mardin and *Deyrü'z-Zaferân* were located, would occasionally have its *mutrân* specifically assume the title of *patrik vekîli.*[245]

That the presence of the uneducated and the immoral amongst the ranks of the lower clergy was a major topic of debate within the community during the early twentieth century suggests that the criteria for selection was not necessarily merit or piety. The laity even criticised the conduct of the upper echelons in the hierarchy for engaging in questionable activities which seemed motivated more by personal gain than the benefit of the community. The Jacobite patriarch, for example, was selected from a list of three candidates presented by a synod of bishops which had, in theory, consulted the community but often received bribes. Official approval of the candidate came from local authorities in Diyarbakır or, when required, from Istanbul.[246]

This system of patriarchal succession did not always proceed smoothly. Rival claims to the seat were frequent; in 1814, for example, four different claimants to the Jacobite Patriarchate

---

[244] Occasionally, he was also referred to as the *patrik vekîl-i umûmîsi* [patriarchal vicar general]: "Cebel-i Tûr ahvâli," *Mürşid-i Âsûriyûn*, 5, no. 5 (Nîsân 1913), 78. At one point in the 1880s the position had been held by Abdünnûr, the future *mutrân* of Harput about whom more information will follow. From 1896 until at least 1914, the *patrik vekîli* in Istanbul was *serepiskopos* Pavlûs. Özcoşar has compiled a list in *Bir Yüzyıl Bir Sancak Bir Cemaat*, 94.

[245] Ibid., 85-88.

[246] Özcoşar, "Osmanlı Devlet'inde Millet Sistemi ve Süryani Kadim-ler," 224-226.

emerged.[247] Influence and money could secure the seat, and consequently, patriarchal duties included a large measure of the temporal in order to recuperate the investment. Both historians and contemporary observers such as Âşûr Yûsuf came to the conclusion that this was the reason behind the lack of attention paid to education or to the spiritual development of the church.

The election following the death of the patriarch in 1894 demonstrates the questionable loyalties that the system produced. When Abdülmesîh prevailed over his rival Abdullah Sattûf in 1895, the latter converted to Catholicism and became the Uniate *Süryânî* bishop of Homs, returning to the Jacobite Church nine years later on the promise that he would be the next patriarch. Abdülmesîh was summarily deposed in 1906 by a governmental decree, and Abdullah was finally able to secure his election through intrigue and the expenditure of some 500 Ottoman lira. The Jacobite metropolitan in Jerusalem actually provided Abdullah with most of this sum – 360 lira according to the *Süryânî* newspaper *İntibâh* – but a dispute over the loan would see a case being brought to an Ottoman court in 1912.[248]

In the meantime, Abdülmesîh followed his rival Abdullah to India and, in an effort to recoup his lost influence, he successfully supported a breakaway faction of the Jacobite Church seeking to become autocephalous. Finally, in 1913, Abdülmesîh abandoned both the separated Indian congregation and the Jacobite Church as a whole and himself converted to Catholicism.[249] The fact that this one protracted succession dispute resulted in schism, multiple instances of apostasy and a public court case over money between the Patriarch and a senior prelate explains the disillusionment many *Süryânî* felt and the exasperated tone of Âşûr Yûsuf's writing.

---

[247] Joseph, *Muslim-Christian Relations*, 31.

[248] "Rüesâ-yı rûhânîlerimiz mahkeme kapısında," *Mürşid-i Âsûriyûn*, 4, no. 10 (Kânûn-ı Evvel 1912), 146. Another contemporary observer gave a figure of 350 lira and reported that "There are discontented Jacobites under [Abdullah Sattûf] who say that His Holiness stains the Patriarchal throne by various faults, of which excessive avarice is the chief. Many hope for and expect his deposition." Fortescue, *The Lesser Eastern Churches*, 339-340.

[249] Joseph, *Muslim-Christian Relations*, 181 n.73.

A second problem was that the mediator between the Porte and the Jacobite populace was not in fact its own patriarch, but rather that of the Armenians. Prior to the 1780s the Jacobite Church had had some direct relations with the Porte, but they were formally attached to the Armenian Patriarchate in Istanbul in 1783, a year in which the supremacy of the Istanbul patriarchates over those outside the capital was reinforced.[250] This process of greater centralisation had begun some years earlier when the government abolished the Orthodox patriarchates in Peć and Ohrid and turned their authority over to the Patriarch of Constantinople. This restructuring in the administration of the non-Muslim communities, however, was largely part of a process of centralisation which began as a response to military defeat by Russia and the Treaty of Küçük Kaynarca in 1774. Theologically, the Armenian and the Jacobite Church were not far removed from one another, neither having recognised the Council of Chalcedon, but geographically the distance between Mardin and Istanbul was great.

Consequently, in Ottoman administrative parlance, a number of different expressions were used in reference to this relationship. Generally, the *Süryânî* were referred to as a *tâife* belonging to the Armenian *millet* in constructs such as: *Ermeni milletine tâbi Süryânî tâifesi* or *Ermeni milleti kullarına bağlı Süryânî tâifesi.*[251] This dependency only really affected the community's interactions with the central state, as opposed to its own internal affairs; nevertheless, tentative activities in the nineteenth century indicated a desire for greater independence from the Armenians and the creation of a separate *millet* for the *Süryânî*. There was much greater insistence that the approval of a new patriarch come from Istanbul and not from a local official. This acquired such importance that newly elected patriarchs would travel to Istanbul for their

---

[250] Seyfeli, "Osmanlı Devlet Salnamelerınde Süryaniler," 68-70. The Jerusalem Armenian Patriarch was responsible for the Jacobite hierarchy in Jerusalem as well as the Coptic and Ethiopian Churches until 1865.

[251] These are taken from Özcoşar, *Bir Yüzyıl Bir Sancak Bir Cemaat,* 61-62.

confirmation as was done for the first time in 1836.[252] This assertion may be seen as a reaction to the internal conflict with the Catholic *Süryânî* which brought about the government's intervention and consequently the Jacobite religious hierarchy's realisation that it needed more direct contact with the central administration.[253]

The perception of a need for independence also coincided with a rise in tensions with the Armenian religious leadership eager to assert itself over the *Süryânî* during a period in which its own authority within the *millet* was being challenged. For example, attempts were made to assert Armenian control over properties and to count the *Süryânî* as Armenians in Ottoman censuses.[254]

A signal of the growing separation was the establishment of an unofficial place of worship for *Süryânî* in the Pera district of Istanbul in 1844. This marked the first permanent residence of a *Süryânî* bishop and patriarchal representative in the city and helped furnish direct relations with the Porte. Perhaps an indication of the benefit of this decision was that the government accepted the Jacobites' request to be known as the *Süryânî-i Kadîm*.[255] The first definitive steps towards complete administrative independence came in the 1870s, when Jacobite leaders from Nusaybin petitioned the Porte for their own *millet*.[256] This was followed in 1878 by the construction of a permanent church building, the *Meryem Ana Kilisesi*.[257] A separate Jacobite community was recognised in 1882, although the first Ottoman *sâlnâme* to list the change was the 1302

---

[252] Özcoşar, "Osmanlı Devlet'inde Millet Sistemi ve Süryani Kadimler," 226-227.

[253] Özcoşar, *Bir Yüzyıl Bir Sancak Bir Cemaat*, 63.

[254] The conflict between the *Süryânî* and the Armenians will be described in more detail below starting on page 195.

[255] Ahmet Taşğın, "Süryani Kadim Ortodoks Kilisesinde Yenileşme Çabaları: Deyru'l-Zafaran Manastırında Patriklik Matbaası," in *Süryaniler ve Süryanilik*, vol. 4, 9-10.

[256] Özcoşar, "Millet Sistemi ve Süryani Kadimler," 226-227.

[257] The *Meryem Ana Kilisesi* in Tarlabaşı is still the primary *Süryânî* church in Istanbul and the seat of the Metropolitanate.

[1884/1885] edition.[258] However, it would appear that final legal status did not occur until at least 1912 and the drafting of a constitution (*nizâmnâme*) for the *Süryânî millet*.[259]

Administratively, in 1830, the Porte entered negotiations on the future of the Ottoman Catholics, laying the foundation for a Uniate Armenian *millet* in 1831 to which the *Süryânî* Catholics were also added.[260] Joseph cites 1843 as the date of the Catholics being granted "civil as well as spiritual jurisdiction" over "a separate and distinct community" while Frazee gives 1845 as the date of autonomy from the Armenians.[261] But recognition of the community apparently did not occur until much later. Ottoman *sâlnâme* may simply have been slow to reflect administrative changes as it was not until the 1305 [1889/1890] edition in which the *Süryânî Katolik Patrikliği* was listed separately from the Armenian Catholics, and not until eight years later was the term *millet* expressly used.[262]

The Protestants were unique in the fact that their *millet* did not separate into separate Armenian, Greek and Syriac bodies. Instead, its administration was always dominated by the Armenians, who comprised the largest number of converts. British pressure prompted the issuing of a *fermân* in 1850 by which the Protestants were granted protection and the creation of an administration with representatives, although it stopped short of granting full *millet* status. The first appearance of a Protestant leader in the state *sâlnâme* did not occur until 1320 [1902/1903], a relatively late date.[263]

---

[258] Joseph, *Muslim-Christian Relations*, 29-30; Seyfeli, "Osmanlı Devlet Salnamelerinde Süryaniler," 71.

[259] Özcoşar, *Bir Yüzyıl Bir Sancak Bir Cemaat*, 66. The text of the *nizâmnâme* may be found in Şimşek, *Süryaniler ve Diyarbakır*, 299-314.

[260] In the pre-*Tanzîmât* period, the Jacobites were the mediators between the two, however.

[261] Joseph, *Muslim-Christian Relations*, 50. Frazee, *Catholics and Sultans*, 294.

[262] Seyfeli, "Osmanlı Devlet Salnamelerinde Süryaniler," 86 and 91-93.

[263] Ibid., 122-126. It was an official *millet* according to Joseph, *Muslim-Christian Relations*, 76.

By comparison, the Nestorians of Hakkâri had an extremely loose relationship with the state most probably because of the isolation and protection afforded by the mountains. Even after the *Tanzîmât* and the granting of *millet* status to other communities, the Nestorians remained nearly unnoticed in the Ottoman administrative structure. Technically, they were bound to the Armenian *millet*, either directly or through intermediaries in Mardin. They had, however, more independence than any other Ottoman community in return for a yearly tithe.[264] Some attempt was made to establish an independent *Nestûrî millet* in 1864, but this did not come to fruition. In the 1840s, the more numerous Chaldeans were recognised as a community within the greater *Katolik milleti*. In 1306 [1888/1889], the *Keldânî Patrikliği* was recognised as separate from the Armenian Catholic Patriarchate.[265]

The object of this discussion is to emphasise the divisions within the *Süryânî* communities and the *ad hoc* manner in which the Ottoman government attempted to administer this most difficult of situations.[266] Administration as part of the Armenian *millet* was much less a theologically based decision – even if it was more or less a correct one – than a decision made out of convenience by the Ottomans seeking an order which could be understood and managed easily. At times there had even been disagreement over whether the *Süryânî* were supposed to be tied to the Greek or the Armenian patriarchates.[267] After the decisive attachment to the Armenian *millet*, some of the terms which are encountered in government documents, such as *Yakûbî Ermenîler*, indicate that

---

[264] Joseph, *The Nestorians*, 34-37; Seyfeli, "Osmanlı Devlet Salnamelerinde Süryaniler," 81-84.

[265] Ibid., 101-103.

[266] The Ottoman administration also used terms such as *Nestûrî Katolikler* and *Keldânî Kadim Ermeniler* during the nineteenth century to describe what it clearly did not understand. See Özcoşar, "Papalığın Müdahalesi ve Süryani Kiliselerinde Bölünme," in *Süryaniler ve Süryanilik*, vol. 1, 277.

[267] Özcoşar, "Süryani Kiliselerinde Eğitim," 199-200. In documents from 1733, 1734, 1839 and 1850 the Georgian, Serbian, Ethiopian, Coptic and Syriac churches were all considered part of the Greek Orthodox hierarchy.

there was still considerable confusion.[268] And yet, it is clear that in the government's eyes, the *Süryânî*, the *Keldânî* and the *Nestûrî* were three distinct communities and consequently did not belong to the same *millet* once the Armenian *millet* began to break down into its constituent denominations.

## Social Participation

The social and economic conditions of the *Süryânî* deserve a few comments. The secondary sources are much better informed about the Persian *vis-à-vis* the Ottoman Syriac Christians, whose economic activities have not been the subject of a comprehensive study. The late nineteenth century was a time of prosperity for the Urmiye Syriacs and there was an increase in the number of professionals and merchants. Previously, their urban population had been small with the majority found in villages, where they mostly laboured as sharecropping peasants. Those in the city of Urmiye worked as masons, carpenters or similar trades, but by the twentieth century, they had became the most prosperous group.

Poor peasants still existed, although many prospered either by moving to one of the urban centres or by using money earned working abroad, usually in Georgia or other parts of the Caucasus, to buy their own farmland. The new wealth and influence enjoyed by the Christians of the Urmiye region was reflected socially in a number of ways; the most important point, however, is that there was a rise of a Syriac bourgeoisie dependent on European imperial powers. It has furthermore been suggested that this group had little inclination to participate in the country's constitutional movement and subsequent legislature. The entry of the imperial powers, namely Britain and Russia, into Persia allowed protected Christians the opportunity to advance into trades from which they had previously been discouraged from entering.[269]

---

[268] Özcoşar gives examples from Ottoman documents in "Papalığın Müdahalesi ve Süryani Kiliselerinde Bölünme," 227.

[269] Ishaya, "Ethnicity, Class, and Politics," 7-15; De Kelaita, "On the Road to Nineveh," 8.

Like those in Urmiye, most Ottoman Syriac Christians were rural agriculturalists.[270] Enough *Süryânî* were involved in such activities that Âşûr Yûsuf saw the value for *Süryânî* farmers of publishing articles concerning agriculture and animal husbandry during the harvest season.[271] On the urban side, there were merchants who exported the products of the rural lands that they owned.[272] Moreover, as in other parts of the Ottoman Empire, the non-Muslim communities were prominent artisans and tradesmen; the *Süryânî* of Diyarbakır, for example, dominated silk weaving industry.[273]

Although there has not been a systematic study of *Süryânî* or Chaldean service in the Ottoman government, some authors have mentioned their presence in the local governmental system in the provinces of Bitlis, Diyarbakır and Mamûretü'l-Azîz, especially on the administrative and municipal councils.[274] I have gathered a few examples of such participation from the primary sources, though this is not an exhaustive study by any means.

In Garzan, for example, one Mûsî Kâzım served as the government's *sandûk emîni* [treasurer].[275] In Cizre, a local *Süryânî* was appointed to replace a Chaldean as a member of the *bidâyet mahkemesi* [first-order court], while Yakûb Fâik sat on the *istînâf mahkemesi* [high court] of Üsküp [Skopje] in the Ottoman province

---

[270] Joseph, *Muslim-Christian Relations*, 24.

[271] For example: "Arpa ve buğday hastalığı," *Mürşid-i Âsûriyûn*, 4, no. 7 (Kânûn-ı Evvel 1912), 112; "Ekin hastalığına dâir," *Mürşid-i Âsûriyûn*, 5, no. 9 (Ağustos 1913), 146; "Agnâm uyuzu yâhûd cereb," *Mürşid-i Âsûriyûn*, 5, no. 10 (Eylûl 1913), 161-163.

[272] There is an example of Syriac landowners residing in Urfa, though the peasants in this case were Armenians: Naayem, *Shall This Nation Die?*, 7-8.

[273] Taşğın, "Süryani Püşiciler," in *Süryaniler ve Süryanilik*, vol. 4, 96-97.

[274] Krikorian, *Armenians in the Service of the Ottoman Empire*, 23 and 30. Kriokorian bases his work on provincial *sâlnâme*. For some notes on Chaldeans working for the government, see Naayem, *Shall This Nation Die?*, 125 and 163-164.

[275] "Abone vusûlü," *Kevkeb Mednho*, 2, no. 5 (7 Teşrîn-i Evvel 1911), 8.

of Kosovo.[276] In the summer of 1910, Cebbûr Boyacı listed the names of *Süryânî* who had been given posts in the latest round of government appointments. These included new members on the *bidâyet* and *istînâf* courts in Mosul, Bitlis, Siverek and Mardin as well as individuals in an number of other positions in Diyarbakır, Meyyâfârkîn and Midyat.[277]

The most senior Syriac Christians directly employed by the Ottoman bureaucracy appear to have been two provincial assistant governors (*vâli muavini*): Abdülkerîm Efendi (*Keldânî*) served in this position in the *vilâyet* of Van while Cercîs Efendi (*Süryânî-i Kadîm*) received perhaps two such appointments.[278] Moreover, a Chaldean, Dâvud Yûsufânî (born in 1858), served on the administrative council in the *vilâyet* of Mosul. Then on 9 Şubât 1908, he was elected as one of two deputies for the *sancak* of Mosul in the Ottoman parliament, the *Meclis-i Mebûsân*.[279] During his time in Istanbul, Yûsufânî also sat as a member of the first executive council of the *Hürriyet ve İtilâf Fırkası*, the influential opposition party mentioned above.[280]

---

[276] "Azil ve tayîn," *Kevkeb Mednho*, 2, no. 8 (16 Kânûn-ı Evvel 1911), 8 and "Abone vusûlü," *Kevkeb Mednho*, 1, no. 21 (22 Nîsân 1911), 8. Çıkkı mentions the existence of two high-ranking members of the Ottoman legal system, but their names are not given: *Naum Faik ve Süryani Rönesansı*, 52.

[277] "Diyârbekir 3 Hazîrân 1910 tensîkât-ı cedîdede tayîn olunan Süryânî memûrîn," *İntibâh*, 1, no. 10 (Ağustos 1910), 8.

[278] Abdülkerîm Efendi was a graduate of two important Ottoman schools, the *Mekteb-i Sultânî* [Galatasaray Lycée] and the *Mekteb-i Mülkiye* [School of Civil Administration], and also worked as a chief translator for the *Bâb-ı Zabtiye* [Office of the Minister of Police]. His appointment to Van came in 1895. See Abdülhamit Kırmızı, "Son Dönem Osmanlı Bürokrasisinde Akraba Ermeniler," *Ermeni Araştırmaları* no. 8 (Winter, 2003).

[279] Naayem, *Shall This Nation Die?*, 112; Ebubekir Hâzim Tepeyran, *Hatıralar* (Istanbul: Pera, 1998), 375-378 and 416; Aykut Kansu, *The Revolution of 1908 in Turkey*, 292 n. 277. Note that Kansu and many others incorrectly list him as being an Arab. A brief biography and a photograph may also be found in İhsan Güneş, *Türk Parlamento Tarihi*, vol. 2 (Ankara: Türkiye Büyük Millet Meclisi Vakfı, 1997), 503.

[280] See page 39 above.

The case of Cercîs Efendi deserves a few extra words since he was highly respected in the *Süryânî* community. In 1895, records show that a Cercîs Efendi was appointed as *vâli muavini* in Mamûretü'l-Azîz after having served as a clerk in the *Süryânî-i Kadîm* patriarchate.[281] In 1910, Naûm Fâik published his answer to a question posed by Cercis Efendi, "the honourable former governor's assistant in Sivas (*Sivas vâli muâvin-i sâbıkı izzetli Cercis* [*sic*] *efendi*)", an expression also used by Âşûr Yûsuf in 1911 and 1912.[282] In late 1911 and early 1912, the subscription records of both *Kevkeb Mednho* and *İntibâh* show that Cercîs Alacacı was in Salonika serving on a government commission.[283] Then, at the end of the same year, there was a request in *Mürşid-i Âsûriyûn* for information from several people including "the honourable Cercîs Alacacı in Samsun (*Samsun'dan izzetli Cercîs Alacacı*)"; there is no indication of the position he held, but his residence in Samsun, a place not traditionally inhabited by *Süryânî*, suggests that he continued to serve in a governmental role.[284]

Several generations of the Catholic *Süryânî* Taşo family also held a number of governmental positions in Mamûretü'l-Azîz.[285] Nazar Taşo was a member of Harput's finance and

---

[281] Kırmızı, "Son Dönem Osmanlı Bürokrasisinde Akraba Ermeniler."

[282] "Cevâb," *Kevkeb Mednho*, 1, no. 2 (31 Temmûz 1910), 1; "Dersaâdet'ten Harpût Mürşid-i Âsûriyûn cerîde-i behiyesine Mamûretü'l-Azîz ve tevâbii Süryânî-i Kadîm murahhası Diyonnosiyus mutrân Abdünnûr efendiye açık mektûb," *Mürşid-i Âsûriyûn*, 3, no. 3 (Mart 1911), 45-47; and "Hukûkumuza sâhib olalım," *Mürşid-i Âsûriyûn*, 4, no. 2 (Şubât 1912), 20.

[283] "Abone vusûlü," *İntibâh*, 3, no. 6 (Nisân 1912), 8 and "Abone vusûlü," *Kevkeb Mednho*, 2 no. 7 (2 Kânûn-ı Evvel 1911), 8.

[284] Âşûr Yûsuf made his appeal following a letter by the newspaper *İntibâh*: "İkinci cevâb İntibâh'tan," *Mürşid-i Âsûriyûn*, 4, no. 10 (Kânûn-i Evvel 1912), 153. I understand الاجه جى to be Ottoman Turkish for *Alacacı*, but this reading may be incorrect.

[285] The information about Piyer Taşo comes from the section on doctors in a listing of famous natives of Harput: Sunguroğlu, *Harput Yollarında*, vol. 2, 450-452.

correspondence offices and later a bureaucrat in the *Régie*.[286] His son Piyer, born in 1867, was educated in the local Catholic school and then in the French *lycée* in Aleppo. He too would work for the *Régie* in Mamûretü'l-Azîz as well as in Lebanon and in Trâblus-ı Garb [Libyan Tripoli] before graduating from the French medical school in Beirut. Returning to Mamûretü'l-Azîz, Piyer Taşo had a regular column in the local Armenian newspaper *Yeprad* in which he edified his readership on hygiene, nutrition, medicine and other subjects related to leading a healthy life.[287] Besides practising medicine, he also had his translations of Montesquieu published in the Istanbul press while serving as assistant editor for the government-run newspaper *Mamûretü'l-Azîz*.[288] The eldest of Nazar Taşo's four children, Karabet Ağa, was "of the merchants [*tüccârân*] and notables [*muteberân*]" of Antep and himself had several sons actively involved in trading activities in the Ottoman Empire and the United States.[289]

Considering that Âşûr Yûsuf looked favourably on success in mercantile activities (when conducted with morals and not greed), it is telling that he makes so little mention of more such leading *Süryânî* figures in his newspaper.[290] Indeed, during the late

---

[286] The *Régie cointéressée des tabacs de l'Empire ottoman* was the foreign controlled monopoly on tobacco. The 1305 [1889/1890] *sâlnâme* for the *vilâyet* of Mamûretü'l-Azîz lists Nazar Taşo as *Reji Zirâat Müfettişi*.

[287] His contributions are mentioned in "Hukûkumuza sâhib olalım," *Mürşid-i Âsûriyûn*, 4, no. 2 (Şubât 1912), 18. Even more information is available in Kılıçdağı, *The Bourgeois Transformation and Ottomanism among Anatolian Armenians*, 14-15.

[288] An article republished from *Mamûretü'l-Azîz* is ascribed to Taşo bin Yakûb. This would make the author the cousin of Piyer as Yakûb was the brother of Nazar: "Hayât-ı insâniyeye bir nazar," *Mürşid-i Âsûriyûn*, 5, no. 6 (Mayıs 1913), 87.

[289] "Vefât," *Mürşid-i Âsûriyûn*, 4, no. 1 (Kânûn-ı Sânî 1912), 16. Elsewhere, Âşûr Yûsuf noted the passing of two other members of the Taşo family: "Tekrâr vefât," *Mürşid-i Âsûriyûn*, 3, no. 1 (Kânûn-ı Sânî 1911), 20. İlyâ Taşo was Cebbûr Boyacı's representative for *İntibâh* in Harput: "Türkiye'de vekîllerimiz," *İntibâh*, 4, no. 1 (Teşrîn-i Sânî 1912), 8.

[290] There was even a call for readers to contribute the names of famous Syriac men of religion, doctors, government officials and merchants

nineteenth and early twentieth centuries, it was the prospect of greater economic opportunities which drove the Ottoman *Süryânî* to either emigrate themselves or send their children abroad.[291]

Settlement in North America was concentrated in specific locations: for those from Harput, the destination was primarily Massachusetts; for Diyarbakır, New Jersey; for Cebel-i Tûr, Central Falls, Rhode Island; and for Mardin, Montreal.[292] By 1913, a compilation made by a youth organisation in Boston, the *Süryânî Gençler Şirketi*, indicated that the total North American population was in excess of a thousand individuals.[293] Additionally, around the turn of the century, *Süryânî* began emigrating to Argentina as part of a larger population movement from present-day Syria and Lebanon to South America.

And yet, despite the search for prosperity abroad, a letter writer to *Mürşid-i Âsûriyûn*, probably İbrâhîm Yûsuf, indicated that the same dire situation was holding true in the United States: "Alas, in the business world, there is not a single outstanding *Süryânî*. As for the Armenians, today you can find their successful shops everywhere."[294] There were, consequently, cases in which immigrants abandoned the United States in order to return to the Ottoman Empire after the 1908 revolution; the *Patrik Vekîli* in Istanbul even appealed to the government for funds to help

---

(*tüccâr-ı sanatkâr*): "1913 senesi takvîmi," *Mürşid-i Âsûriyûn*, 5, no. 8 (Temmûz 1913), 129-130.

[291] This is stated in numerous articles from *Mürşid-i Âsûriyûn*.

[292] Paterson was a major centre of silk production, like Diyarbakır, where the *Süryânî* dominated the industry. Edip Aydın, *The History of the Syrian Orthodox Church of Antioch in North America: Challenges and Opportunities*. (Master's thesis, St. Vladimir Orthodox Seminary, 2000). Also see Kiraz, "Suryoye and Suryoyutho."

[293] The group published the names and addresses of some 1060 *Süryânî* in the United States and Canada. Cebbûr Boyacı noted that at least 100 more, either newcomers or those missed in the survey, were known to exist: "Amerika'daki Süryânîlerin nüfûs defteri," *İntibâh*, 4, no. 10 (Ağustos 1913), 8.

[294] In print, the letter is signed only by the initials "" l‏ – ‏.: "Amerika'dan diğer bir mektûb," *Mürşid-i Âsûriyûn*, 4, no. 10 (Kânûn-ı Evvel 1912), 159-160. Although the writer refers to "Amerika" throughout, the situation described is probably that of Worcester alone.

poverty-stricken *Süryânî* who had emigrated from the provinces of Mamûretü'l-Azîz, Diyarbakır and Bitlis but were now in the process of returning to their homes.[295] Instead, according to another disillusioned observer, the *Süryânî* in the United States worked as simple labourers and aspired to nothing greater, much unlike their hard-working Armenian neighbours.[296] The latter information also came from İbrâhîm Yûsuf, who was a native of Harput and one of the first *Süryânî* to emigrate to the United States. Born in 1866, İbrâhîm Yûsuf was educated at the Central Turkey College in Antep before moving to Baltimore in 1889 to study medicine. He eventually settled in Worcester, Massachusetts and began practising as a doctor. İbrâhîm Yûsuf would become probably the most famous of the early *Süryânî* immigrants to North America, something which will be examined in greater detail in Chapter 3.[297]

I have been unable to locate any Syriac Christians who had managed to obtain foreign consular protection, something prevalent in the coastal regions of the Ottoman Empire with other non-Muslim communities. Part of the difficulty in identifying *Süryânî* from Ottoman historical records that do not explicitly state religious affiliation is the tendency of *Süryânî* to use names which were identical to those used by Armenians, Arabs or Catholics.[298] In all probability, notable Syriac Christians have been counted as belonging to other communities, but this does not negate the fact that there was no *Süryânî* parallel to the wealthy and influential Armenian, Greek and Jewish individuals of the Ottoman Empire.

---

[295] Özcoşar, *Bir Yüzyıl Bir Sancak Bir Cemaat*, 177.

[296] "Amerika'da Worcester'de bulunan Süryânî ahvâli," *Mürşid-i Âsûriyûn*, 4, no. 2 (Şubât 1912), 23-26.

[297] See Aydın, *The History of the Syrian Orthodox Church of Antioch in North America*. Eden Naby incorrectly calls him a dentist in "The Assyrian Diaspora," 221.

[298] Carter Findley's survey of non-Muslims in the Ottoman bureaucracy turned up a number of Arab Christians, but it is impossible to establish whether any of these – or indeed any of the presumed Muslims – were in fact Syriacs: "The Acid Test of Ottomanism: The Acceptance of Non-Muslims in the Late Ottoman Bureaucracy," in *Christians and Jews in the Ottoman Empire*.

Nor can we pinpoint an emergent middle class or a powerful guild structure.

The lack of any lay parallel – both in terms of a traditional authority within the community and a presence in the Ottoman capital – helps to explain the lack of a challenge to the religious hierarchy prior to the twentieth century: it was simply never in doubt. Moreover, the conflict between the Armenian Church and the nascent *Süryânî-i Kadîm millet* further allowed the Jacobite hierarchy to be at the fore since this was, by official definition, a religious issue. The final chapters of this work will elaborate on the *Süryânî* intellectuals of the early twentieth century and will explore the claims that it was they who finally did mount a secular challenge, through Assyrian nationalism, to the Jacobite leadership in the manner of the Urmiye communities and of the other Ottoman non-Muslims.

This chapter has highlighted the divisions which emerged in the non-Muslim communities over the nineteenth century and has examined non-Muslim participation in Ottoman politics in the second constitutional period. During the *Tanzîmât* there was a general trend of moving away from *millet* administration and institutions being concentrated in the hand of the religious authorities and a small group of wealthy individuals. These were challenged by a middle class composed of intellectuals, merchants or the guilds.

The ensuing cleavages outwardly took the form of a conflict between secular and lay, or between conservative and progressive, forces. There were many anti-clerical activists in the Armenian community, for example. The tension between the religious authorities of the Jacobite Church and Assyrian nationalists over the twentieth century has meant that many historians have sought to find examples of tensions between the two groups in the nineteenth and early twentieth centuries. But in the Ottoman Empire, divides were not necessarily predicated on conflict between the secular and the spiritual. Greek and Jewish examples have shown how even the leading religious figures could come down on the side of "the reformers" rather than "the conservatives".

As for non-Muslim attitudes towards the Young Turk revolution and the new constitutional era, Bernard Lewis has written that, the "Armenians and Christian nationalities ... found little to attract them in the Ottoman federation, and preferred to seek the fulfilment of their political aspirations outside the Empire."[299] But as we have seen, there were non-Muslims who were not only prepared to cooperate with the CUP, but who were passionate supporters of realising Ottomanism. Emmanouēlidēs was obviously but a single example from the largest non-Muslim community of the Ottoman Empire. But like Krikor Zohrab, he embodies the spirit of the early years of the second constitutional era, during which there was a real belief in the Ottoman Empire. If nothing else, the establishment of the parliament allowed certain figures outside the traditional elites to negotiate with the Ottoman political leadership and represent their communities.[300] No *Süryânî* ever served in the parliament. But this does not mean that we do not have any insight into their political beliefs and their attitudes towards Ottomanism.

---

[299] Bernard Lewis, *The Emergence of Modern Turkey*, 3rd edition (New York: Oxford University Press, 2002), 204.

[300] Kechriotis, "On the Margins of National Historiography."

# 3 IDENTITY IN THE *SÜRYÂNÎ* PRESS

At the outset of this work, I endeavoured to establish a consistent set of terms which would serve to facilitate a historical discussion while avoiding the accompanying historiographical pitfalls. In part, I arrived at my particular decisions based on the use I encountered in the pages of *Kevkeb Mednho, Mürşid-i Âsûriyûn* and *İntibâh*, but the precise way in which Naûm Fâik, Âşûr Yûsuf and Cebbûr Boyacı employed key words deserves further attention. Of particular importance are the terms *vatan*, *millet* and *cemâat*, usually translated as "fatherland", "nation" and "congregation" respectively, as well as the word *Süryânî* itself.

Since both men were writing in an Ottoman environment and in the Ottoman language, I fully subscribe to the argument that "it is within the framework of the Ottoman reality that these terms must above all and first and foremost be seen."[301] Such warnings must be heeded to properly understand the meaning of Ottoman-era writers, something, it should be noted, which has not always been the case with scholarship dealing with Naûm Fâik, Âşûr Yûsuf and the other *Süryânî* intellectuals.

## *VATAN, MILLET* AND *CEMÂAT*

In the second issue of *Kevkeb Mednho*, an announcement appeared stating that "our goal consists of humbly serving the sons of the *vatan* and of the *millet*."[302] Cebbûr Boyacı exclaimed that, "yes, the

---

[301] Anagnostopoulou, "The Terms *Millet, Génos, Ethnos, Oikoumenikótita, Alytrotismos* in Greek Historiography," in *The Passage from the Ottoman Empire to the Nation-States* (Istanbul: Isis Press, 2004), 38.

[302] "Maksadımız ibnâ-yı vatan ve millete bir hidmet-i nâçiz îfâ etmekten ibâret olup mâddeten istifâde almaktan ziyâde onları manen müstefîd

light of freedom has risen in our *vatan*."[303] And *Mürşid-i Âsûriyûn*'s synopsis of 1912 and introduction to 1913 concluded by saying, "We hope to God that this new year will be a fruitful and blessed one for our *vatan*, our *millet* and ourselves."[304] What then were the *millet* and the *vatan*? Was the *millet* the *Süryânî-i Kadîm* community alone or something larger? Was the *vatan* the Ottoman Empire or a newly conceptualised homeland of the Assyrian people?

First of all, *vatan* had, by the mid-nineteenth century, begun to take on a meaning inspired more by European nationalist thought. The Arabic original was more parochial, referring to a place of birth, but *vatan* in the Ottoman context was also often used in the sense of "country" or "the fatherland", that is to say, the Ottoman Empire.[305] No learned Ottoman in the twentieth century could have been ignorant of this concept, but it should not be taken as granted that it had the same meaning to the *Süryânî*.

The first cautionary note is that *vatan* is not a word encountered with the same frequency as *millet* or *cemâat* in *Kevkeb Mednho*, *Mürşid-i Âsûriyûn* or *İntibâh*. The second is that the word may have carried a different meaning from author to author or from article to article. And yet, there is enough evidence to be able to speculate on how the *Süryânî* intellectuals were interpreting it.

---

kılmak ârzûsuyla meşâgil-i kesîremize ilâveten bu bâr-ı girânîde üzerimize almak meşakkatına giriştik.": "İfâde-i mahsûsa," *Kevkeb Mednho*, 1, no. 2 (31 Temmûz 1910), 1. A nearly identical use of these two terms accompanied Naûm Fâik's notice of the founding of *Şifuro* a year later, in 1911: "Vatan ve millete nâfi ve hakîkata hâdim olacağı emel-i kavîsindeyiz." See "Şifuro yani Boru cerîdesi," *Kevkeb Mednho*, 1, no. 24 (3 Hazîrân 1911), 28.

[303] "İlân-ı hürriyet ve biz Süryânîler," *İntibâh*, 1, no. 3 (Kânûn-ı Sânî 1910), 2: "İşte bu esbâba mebnîdir ki diyoruz evet vatanımızda hürriyet nûru doğmuş. Bu nûru görenleri ihyâ ediyor. Bu nûr daha bir buçuk senedir doğmuş ama güneş dünyâ kurulalı her gün doğur ama körler güneşin nûrundan ne vakt istifâde edebilmişler ki biz hürriyetin nûrundan istifâde edebilelim."

[304] "Rabden temennî ederiz ki işbu yeni sene, vatanımız, milletimiz ve kendi şahsımız için müsmir ve mübârek bir sene olsun.": "1912 senesi," *Mürşid-i Âsûriyûn*, 5, no. 1 (Kânûn-i Sânî 1913), 15-16.

[305] Lewis, *The Emergence of Modern Turkey*, 334-340.

For example, on the second anniversary of the ascension of Sultan Mehmed Reşâd to the Ottoman throne, Naûm Fâik related reports of the celebrations at the patriarchate, included the singing of "hymns to the fatherland (*vatan besteleri*)" by *Süryânî* youths.[306] Here Naûm Fâik was clearly referring to the Ottoman Empire just as Beşâr Hilmî was when he wrote in *Kevkeb Mednho* of "securing the future of the *millet* and the *vatan* in which we take so much pride."[307]

Returning to the case of İbrâhîm Yûsuf, the *Süryânî* doctor residing in Worcester, we encounter instances of Âşûr Yûsuf too using the word *vatan* in much the same way. *Mürşid-i Âsûriyûn* began following the progress of İbrâhîm Yûsuf in 1912, when he left the United States to spend time at hospitals in London and Vienna. Then, as was reported, "for the purpose of visiting his *vatan*," he arrived in the Ottoman Empire, making stops in Istanbul and Harput amongst other places.[308] Here, the usage of *vatan* could be understood to be either the Ottoman Empire or his birthplace of Harput, but when İbrâhîm Yûsuf arrived back in the United States, Âşûr Yûsuf published an article entitled "Doctor Yûsuf's return to his *vatan*."[309] This *vatan* was not, therefore, some immutable

---

[306] "Süryânî gençleri tarafından vatan besteleriyle intibâh neşîdeleri terennüm ... edilmiştir.": "Cülûs-ı hazret-i pâdişâhî," *Kevkeb Mednho*, 1, no. 22 (6 Mayıs 1911), 20.

[307] "Mârdîn'den mevrûd havâdis," *Kevkeb Mednho*, 1, no. 2 (31 Temmûz 1910), 2: "Heyet-i idâremiz tarafından karârgîr olduktan sonra cumartesi günü Diyârbekir'den hareket târîhinde musâdif pazar günün Mârdîn'e muvâsalat eylediğimde nâmıyla iftihâr eylediğimiz vatan ve milletin temîn-i istikbâli için bir muhabbet-i samîme, bir ittihâd-ı kavî ile Süyânî-i Kadîm cemâatimize intibâh unvân-ı hikmet beyânıyla teşekkül eden cemiyetlerin merkez-i umûmîsine hakîkî bir revnak veren Mârdîn İntibâh cemiyet-i muhteremesinde bulunduğum cihetle kendimiz bahs [illegible] ederim."

[308] "Aldığımız habere nazaran, doktor Yûsuf efendi vatanını ziyâret etmek üzere bir kaç gün sonra Harpûtlu millettaşlar ile eğer mâniler zuhûr etmez ise Harpût'a avdet etmek niyetindedir.": "Avdet," *Mürşid-i Âsûriyûn*, 4, no. 2 (Şubât 1912), 32. A summary of his later activities is in "Doktor İbrâhîm Yûsuf," *Mürşid-i Âsûriyûn*, 4, no. 8 (Teşrîn-i Sânî 1912), 128.

[309] "Doktor Yûsuf Türk ve Balkan muhârebesinde îfâ-yı hidmet ettikten sonra vatana avdeti," *Mürşid-i Âsûriyûn*, 5, no. 10 (Eylûl 1913), 159-160.

fatherland of a nation but was rather one which was dependent on citizenship and residence.

An additional occurrence from Âşûr Yûsuf reinforces this argument. His "interview with a correspondent who travels our *vatan*" describes the activities of Armenians in building schools, publishing books and establishing charitable organisations.[310] It concludes with the interviewer asking "and what about the *Süryânî*?", to which he receives a reply denigrating their lack of efforts.[311] But the *vatan* was not just the lands inhabited by the *Süryânî*, for the interviewee discusses regions, such as Izmir and Erzurum, well outside their range of settlement. In addition, by speaking of "our *vatan*", Âşûr Yûsuf suggests that in the language of the early twentieth century *Süryânî* intellectuals, one's *vatan* was one's state, one's country.

But it could also refer to a non-state national homeland. Of this usage, *Mürşid-i Âsûriyûn* provides an example in Âşûr Yûsuf's translation of a manifesto by Max Nordau (born Südfeld Simon Miksa), co-founder of the World Zionist Organization with Theodor Herzl.[312] Nordau wrote that "The objective of Zionism is, as its agenda of ten years ago announced, to prepare in Palestine a *vatan* for the Jewish people, secured by the laws of mankind."[313] Nordau was not, however, suggesting that this *vatan* be independent from the Ottoman Empire: "We want to be Ottomans

---

[310] "Vatanımızı dolaşan bir muhabiri isticvâb," *Mürşid-i Âsûriyûn*, 3, no. 8 (Eylûl 1911), 128-130. The fact that the name of the traveller is not given and that the interview feels contrived leads me to suspect that Âşûr Yûsuf is both asking and answering the questions, especially when we consider that he is known to have resided Izmir.

[311] "Suâl - Ermenîler ne yapıyorlar? Cevâb - Ermenîler kendi milletlerini tenvîr ve ifâze etmeğe çalışırlar ... S - Ya Süryânîler ne yapıyorlar? C - Bunlar yamık bir millet olup hâb-ı gaflette derin bir uyku çekmektedirler."

[312] "Yahûdîler ve Balkan meselesi," *Mürşid-i Âsûriyûn*, 5, no. 2 (Şubât 1913), 27-30.

[313] Ibid., 29: "Siyonizmin maksadı 10 sene evvel programında ilân olunduğu gibi Bagesdin'de Yahûdîlere kânûn-ı beşer ile temîn edilmiş bir vatan hâzır etmektir."

like all the other peoples there."[314] In translating Nordau from Armenian[315] Âşûr Yûsuf chose *vatan* with the meaning of a homeland or fatherland for a people. He repeated this usage in his own words several months later when he spoke of the Jewish people "whose *vatan* is Palestine and Jerusalem."[316]

The second such instance is similar but more significant for the purpose of this work despite being another translation, this time by Livengood, "a graduate of Harvard University".[317] The article concludes by stating that "today's province of Syria contains but a small portion of the original *vatan* of the *Süryânî*."[318] While there is nothing particularly striking about references to these ancient homelands, the fact that neither Naûm Fâik nor Âşûr Yûsuf ever spoke of a *Süryânî* or Assyrian *vatan* themselves or in a contemporary context stands in contrast to their portrayals in the nationalist historiography. Only when translating from other languages did they employ *vatan* in reference to a homeland of an ancient people; in their own words, *vatan* meant the Ottoman Empire, and throughout the remainder of this work, references to it will continue to carry the same meaning.

Unlike *vatan*, *millet* was an extremely common word, and although there were some inconsistencies, its meaning can be established with a high degree of certainty. As we have seen, *millet*

---

[314] Ibid., 30: "Biz hep oradaki milletler gibi Osmânlı olmak isteriz."

[315] We can tell that Âşûr Yûsuf translated from Armenian based on the fact that in the article there are repeated references to a place by the name of باغسدين, which is in fact the Armenian name for Palestine. In other articles, he uses Filistîn, the normal Arabic and Turkish term.

[316] "Dünyânın çâr köşesinde dağılmış olan Yahûdîler, millettaşlarını kayırmak ve vatanları olan Filistîn ve Ûrişlem'i Yahûdî mühâcirin vâsıtasıyla imâr etmekte gösterdikleri faâliyet şöyle dursun, ...": "Süryânî lisânının kesb-i hayâtı," *Mürşid-i Âsûriyûn*, 5, no. 13 (Kânûn-ı Evvel 1913), 200.

[317] "Âşûr diyârı, Sûriye ve Süryânîler," *Mürşid-i Âsûriyûn*, 5, no. 3 (Mart 1913), 39-41. The attribution is to "Harvard Dârü'l-fünûnu mezûnlarından fazîletli Livengood". His full name is given at the end of the article in the Latin alphabet, but unfortunately it is largely obscured in copy. In any case, there was a Mr. Livengood in the area at the time: Atkinson, *The German, the Turk and the Devil Made a Triple Alliance*.

[318] "Şimdiki Sûriye tabir olunan vilâyet Süryânîlere aslî olan vatanın küçük bir kısmı hâvîdir."

was a term employed by the Ottoman administration to designate a community defined by religion rather than, say, ethnicity. However, while in modern Turkish *millet* has taken on the meaning of "nation", Naby's equation of the two terms for nineteenth-century Persia is abrupt and not backed by any analysis of the terminology.[319] As we will see, if by *millet* Âşûr Yûsuf and Naûm Fâik did mean the "nation", then by implication, the Nestorians and Chaldeans were not of the same nation as the *Süryânî*.

At a first glance, Âşûr Yûsuf and Naûm Fâik appear to use *millet* to speak of their *Süryânî-i Kadîm* co-religionists in the standard Ottoman parlance, but on closer examination we may see that its meaning was, in fact, more expansive, covering all *Süryânî* irrespective of church affiliation. Contrasting *millet* with the term *cemaât* illustrates their reliance on secular and spiritual definitions respectively. In a single sentence, Âşûr Yûsuf wrote of both the *Süryânî Protestan cemâati* and the *Süryânî-i Kadîm cemâati*, and then followed this by describing a respected *Süryânî* figure as "our Protestant *millettaş*".[320] A *cemâat* concerned only one's church – Protestant or Jacobite – while *millet* was a term which encompassed something larger. Nor were Catholics excluded from belonging to the same *millet*: Piyer Taşo (described above on page 107) was also referred to as a *millettaş*.[321]

In all of these examples the language is constant, with *millet* being a secular term used to speak of a community no longer defined by church affiliation. Naûm Fâik called the Indian Jacobite community "our *cemâat*", but in all the articles that I have examined, neither he nor Âşûr Yûsuf ever suggested that the

---

[319] See Naby, "The Assyrians of Iran," 245 for a specific example.

[320] "Harpût Protestan cemâatinden şemmâs Barsûm mahdûmî şemmâs Avagîm ağa maâile bugün Amerika'da olup Harpût'da mülkü bulunan bir bâb hâne ile bir bâb dukkânını Harpût Süryânî-i Kadîm cemâatine mensûb bulunan Meryem Ana kilisesine hediye etmek olduğu maatteşekkür mesmûumuz oldu. Şu Protestan millettaşımız ...": "Harpût Meryem Ana kilisesine hediye," *Mürşid-i Âsûriyûn*, 3, no. 4 (Hazîrân 1911), 17. The Turkish suffix *-daş* indicates fellowship in the same class of people, whether they be fellow citizens (*vatandaş*) or travelling companions (*yoldaş*).

[321] "Millettaşlarımızdan doktor Piyer efendi Taşo ...": "Hukûkumuza sâhib olalım," *Mürşid-i Âsûriyûn*, 4, no. 2 (Şubât 1912), 18.

Indians were from the same *millet* as the *Süryânî* in the Ottoman Empire.[322]

The sole caveat to this discussion would be their usage of the Ottoman Turkish terms for the Ottoman people as a whole – *millet-i Osmâniyân*[323] and *millet-i Osmâniye*[324] – but aside from these set phrases, they reserved *millet* to speak of their community based on a common heritage and not on citizenship or religious affiliation. And yet, there is not a single instance of Âşûr Yûsuf, Cebbûr Boyacı or Naûm Fâik describing a Nestorian or a Chaldean as a *millettaş* or as being from the same *millet* as the *Süryânî*. Consequently, I argue that while *millet* did indeed have a secular meaning, it meant only *Süryânî-i Kadîm* as well as the members of the break-away Catholic and Protestant *Süryânî* churches. It certainly did not refer to the "Assyrian nation" – even if Âşûr Yûsuf, Cebbûr Boyacı and Naûm Fâik clearly believed that they, and indeed all *Süryânî*, were the descendants of the ancient Assyrians.

## *SÜRYÂNÎ*, *ÂSÛRÎ* AND *ÂRÂMÎ*

The second facet of the question of identity centres around the belief that the *Süryânî*, as Assyrians, were ethnic kindred of the Nestorians and Chaldeans as well as the Melkites and Maronites. But, as I have already emphasised, to equate *Süryânî* with Assyrian would be erroneous, and not only because there existed separate Ottoman Turkish, Arabic and Syriac terms for Assyrian.[325] *Mürşid-i Âsûriyûn*, *İntibâh* and *Kevkeb Mednho* expressly use *Âsûrî* to speak of Assyrians as a whole, while *Süryânî* has only the limited scope used

---

[322] "Hindistân'daki ihtilâflarımız," *Kevkeb Mednho*, 2, no. 3 (Ağustos 1911), 8.

[323] "Hukûkumuza sâhib olalım," *Mürşid-i Âsûriyûn*, 4, no. 2 (Şubât 1912), 18.

[324] "Cülûs-ı hazret-i pâdişâhî," *Kevkeb Mednho*, 1, no. 22 (6 Mayıs 1911), 8.

[325] A common error is to argue that since the two words share a common origin, then they refer to the same people. Etymological relationships (something which is disputed in this case) do not *ipso facto* mean synonymity, so whatever the roots of these two words, they did not mean the same thing in Ottoman times and nor do they today.

in this work. This is most easily demonstrable by observing the juxtaposition between the terms: Âşûr Yûsuf requested information about the "newspapers published in Turkish or Arabic or Chaldean (*Keldânîce*) amongst the *Süryânî* and the *Keldânî*."[326] Not only were the *Keldânî* not *Süryânî*, but Âşûr Yûsuf even considered the languages of the two groups deserving of separate terms. Elsewhere in *Mürşid-i Âsûriyûn*, he wrote of the Maronites, Nestorians, Chaldeans and *Süryânî*, each group denoted individually.[327] This pattern holds true throughout the pages of *Mürşid-i Âsûriyûn*, *İntibâh* and *Kevkeb Mednho*.

Naûm Fâik and Âşûr Yûsuf also used the word in a few compounds. We have already seen *Süryânî-i Kadîm*, *Süryânî-i Cedîd* and *Süryânî Protestan*, but what should we make of *Arab Süryânî*, *Türk Süryânî*, *Kürd Süryânî* or *Hindistân Süryânî* – all expressions found in *Mürşid-i Âsûriyûn*? The first three were simply used to describe the speakers of Arabic, Turkish and Kurdish respectively and were not used to suggest an ethnic connection to the Arab, Turkish or Kurdish people.[328] *Hindistân Süryânî* and *Hind Süryânî* are perhaps more problematic in the sense that Âşûr Yûsuf could consider a separate ethnic group – the Malabar Indian Jacobites – as *Süryânî* in their own right.[329] It is possible that Âşûr Yûsuf believed the Indian congregation to be, in fact, of the same

---

[326] "(4) Süryânîlerde ve Keldânîlerde, Türkçe ve Arabça yâhûd Keldânîce neşr olunan cerîdeler ve onların târîh-i intişârı ve onların hidmetlerine dâir malûmât.": "1913 senesi takvîmi," *Mürşid-i Âsûriyûn*, 5, no. 8 (Temmûz 1913), 129-130.

[327] "Hukûkumuza sâhib olalım," *Mürşid-i Âsûriyûn*, 4, no. 2 (Şubât 1912), 18-20.

[328] "Ve diğeri (el-Hikmet) nâmla Arabiyü'l-ibâre Arabî hurûfâtıyla müellefi Mîhâîl Hikmet Çıkkı Efendi Mârdîn'de Deyrü-z'Zaferân matbaasından sâha-ı vücûda gelmekte ve memûl ederiz ki muhteviyâtıyla Arab Süryânîlerine pek çok fâideli olacaktır.": "Süryânîler için iki yeni cerîde dahâ," *Mürşid-i Âsûriyûn*, 5, no. 9 (Ağustos 1913), 148. "Lakin şunu da ilâve etmeliyiz ki şu eserler Türkî ve Arabî lisânlar ile mahlût olmalı yoksa Türk Süryânîleri için manâsız ve fâidesiz olacaktır.": "1913 senesi takvîmi," *Mürşid-i Âsûriyûn*, 5, no. 8 (Temmûz 1913), 130. For Kurdish, see page 74, note 189.

[329] For example, see "Hindistân Süryânî hıristiyânları," *Mürşid-i Âsûriyûn*, 5, no. 7 (Hazîrân 1913), 111-112.

ethnicity as those in the Ottoman Empire since a minority were indeed descendants of missionaries from several centuries earlier.[330] More probably, referring to the Indian Jacobites as *Hind Sûryânî* reflects a practice accepted by tradition, even if the word *Sûryânî* on its own had taken a secular meaning by the twentieth century. Nevertheless, we have already seen that the Indian Christians were considered to be another *cemâat* of the *Sûryânî-i Kadîm* but not from the same *millet* as the *Sûryânî*.

There is also one instance in which Âşûr Yûsuf may have used the appellation *Sûryânî* when referring to Nestorians and Chaldeans, but even in this case his intentions are not entirely clear. A single sentence from *Mürşid-i Âsûriyûn* stated that in Persia, "*Sûryânî*, Jewish and Armenian children, together with over a thousand Persian children, are being educated in thirteen schools belonging to Christians."[331] Here, *Sûryânî* may have meant the indigenous Nestorians and their converts to the Catholic, Protestant or Orthodox Churches, but there were in fact also small Jacobite settlements in Persia, such as those in Shiraz and Isfahan, where both Armenians and Jews could also be found.[332] More probably, Âşûr Yûsuf was translating from English and that the term in question was "Syriac", which he mistranslated as *Sûryânî*.[333] In any case, this would be the sole possible exception that I have located in the primary sources and the uncertainty surrounding the usage does not change any of my conclusions.

Unlike *Sûryânî*, *Âsûrî* is exceedingly rare in the works of Âşûr Yûsuf and Naûm Fâik, although there is no reason to doubt that when it was used, it referred to all Assyrians, irrespective of denomination. Naûm Fâik, for example, spoke of the "patriotism of the *Sûryânî* and pride of the Assyrians (*hamiyet-i Sûryâniye ve*

---

[330] Joseph, *Muslim-Christian Relations*, 139.

[331] "Malûmât-ı müfide," *Mürşid-i Âsûriyûn*, 5, no. 7 (Hazîrân 1913), 112: "Acemistân'da Hristyânlara mahsûs olan on üc mektebde, Sûryânî, Yahûdî, ve Ermenî çocuklarıyla berâber binden ziyâde Acem çocukları da talîm edilmektedirler."

[332] Joseph, *Muslim-Christian Relations*, 21.

[333] A similar process by which I believe *Âsûrî* erroneously entered Ottoman Turkish writings will be described below.

*nahvet-i Âsûriye*)."[334] There can be no question that despite speaking of them separately, Naûm Fâik believed the *Süryânî* to be Assyrians. This opinion he shared with his readership, with Naûm Beşârûf in the United States, for example, praising the author's "noble Assyrian sentiments".[335] In arguing against their claims to *Süryânî* property, Naûm Fâik also stated that Armenians "would not let an Assyrian tread on even a single stone of their church", but these sentences contain some of the only instances of the word *Âsûrî* appearing in *Kevkeb Mednho*.[336]

Furthermore, I have catalogued over 250 articles from *Mürşid-i Âsûriyûn* and read several dozen more, and yet, I have found only two instances of Âşûr Yûsuf using the word *Âsûrî* himself. Requesting more examples of the Syriac vernacular spoken in Cebel-i Tûr, Âşûr Yûsuf wrote that "we even hope to find examples of the Assyrians amongst these."[337] Secondly, he prefaced a discussion of an archaeological discovery, again in Cebel-i Tûr, believed to show the relationship between the *Süryânî* and the ancient Assyrians, saying "[h]ere is proof that we are Assyrians."[338]

---

[334] "Cerîdeler âlem'nde cerîdelerimiz, ve zavâllı nâşirleri," *Kevkeb Mednho*, 1, no. 19 (25 Mart 1911), 3.

[335] Ibid.: "Hamiyet-i Süryâniye ve hissiyât-i şerîfe-i Âsûriyenizden son derece memnûn olup Süryânî milletimize şarkta bu gibi şâyân takdîr olan bir gazetenin neşrine muvafık olmanızdan sizleri ne gibi elfâz ile tebrîk edeyim bir türlü bilemiyorum." Naûm Beşârûf would later be involved in the publishing of the periodical *Babil* out of Boston; although in Armenian, *Babil* was specifically for the *Süryânî* community.

[336] "İyi bilmiş olalım ki onlar kiliselerinin bir taşı üzerine basmağa bile Âsûrîlerden kimseyi bırakmazlar. Hâl böyle iken mutrân Tûmâ efendi hazretleri nasıl olur da Erbaîn Kilisesi'nde onlara mahal-i tahsîs ediyor. Lice kazâsı dâhilinde (ﺣﺰﻨـ ﺳﻤﺒ) yani Ak Kilise'nin davâsı hâlâ meydânda iken ve onu hemân hemân Süryânîlerin elinden almalarına [?] gurûşta otuz para istimâli var iken artık çeşm-i tamalarını mâlimize her vakt dert açan böyle bir millete nasıl emîn oluyor." See "Devr-i intibâhta bir azîm gaflet," *Kevkeb Mednho*, 1, no. 22 (6 Mayıs 1911), 1.

[337] "Beyne'n-nâs mesel makâmında tedâvül olunur," *Mürşid-i Âsûriyûn*, 3, no. 10 (Teşrîn-i Sânî 1911), 164: "Biz bunlarda Âsûrîler eserini bile bulmak memûlindeyiz."

[338] "Cebel-i Tûr ahvâli," *Mürşid-i Âsûriyûn*, 5, no. 6 (Mayıs 1913), 92-94. The article is split into three parts, the final section, "İşte Âsûrî

To these we may add a handful of other times in which the word *Âsûrî* was used in *Mürşid-i Âsûriyûn* but not by Âşûr Yûsuf himself. The exceptional case was a single issue from 1911 which contained four such examples, two in reports from the United States, one in a letter from *serepiskopos* Pavlûs in Istanbul and one in a translation of Leo Tolstoy's *Esarhaddon, King of Assyria*.[339] This issue is also notable for containing the only two articles which use *Âsûrî* when referring to contemporary *Süryânî*, and not merely the historical Assyrian people. First of all, Âşûr Yûsuf published a translation of an article from an unnamed English-language newspaper discussing a conference by the *Âsûrî Şirket-i İlmiye* or *Âsûrî İlmî Cemiyeti* [Assyrian Scholarly Association] in Fitchburg, Massachusetts.[340] From the names of the participants and the subjects discussed, it would appear that *Süryânî* alone attended the event, although Chaldeans and Nestorians may well have also been present. Second of all, Lusi Donabed's letter in Ottoman Turkish detailed the activities of the *Worcester Âsûrî Kadınlar Şirketi* [Worcester Assyrian Ladies Association].[341] This letter also makes no mention of Nestorian or Chaldean participation, and so it is plausible that both of these organisations had simply adopted the English term "Assyrian" as the translation of the Ottoman Turkish *Süryânî*, which was then retranslated from English as *Âsûrî* in *Mürşid-i Âsûriyûn*, something which still occurs today.

---

olduğumuza bir ısbât", briefly describes the discovery from the village of Harmîs.

[339] *Esarhaddon, King of Assyria* actually began in the previous issue: "Âsûrîlerin Esârhâddûn pâdişâhı," *Mürşid-i Âsûriyûn*, 3, no. 1 (Kânûn-ı Sânî 1911), 13-17 and "Âsûrîlerin Esârhâddûn pâdişâhı," *Mürşid-i Âsûriyûn*, 3, no. 2 (Şubât 1911), 24-27.

[340] Both *Âsûrî Şirket-i İlmiye* and *Âsûrî İlmî Cemiyeti* were used in the article; my English translation may not reflect the actual name of the organisation. See "Amerika'da Âsûrîlerin Şirket-i İlmiye senevi tecemmuu," *Mürşid-i Âsûriyûn*, 3, no. 2 (Şubât 1911), 32-33.

[341] See "Worcester Âsûrî kadınlar şirketi," *Mürşid-i Âsûriyûn*, 3, no. 2 (Şubât 1911), 34-35. The same organisation had earlier been recorded as the *Worcester Süryânî Kadınlar Muâvenet-i Hayriye Cemiyeti* [Worcester *Süryânî* Ladies Charitable Aid Association]: "Worcester Süryânî Kadınlar Cemiyeti," *İntibâh*, 2, no. 3 (Kânûn-ı Sânî 1911), 8.

Unlike his compatriots in the Ottoman Empire, Cebbûr Boyacı was more liberal in his use of the term *Âsûrî*. Beginning in the first issue of its second year, *İntibâh*'s English subtitle "Assyrian's [*sic*] monthly newspaper" whereas before it had been "our pages are open to all works beneficial to the *Süryânî millet* (*menâfi-i millet-i Süryâniye için âsâra sahîfelerimiz açıktır*)". Although these former was obviously not a translation of the latter, the progress from the original term *Süryânî* to the English "Assyrian" is again what I believe to have been occurring.[342]

This is further evident in cases where Cebbûr Boyacı commented on articles in Armenian-language publications, where the term used to refer to the *Süryânî* closely resembles the Ottoman Turkish *Âsûrî*; in such instances, Cebbûr Boyacı's language reflects the source and he speaks of Assyrians.[343] It is probably no coincidence that in the Ottoman Empire, it was particularly in Harput that the *Süryânî* referred to themselves as *Âsûrî* when speaking Ottoman Turkish, Harput being the most heavily Armenian of all the areas inhabited by *Süryânî*.[344]

While Cebbûr Boyacı did on occasion use *Âsûrî* to speak of a modern, and not an ancient people, for the most part, *İntibâh* retained the standard Ottoman Turkish practice of using *Süryânî*.[345]

---

[342] George Kiraz has noted that Arabic-speaking Greek Orthodox (that is to say, Orthodox Melkite) immigrants to North America had already begun calling themselves "Syrian Orthodox" even before the arrival of the first *Süryânî*. Both the unavailability of that appellation as well as the similarity between their Arabic name, *as-Suryân*, and "Assyrian" may have dictated why there was a preference for the latter form in English amongst the *Süryânî*. See Kiraz, "Suryoye and Suryoyutho."

[343] According to Joseph, Armenian has separate terms for *Süryânî* (*Asori*) and Assyrian (*Asorestants'i*): "Assyria and Syria: Synonyms?," 39. Frye sees the Armenian name to be evidence of the *Süryânî*'s Assyrian heritage: "Assyria and Syria: Synonyms." For an example of drawing on Armenian in *İntibâh* see "Hürr-i beyâz kimseler," *İntibâh*, 1, no. 2 (Kânûn-ı Evvel 1909), 2-3.

[344] For the comment that it was the Harput *Süryânî* who used *Âsûrî*, see question number five in "Süryânî bir kız tarafından suâller," *İntibâh*, 2, no. 2 (Kânûn-ı Evvel 1910), 6.

[345] See, for example, his article "İlân-ı hürriyet ve biz Süryânîler," *İntibâh*, 1, no. 3 (Kânûn-ı Sânî 1910), 1-2.

Indeed, he was quite open about his rational for not using "Syrian" when speaking English: it was already being employed to refer to Muslims, Greek Orthodox, Druze and others who had emigrated from Syria to the United States. He drew a parallel with the Armenians, saying that in their own language they call themselves *Hay*, while in Arabic and Ottoman Turkish, the term *Ermenî*. Consequently, he argued, the English term "Assyrian" or the Ottoman Turkish *Âsûrî* need not be avoided simply because they do not resemble the *Süryânî* self-designation *Suryoye*.[346]

Considering the extremely divisive polemic over the origins of the Syriac Christians – Assyrian or Aramaean – it is also interesting to notice the frequency with which the word *Ârâmî* also makes an appearance in *Mürşid-i Âsûriyûn*. The articles by Livengood and *serepiskopos* Pavlûs made contrasting arguments as to the origins – etymological and ethnic – of the *Süryânî*.[347] Pavlûs in particular stated outright that "... in Syria and Mesopotamia they are *Süryânî*, around Mosul, *Âsûrî*, in Baghdad, *Keldânî*, and all are originally *Süryânî*, that is to say, *Ârâmî* ... the Nestorians and Melkites too are *Ârâmî*."[348] Another reader spoke of the Aramaeans several times in praising *Mürşid-i Âsûriyûn* and the efforts of Âşur Yûsuf to "wake the oppressed *Süryânî millet* and the unfortunate *Ârâmî* from their ignorance."[349] Unfortunately, Âşur Yûsuf provided no commentary

---

[346] These comments may be found in Cebbûr Boyacı's response to "Süryânî bir kız tarafından suâller," *İntibâh*, 2, no. 2 (Kânûn-ı Evvel 1910), 6.

[347] "Âşûr diyârı, Sûriye ve Süryânîler," *Mürşid-i Âsûriyûn*, 5, no. 3 (1 Mart 1913), 39-41 and "Süryânî ismleri hakkında beyânât," *Mürşid-i Âsûriyûn*, 3, no. 2 (Şubât 1911), 30-32.

[348] "Bınâberîn Sûriye'de ve Beyne'n-nehreyn'de olanlara Süryânîler, Mûsul tarafında olanlara Âsûrîler, Bağdâd tarafında olanlara Keldânîler ki hep bunların da aslî Süryânîdirler yani Ârâmî ... Nastûrîler ve Melkîtler dahî Ârâmîlerden yani asllerî Süryânîdirler."

[349] "Millet-i mazlûme-i Süryânîye'yi ve tâli-i makûs Ârâmî'yi hâb-ı gâfletten inbâh ve ikâz ve tarîk-i incâh ve felâh-ı sevk ve irşâde hâdim ol-mak üzere âlem-i Süryâniyân ve Ârâmiyân'da ilk evvel tahûr ve tulû eden Mürşid nâm-ı celîlle yâd ve tesmiye kılınan cerîde-i ferîdenizi sâha-ı in-tikâra vaz edile geleli günden beri birinci nüshasından beden mutâlaa ..." Note how *Âsûriyûn* is avoided, while *Ârâmî* appears twice in the opening

on this contribution, so it is difficult to gauge his reaction to the notion of an Aramaean ancestry for the *Süryânî*.[350] Naûm Fâik, like *serepiskopos* Pavlûs, illustrates how no distinction was made between an Assyrian and Aramaean past:

> "If those who do not trust in this truth examine our *Süryânî millet*, then first of all they shall see a low, base and unimportant place in society for this people which derived from the stock of those once worthy of the names *Âsûrî* and *Ârâmî* and which later split into five groups – the *Süryânî*, Nestorians, Chaldeans, *Süryânî* Catholics and Maronites – out of ignorance and zealotry."[351]

In another article, Naûm Fâik used the same two terms – *Âsûrî* and *Ârâmî* – interchangeably in successive sentences to refer to the same people.[352] These examples offer varying views of *Süryânî* history but show none of the vitriol which characterises the debates today, and even the views which go against the modern Assyrian thesis went unchallenged in *Mürşid-i Âsûriyûn*, *Kevkeb Mednho* or *İntibâh*, in which Cebbûr Boyacı used *Ârâmî* in his

---

sentence. "Mürşid-i Âsûriyûn'a hitâb," *Mürşid-i Âsûriyûn*, 5, no. 8 (Temmûz 1913), 130-132.

[350] By comparison, the article following the Livengood piece, a short letter concerning the purchase of metal type, was followed by a page-long response. It was common practice for Âşûr Yûsuf to write his reaction to any submission he considered to be important or controversial.

[351] "Bu hakîkata itimâd etmeyen kimseler bizim Süryânî milletimize imâle-i nazar buyursalar, Âsûrî veyâhûd Ârâmî ismi tahtında şâyân, ve cinsten neşet edip teşaub eden ancehl ve sâika-ı taassubla beş fırkaya ayrılan Süryânî, Nestûrî, Keldânî, Süryânî Katolik, Mârûnîlerin bugün heyet-i ictimâiyedeki mevkileri pek dûn, pek zelîl, pek ehemmiyetsiz olduğunu vehle-i ulâda görürler.": "Terakkiyât-ı fikriye," *Kevkeb Mednho*, 1, no. 4 (27 Ağustos 1910), 1-2.

[352] "Bunlardan birinci hâli Ârâmîlerde mevcûd diğeri ise büsbütün mefkûddur. Demek ki Âsûrîlerin cehâletini izâle etmek muhabbet ve ittihâd ve gayretle mümkün olabilir başka çâre yok.": "Cehâletimiz ne ile zâil olur," *Kevkeb Mednho*, 1, no. 3 (13 Ağustos 1910), 6.

translation of a poem by *şemmâs* Dâvûd from Syriac to Ottoman Turkish.[353]

In some ways, Âşûr Yûsuf, Cebbûr Boyacı and Naûm Fâik write as one would expect an Ottoman to do, but their use of *millet* shows that they had accepted a more modern definition for a term traditionally reserved for religious congregations. However, the Assyrian nationalist scholarship, which has emphasised the secularist tendencies of these individuals, is misguided in assuming that their focus was on the Assyrian rather than the *Süryânî* communities. Not only are the two terms clearly distinguished, but Âşûr Yûsuf – in three volumes of *Mürşid-i Âsûriyûn* – did not see much need to address the relationship he clearly saw between the ancient Assyrian people and the contemporary *Süryânî*. Indeed, little mention was ever made of Chaldeans or Nestorians: from *Mürşid-i Âsûriyûn* there were six occurrences of the former and only three of the latter. From *Kevkeb Mednho*, I have found but a single one.

## OTTOMANS, ASSYRIANS OR *SÜRYÂNÎ*?

We have already seen that Naûm Fâik had credited the revolution of 1908 with providing the *Süryânî* with the means to better themselves; we have seen that in 1908, Harput was the scene of great celebrations attended by Turks, Armenians, *Süryânî* and others. But how did Âşûr Yûsuf and Naûm Fâik envisage their place in Ottoman society? Did they see themselves as Ottomans? The significance of the preceding discussion of terminology lies in the examination of other passages which provide answers to these questions while further challenging the assumptions in Assyrian historiography.

Naûm Fâik, who is said to have fled the Ottoman Empire in fear of his own personal safety, exhibits no such concern in *Kevkeb Mednho*, which he stated was being written to serve both *millet* and *vatan*. Indeed, Naûm Fâik saw one of *Kevkeb Mednho*'s objectives to "express the pride of having been part of the Ottoman [Empire]

---

[353] "Şemmâs Dâvûd üskuf efendi tarafından tanzîm edilmiş bir beyttir," *İntibâh*, 1, no. 3 (Kânûn-ı Sânî 1910), 3.

for six centuries."[354] Likewise, the full text of his account of the anniversary of Sultan Abdülhâmîd's deposition and Mehmed Reşâd's ascent to the Ottoman throne, read:

> "On this fortuitous day, as the Ottoman public engaged in joyful celebrations, the gates of our *Süryânî* patriarchate were decorated in a most [illegible] fashion and left open until three or four in the morning, with honoured guests being served drinks, *Süryânî* youths singing hymns to the *vatan* and reciting poems of our reawakening (*intibâh*), and prayers being said for the longevity of the Sultanate of our beloved monarch, Sultan Mehmed Reşâd Han, the Sultan of liberty (*sultân-ı hürriyet*) and emperor of the constitution (*hâkân-ı meşrûtiyet*), in health and happiness, and of the Ottoman people for eternity."[355]

It is not, however, exclusively in the pages of *Kevkeb Mednho* that Naûm Fâik's Ottomanist sentiments may be felt, but in his poetry as well. The community has preserved several poems he penned in Ottoman Turkish prior to his emigration to the United States, teaching them to students at the T.M.S. *Süryânî* school in Beirut during the 1930s.[356] One of these stands out for imploring the *Süryânî* youth to take up arms to defeat the enemies of freedom

---

[354] This was printed in the first issue of *Kevkeb Mednho*. See Çıkkı, *Naum Faik ve Süryani Rönesansı*, 58-59.

[355] "Cülûs-ı hazret-i pâdişâhî," *Kevkeb Mednho*, 1, no. 22 (6 Mayıs 1911), 20. "Bu rûz-ı fîrûzda umûm-ı Osmânlılar merâsim-i şâdmânî ifâ ettikleri gibi Süryânî patrikhânemizin kapısı dahi pek [illegible] bir sûretle tezyîn, ve gece sâat üç dörde kadar patrikhâne açık bırakılarak teşrîf eden zevâta meşrûbât takdîm, ve Süryânî gençleri tarafından vatan besteleriyle intibâh neşîdeleri terennüm, ve sultân-ı hürriyet ve hâkân-ı meşrûtiyet olan sevgili pâdişâhımız sultân Mehmed Reşâd Han efendimiz hazretlerinin serîr-i sultanatlarında sıhhat ve ikbâl ile dâim, ve millet-i Osmâniyenin ebed kadar kâim olmasının ediye-i samîmiyesi tezkâr edilmiştir."

[356] See Appendix B for more information and the full text of the poems.

and to resist oppression.[357] A second poem both extols the *vatan*, expressing the devotion of the *Süryânî* – and all Assyrians – to its continued existence.[358] These sentiments are poignant, and even more so once we situate them historically; Naûm Fâik wrote the first on 1 May 1909 – roughly the time of the counter-revolution and the Adana massacres – and dated the second to 27 August 1909, once order had been fully restored.

Ottomanist sympathies were even more pronounced in articles from *Mürşid-i Âsûriyûn* than from *Kevkeb Mednho*, with issues from 1911 to 1913 providing many such examples, despite this being the period in which anti-Christian sentiments in the Ottoman Empire were said to be increasing as a result of international events. It was Âşûr Yûsuf's belief that the *Süryânî* in the United States would be returning to the Ottoman Empire, bringing civilisation (*medeniyet*), culture (*terbiye*) and knowledge (*ilm ve marifet*) back with them as a gift to share with their *vatan* and their fellow Ottomans (*vatandaş*).[359] This and other similar references indicate that the *Süryânî* intellectuals had a vision of being a contributing element in Ottoman society, even if there was ample acknowledgement that their current conditions placed them far behind others, and the Armenians in particular.

Non-Muslim participation extended beyond simply being the educated and cultured segment of the Ottoman population, however. Immediately after the outbreak of the first Balkan War, a lengthy article republished from *İkdâm* appeared on the front page of *Mürşid-i Âsûriyûn*. Written by Rızâ Tevfik [Bölükbaşı], a deputy

---

[357] This poem was on pages 10 and 11 of the collection. The third stanza reads, in rough translation: "Brothers, with courage / Come forth into the age of glory. / It is the day to take up arms / The enemies of freedom (*hürriyet*) and brotherhood (*uhuvvet*) / It is time to bravely slay."

[358] See page 14, stanza 2. Also see pages 10-11, stanza 6.

[359] "Amerika'daki millettaşlara mektûblarım," *Mürşid-i Âsûriyûn*, 3, no. 9 (Teşrîn-i Evvel 1911), 143-146: "Lakin daha doğrusu evvel medenî diyârda merâm ve maksadınız yalnız akçe kazanmak olmalı değildir. Bununla berâber daha ziyâde oranın medeniyet ve terbiyesinden, ilm ve marifetinden istifâde etmeğe çalışmalısınız şöyle ki avdetinizde vatanınıza ve vatandaşlarınıza bir armağân ve bir hediye diye istifâde olunacak bir sanat veyâ bir yeni marifet getirmeğe muktedir olasınız."

for Edirne and a former CUP member who had joined the opposition *Hürriyet ve İtilâf Fırkası*, the article called on the Ottoman people to set aside their political differences in light of the danger to the Ottoman *vatan*.[360] The country had a duty to obey the government's orders and to remain hard at work while the army fought the Balkan countries. Rızâ Tevfîk continued:

> "There is a third important point. Do not forget that this is thankfully not a religious conflict. In this day and age, there can be no religious conflicts. Were they possible, half the world would be our enemy. This conflict is a conflict over land ... For now I wish only to ask of everyone, of every *vatandaş*, not to heed the words of hypocrites or look down on the Christians with whom we live, with whom we work side by side, who pay their taxes with us and who are soldiers [alongside us]; and do not forget that the state, the Ottoman state and *millet* recognises them, and our law protects their rights just as it protects ours."[361]

---

[360] Rızâ Tevfîk and the Chaldean deputy Dâvud Yûsufânî were part of the same circle in Istanbul. Besides belonging to the *Hürriyet ve İtilâf Fırkası*, both men participated in the publishing of the party's unofficial organ, *Tanzîmât*. Primarily the work of Lütfî Fikrî Bey, a deputy representing the *sancak* of Dersim in the *vilâyet* of Mamûretü'l-Azîz, *Tanzîmât* was closed and reopened numerous times under a variety of names (usually built on the Arabic root *tefîlât*); one of these, *Temînât*, is mentioned on page 142, footnote 398 and another, *İfhâm*, on page 208, footnote 570. Both Rızâ Tevfîk and Dâvud Yûsufânî were at one time or another responsible for obtaining official permission for the opening of *Tanzîmât* or one of its incarnations. See Duman, *Başlangıcından Harf Devrimine Kadar Osmanlı-Türk Süreli Yayınlar ve Gazeteler Bibliyografyası ve Toplu Katalogu*, 820; Tarık Zafer Tunaya, *Türkiye'de Siyasal Partiler*, vol. 1 (Istanbul: İletişim Yayınları, 1998), 244 and 294-295; and Ahmet Ali Gazel, *Osmanlı Meclis-i Mebusanı'nda Parlamenter Denetim (1908-1912)* (Konya: Çizgi Kitabevi, 2007), 60.

[361] "Şimdiki vazîfemiz," *Mürşid-i Âsûriyûn*, 4, no. 8 (Teşrîn-i Sânî 1912), 114-118: "Üçüncü bir mühim nokta daha var. Unutmamalıyız ki bu gavgâ hamd olsun bir dîn gavgâsı değildir. Dîn gavgâları bu asrda olamaz. Eğer olsaydı dünyânın yarısı düşmânımız olurdu. Bu gavgâ toprak gav-

As we have seen in Chapter 2, it was not, however, just Muslims who wished to see Ottoman Christians performing their military service. *İntibâh* provides the clearest example of how in the period immediately following the 1908 revolution, *Süryânî* intellectuals also saw their coreligionists' participation as necessary. On 29 Teşrîn-i Sânî 1325 [12 December 1909] a large crowd composed of civilians, government officials, military officers and religious leaders assembled at the military barracks in Mardin to hear the reading of an imperial *fermân* announcing the institution of general conscription:

> "... and after that an impromptu speech in Arabic and of superior eloquence was delivered by Mosul-native *râhib* Efrâm from the *Süryânî-i Kadîm* community ... and drew the applause and cheers from all the spectators. And following that *kas* Pavlûs from Harput read a prepared speech in Turkish and then Turkish and Arabic speeches were given by members of the police force and students at the *Mekteb-i İdârî* and then Hannâ Sırrı, professor of the Ottoman language at the American college, delivered the short written speech [transcribed] below, and all the Christians received the notion of military service with great content."[362]

---

gâsıdır ... Şimdilik yalnız şunu herkesten her vatandaştan ricâ ederim ki burada bizim ile berâber yaşayan, bizim ile yan yana çalışan, bizim ile vergi veren, askere giden Hıristiyanlara kem gözle bakmasınlar ve münâfık sözüne uymasınlar, unutmasınlar ki onları devlet, millet ve Osmânlı tanır ve bizim hukûkumuz gibi onların da hukûkunu kânûn muhâfaza eder."

[362] "Nefs-i Mârdîn'de milel-i gayr-ı Müslimeden ahz-ı asker bir fermân-ı celîlü'l-unvânın kırâati," *İntibâh*, 1, no. 4 (Şubât 1910), 4: "Hidmet-i filiye-i askeriyenin tamîmine dâir fermân-ı âlîşân-ı pâdişâhî 29 Teşrîn-i Sânî sene 325 Rûmî târîhinde musâdif pazar günü sâat altı râddelerinde askerî kışlası pişgâhında erkân-ı livâ ve ümerâ-yı askeriye, milel-i muhtelifenin rüesâ-yı rûhâniyesi ve ehâliden bir cem-i gafîr hâzır bulunduğu hâlde kemâl tazîm ve tebcîl ile okundu. Fermân kırâati müteâkib kur'a memûru kul ağası tarafından bir nutk îrâd olunup ve onu müteâkib Süryânî-i Kadîm cemâati ruhbân [illegible] Mûsüllü râhib Efrâm efendi tarafından mürtecilen Arabiyü'l-ibâre gâyet belîğ bir nutk îrâd olunarak cümle huzzârın

In his oration, Hannâ Sırrı Çıkkı, whose letters often appeared in *Kevkeb Mednho* and *Mürşid-i Âsûriyûn*, was even more direct in enjoining the non-Muslims to perform their duty as Ottoman citizens:

> "Individuals from all the various elements, being loyal subjects, have received with great content this imperial *fermân* concerning the general military service by all, without exception, as being one of the select fruits and natural results of this felicitous constitution. I am sure that every Ottoman individual from a non-Muslim *millet* is ever prepared to be part of this glorious military and shield with his own body each stone of our sacred *vatan*."
>
> "My honourable citizens ... let us be ready to perform this great service. We ought to love our great *vatan*, for it is by the *vatan*'s grace that there exists freedom, peace and justice. When the various elements who comprise the peoples of the *vatan* eat in one canteen and sleep in one [illegible], then it is only natural that between them there will emerge, through an entering into dialogue, a unity of interests and an abundance of companionship, a meeting of the hearts and a fraternity of ideas. Since love for the *vatan* is, in every religion, in every culture, in every part of the world, counted amongst the a most exalted virtues of the highest order and of the highest sanctity, we ought to hold this love to be the most venerable of natural feelings and the most sacred of all necessary functions. Just as we love our parents, our children, our relatives and relations, we should love that which has provided us with these and which nourishes us – our great *vatan* and sacred domains! For the sake of this we must lay down our lives. Those

---

tahsin ve âferînini celb etmiştir. Ve ondan sonra Harpûtlu kas Pavlûs efendi dahi ezberden Türkçe bir nutk okuyup ve zâbıtândan ve Mekteb-i İdârî şâgirdânından dahi Türkçe Arabca nutklar okunduğu dahi Amerikan Mektebî lisân-ı Osmânî muallimi Hannâ Sırrı efendi tarafından zîrde muharrer muhtasar bir nutk îrâd olunduğu ve hidmet-i askeriye, umûm Hristyânlar tarafından kemâl-i sürûr ile telakkî olunmuştur."

who seek to avoid performing this great service may be said to have committed a great crime against their *vatan*. They shall be remembered for this crime and counted amongst the ungrateful ... Long live the military, long live the constitution, long live freedom and long live the Sultan."[363]

Similarly, Âşûr Yûsuf saw the *Süryânî* role in the Ottoman military as a positive step, describing it as a notable accomplishment for the community:

"The other notable matter in the life of our *millet* was that for the first time, our youths joined the ranks of the professional soldiers last year [1910]. For the benefit of these youths, we will be writing some useful articles about this military duty under the heading '*Hediye*'. We hope that our *millet* will endeavour to undertake even

---

[363] "Meşrûtiyet-i mesûdenin esmâr-ı bergüzîde ve netâic-i tabîiyesinden olarak hidmet-i filiye-i askeriyenin bilâ-istisnâ tamîmine dâir şimdi okunan fermân-ı celîlü'l-unvân-ı pâdişâhî, tebaa-i sâdıkadan olan umûm anâsır-ı muhtelife efrâdından kemâl sürûrıyla telakkî olundu. Milel-i gayr-ı müslimeden her ferd-i Osmânî silk-i celîl-i askeriye dâhil olup mukaddes vatanımızın bir taşına vücûdlarını siper etmeğe her zamân âmâde olduklarına emînim. Muhterem vatandaşlarım ... bu silk-i celîle gireceğe hâzır olalım. Vatan-ı azîzimizi sevmeliyiz çünkü hürriyeti, râhatı, hakkı vatan sayesinde kâimdir. Anâsır-ı muhtelifeden müteşekkil ebnâ-yı vatan bir karavanada yiyip bir [illegible]da yattıkça aralarında iştirâk-ı lisân, ve ittihâd-ı menfaat, ve kesret-i müânese cihetiyle bir karâbet-i kalb, ve bir uhuvvet-i efkâr hâsıl olacağı tabîîdir. Muhabbet-i vataniye her dînde her terbiyede dünyânın her yerinde fezâil-i âliyenin en azîzlerinden en mukaddeslerinden madûd oladuğu için bu muhabbeti hissiyât-ı tabîiyenin kâffesinden muhterem ve havâss-ı lâzımenin cümlesinden mukaddem tutmalıyız. Ebeveynimizi evlâdlarımızı akrabâ, taallukâtımızı sevdiğimiz hâlde ya bunları bize bahş eden ve bizi beslemekte olan vatan-ı azîzimizi mülk-i mukaddesimizi ne kadar sevmeliyiz! Bu uğur da fedâ-yı cân etmeliyiz. Bu hidmet-i celîleden kaçınmak isteyenler vatana karşı büyük bir cinâyet işlemiş olurlar. Cinâyet ile yâd olunup nânkûr add olunurlar. ... Yaşasın askerî, yaşasın meşrûtiyet, yaşasın hürriyet, pâdişâhım çok yaşa.": "Sûret-i nutk," *İntibâh*, 1, no. 4 (Şubât 1910), 4.

greater feats so that we may record more such lofty achievements of our *millet*."[364]

In January of 1911 he was praising the entry of *Süryânî* into the army, but by 1913 he was expressing his displeasure that that none of these soldiers had died in the course of their service:

> "In the midst of this [Balkan] war, we have no news of any self-sacrificing *Süryânî* fighting and dying so that we may recognise their glorious and honoured deaths and grace our *millet* with their graves."[365]

Âşûr Yûsuf may have lamented the lack of participation by his brethren in the Balkan Wars, but it would appear he overlooked one local example, Piyer Taşo, the Catholic *Süryânî* mentioned above.[366] Over the course of the Balkan Wars, Piyer Taşo volunteered as a doctor in the Ottoman army and continued his service in Erzurum and Erzincan during the First World War.[367]

There was, on the other hand, one figure who became probably the most frequently named lay *Süryânî* in *Mürşid-i Âsûriyûn*

---

[364] Hayât-ı milliyemizde kayd edecek diğer bir husûs gençlerimizin geçen sene ilk defa olarak silk-i askeriyeye dâhil olmalarıdır. Gençlerimizin istifâde etmesi için Süryânî askerlerine "hediye" sernâmesiyle askerlik vazîfesine dâir bazı müfid şeyler yazılacaktır. Hayât-ı milliyemizde daha âlî şeyler kayd etmek için memûl ederiz ki milletimiz daha büyük işler icrâsına mübâşeret etmeğe say ve gayrette bulunacaktır.": "Geriye doğru bir atf-ı nikâh," *Mürşid-i Âsûriyûn*, 3, no. 1 (Kânûn-ı Sânî 1911), 3.

[365] "... şu muhâbere meydânında cânsipârâne muhârebe edip de vefât eden Süryânîlerden de haberdâr değiliz ki hiç olmaz ise onların izzetli ve şerifli ölümünü kayd ve hayât-ı milliyemizi onların mezârı ile tezyîn edelim.": "1912 senesi," *Mürşid-i Âsûriyûn*, 5, no. 1 (Kânûn-ı Sânî 1913), 15.

[366] See page 106.

[367] In the early 1920s, Piyer Taşo continued his activities, working for *Fırât Mecmûası* [Euphrates Journal] and *Satvet-i Millîye* [Strength of the Nation], Elâzığ-based newspapers supportive of the Turkish nationalist struggle. The "Türk dostu" Taşo family was targeted during the Şeyh Saîd rebellion against the new Turkish Republic in 1925, suffering material losses. Following the uprising, they were forced to leave Elâzığ for reasons unspecified and elected to relocate to Pangaltı in Istanbul. Sunguroğlu, *Harput Yollarında*, vol. 2, 450-452 and 538-539.

by virtue of his actions during the Balkan Wars. The visit of İbrâhîm Yûsuf to his native Harput coincided with the outbreak of hostilities, and Âşûr Yûsuf closely followed his time as chief surgeon for the Ottoman army and the *Hilâl-i Ahmer* [Red Crescent]. İbrâhîm Yûsuf became, in fact, something of a minor celebrity in the Ottoman capital for his service at the *Dârü'l-Fünûn* and military hospitals, with newspaper reports of his exploits appearing in the Ottoman, Armenian and American press.[368]

He was, for example, the doctor brought to treat the Ottoman minister of War, Nâzım Paşa after he was shot during the *Bâb-ı Âlî* coup.[369] He would later tend to Mahmûd Şevket Paşa, *sadr-ı âzam* [Grand Vizier] in the post-coup CUP government, when he too was assassinated, and attended his funeral as the chief doctor.[370] After the conflict, he returned to the United States, where a large crowd of "Turkish nationals" (*Türkiyeli*) gathered at the train station in Worcester to greet him on his arrival.[371] İbrâhîm Yûsuf's death in 1924 was even reported in the *New York Times*, although by then he had achieved recognition for other activities.[372]

The language surrounding these articles is also noteworthy since it centres around sacrifice and service to the Ottoman cause: "... while many doctors had fled due to the war, our self-sacrificing (*fedâkâr*) doctor applied as a volunteer (*hayr ârzûsuyla*) to the Red Crescent in order to aid the Ottoman army's wounded arriving

---

[368] This was noted in an untitled article: *Mürşid-i Âsûriyûn*, 5, no. 6 (Mayıs 1913), 95.

[369] İbrâhîm Yûsuf was summoned to attend to Nâzım Paşa, but the patient died prior to his arrival. "Doktor İbrâhîm Yûsuf Türk ve Balkan muhârebesinde sekiz buçuk ay îfâ-yı hidmet ettikten sonra yine Amerika'ya avdeti," *Mürşid-i Âsûriyûn*, 5, no. 12 (Teşrîn-i Sânî 1913), 194.

[370] Ibid.

[371] "Doktor Yûsuf Türk ve Balkan muhârebesinde îfâ-yı hidmet ettikten sonra vatana avdeti," *Mürşid-i Âsûriyûn*, 5, no. 10 (Eylûl 1913), 159-160. The use of the very modern term *Türkiyeli* is unusual, but Âşûr Yûsuf did so elsewhere to speak of "the [*Süryânî*] priests of Turkey (*Türkiyeli ruhbânlar*)": see page 158, footnote 433.

[372] "Dr. Arthur [*sic*] K. Yoosuf Dies Suddenly," *New York Times* (27 December 1924), 9.

[from the front]."[373] Âṣûr Yûsuf also repeated İbrâhîm Yûsuf's assessment of the superiority of Turkish soldiers' nature with respect to those of other countries which had originally been published in an American newspaper. He lauded them for their great endurance, patience and superior powers of recovery as well as their forthright character in, for example, avoiding alcohol.[374]

Other support from the Ottoman *Süryânî* community came in the form of monetary donations. Abdünnûr, the *mutrân* of Harput, spent November of 1912 travelling his diocese collecting money (*harb iânesi*) for the war effort.[375] Cebbûr Boyacı called on the *Süryânî* to participate in the collection of funds for the expansion of the Ottoman fleet (*donanma iânesi*), first printing an article from the newspaper *Yozgad* on such acitvities by Armenians which stated: "Muslim, Greek and Armenian, we are the sons of a single *vatan*, to be separate from one another in any way whatsoever is to invite disaster."[376] *İntibâh*'s commentary on this article ran: "Read, O Assyrians, how people are deserving of praise! For God's sake. Are we *milletperver*? Are we *vatanperver*? Let us show what we are."[377]

---

[373] "Doktor İbrâhîm Yûsuf," *Mürşid-i Âsûriyûn*, 4, no. 8 (Teşrîn-i Sânî 1912), 128: "Harpût'u ziyâret etmek üzere Dersaâdet'e müvâseletinde bir takım doktorlar harb yüzünden mahâl-i ahıre firâr etmekte iken şu bizim fedâkâr doktor Osmânlı ordusundan gelen mecrûhlara muâvenet etmek hayr ârzûsuyla Hilâl-ı Ahmer'e heyetine mürâcaat ve evvel heyet tarafından maalmemnûniye davet olunup beş altı haftadan beri ve Dârü'l-Fünûn'daki hastehâne operatör hâlinde fedâkârâne mecrûhları tedâvi etmektedir."

[374] "Doktor İbrâhîm Yûsuf Türk ve Balkan muhârebesinde sekiz buçuk ay îfâ-yı hidmet ettikten sonra yine Amerika'ya avdeti," *Mürşid-i Âsûriyûn*, 5, no. 12 (Teşrîn-i Sânî 1913), 194: "Türk askerlerinde başka bir hâl vardır ki sâir memleketlerin askerlerinde bulunmaz ..."

[375] [untitled article], *Mürşid-i Âsûriyûn*, 4, no. 9 (Kânûn-ı Evvel 1912), 144.

[376] "İslâm, Rûm, Ermenî, hep bir vatanın evlâdıyız, herhangi histe yekdîğerimizden ayrı bulunmak biz felâket davet eder."

[377] "İnsânların nasıl âferîne lâyık olduklarını mutâlaa ediniz ey Âsûriler! Allah aşkına olsun. Milletperver miyiz? Vatanperver miyiz? Ne isek gösterelim." See "Âferîn," *İntibâh*, 2, no. 5 (Mart 1911), 7. The Farsi suffix *-perver* translates as "nuturing" or "supporting"; *vatanperver* usually glosses as "patriotic", but it is not easy to express the subtle differences between *milletperver* and *vatanperver* succinctly.

Additionally, one *Süryânî* youth from Diyarbakır would be, on the eve of war, attending an elite military academy in Istanbul after he had proven to be one of the top students in his class.[378] *İntibâh* was applauding the student's successes in the summer of 1914, but Cebbûr Boyacı's tone had soured by February of 1915, when the first reports of the suffering being endured by Christians in the Ottoman Empire began reaching the United States.[379]

Âşûr Yûsuf's own contribution was limited to publishing articles about these events as well as a fiercely patriotic poem, *Yeni Ay Gâziler* [Soldiers of the New Moon]. Dated to 18 October 1912 and attributed to Ebû Rıdvân Sadık Vicdânî, the five verses speak of "marching on Belgrade to teach the Serbs a great lesson", "putting an end to the Bulgarian race" and fighting the "treacherous Greeks" (*kahbe Yunanlar*), all the while repeating the refrain, "O Rumelia! Anatolia has risen up and come to your succour!"[380]

For all the support of the Ottoman state, its army and its constitution, one notable absence is that of the Committee of Union and Progress.[381] In *Mürşid-i Âsûriyûn*, the party itself received no coverage, either positive or negative, although Âşûr Yûsuf did report "with sorrow" the wounding of Enver Paşa, "warrior of liberty (*mücâhid-i hürriyet*)", during an armed clash outside Edirne in early 1912.[382] In *İntibâh*, we do read about current events involving

---

[378] "İbretâmiz," *İntibâh*, 5, no. 8 (Temmûz 1914), 5. The unnamed youth finished in the top 25 of 750 students, a result which earned him to right to attend the more prestigious programme for the training of officers (*erkânı harb zâbıt*).

[379] See "Türkiye'deki Hıristiyânların ahvâli," *İntibâh*, 5, 9 (Ağustos 1914 – Şubât 1915), 7.

[380] "Ey Rûmeli! Coştu geldi Anadolu imdâdına!": "Yeni ay gâziler," *Mürşid-i Âsûriyûn*, 4, no. 9 (Kânûn-ı Evvel 1912), 141-142. Note that Ebû Rıdvân makes the normal Ottoman Turkish distinction between the Greeks of Greece (*Yunan*) and the Ottoman Greeks (*Rûm*).

[381] It can, however, be found in *Kevkeb Mednho* in a list of organisations active in Diyarbakır: "İntibâh-ı İlmî cemiyetlerinin ictimâ-ı umûmîsi," *Kevkeb Mednho*, 1, no. 3 (13 Ağustos 1910), 1-3.

[382] "Edirne civârında İtalyanlı ile Osmanlı askeri miyânesinde vukû bulan bir muhârebede mücâhid-i hürriyet Enver Beğ ağır sûretle yaralan-

the CUP, though these were typically translations of articles that had appeared in the American press and not a reflection of Cebbûr Boyacı's personal views on the party. There was apparently at least one *Süryânî* member of the CUP, but the lack of public support for the CUP in the *Süryânî* press should not be understood as a rejection of Ottomanism or the post-Abdülhamîd constitutional era.[383] It it my hypothesis that Âşûr Yûsuf may have, in fact, been more sympathetic to the *Hürriyet ve İtilâf Fırkası*, about which far more news appeared in *Mürşid-i Âsûriyûn*.

Praise for the constitution, on the other hand, came from all three authors as well as their readership; it was "the glorious Ottoman constitution (*meşrûtiyet-i muazzeze-i Osmâniye*)" to Naûm Fâik[384] while Âşûr Yûsuf reported on *Süryânî* reciting poems to laud it during their congress at Fitchburg, Massachusetts.[385] In *Kevkbo d-Suryoye*, *mutrân* Abdünnûr described it as the heroic (*kahramân*) constitution.[386] Damning the preceding period of oppression under Abdülhamîd, Cercîs Alacacı wrote of the "beloved era of the constitution (*devr-i dilârâ-yı meşrûtiyet*)" during

---

mış olup komandanlıktan çekilmiş olduğu maatteessüf cerîdelerde okunmuştur.": [untitled article], *Mürşid-i Âsûriyûn*, 4, no. 4 (Nîsân 1912), 63. Âşûr Yûsuf's sources incorrectly described the event as a clash between the Ottoman and Italian armies. In fact, it was the product of a dispute between Young Turk officers and officers loyal to the assassinated former Minister of War, Nâzım Paşa. See "Enver Wounded in Fight: Five Turkish Officers Killed in a Quarrel at Adrianople," *New York Times* (10 September 1913), 1.

[383] de Courtois, *The Forgotten Genocide*, 47 n.3. A Sultan – presumably Mehmed Reşâd – awarded to the same unnamed figure a "uniform with golden buttons".

[384] "Dicle cerîde-i ferîdesi," *Kevkeb Mednho*, 1, no. 19 (25 Mart 1911), 8.

[385] "Amerika'da Âsûrîlerin Şirket-i İlmiye senevi tecemmuu," *Mürşid-i Âsûriyûn*, 3, no. 2 (Şubât 1911), 33: "... hâzırûn tarafından meşrûtiyet-i Osmâniye hakkında yazılmış bir medhiye terennüm edildi."

[386] "Kevkbo d-Suryoye, yani Kevkebü'l-Süryân cerîdesi," *İntibâh*, 1, no. 8 (Hazîrân 1910), 7.

which every man ought to work to spread kindness and generosities for the good of the *millet* and the *vatan*.[387]

Âşûr Yûsuf's Ottomanist sentiments are also visible in his reporting of events and in his selection of other people's works to be printed in his newspaper. In 1911, the local *Süryânî* Catholic leader gave a speech in Arabic during celebrations at the government building in Mamûretü'l-Azîz; speaking to a large crowd of bureaucrats and civilians alike, the priest called for a union of "ideas, hearts and actions" and was received with repeated applause.[388] Âşûr Yûsuf also printed the complete text of a lengthy monologue by Mehmed Şükrî Bey, *kaymakam* of the *kazâ* of Çarsancak in the *vilâyet* of Mamûretü'l-Azîz.[389] The impromptu (*irticâlen*) oration in a Protestant church contained Ottomanist and humanist themes throughout as well as, in the words of Âşûr Yûsuf, incorporating ideas from the Bible (*İncîl-i şerîfin âlî fikrleriyle memzûc*):

"... Turks, Arabs, Kurds, Armenians, Greeks, Jews, Albanians, Laz, Vlachs, Bulgarians, Serbs, Montenegrans, Druzes, Persians, in short the Ottomans, who recognise no white or black, saying 'my country is the world, my nation is humanity' and who show a tranquil face to the world, living as one single body, one soul, will all dignify

---

[387] "Devr-i sâbık-ı istibdâdın efâl-i kerihesinden olan böyle iftirâlarla tehdîdlere bu devr-i dilârâ-yı meşrûtiyette herkes tarafından nazar-ı lanet ve nefret ile bakılacağından bu devr-i celîl-i teceddüdde her adam mümkün mertebe etrâfına muhitine neşr-i mekârim ahlâkla nûrlar, şefkatlar, iyilikler serpmekle millet ve vatana fâide bahş olmağa çalışmalıdır.": "Diyonnosyus mutrân Abdünnûr efendiye açık mektûb," *Mürşid-i Âsûriyûn*, 3, no. 3 (Mart 1911), 46.

[388] "Geçen Îd-i Millî'de Mamûretü'l-Azîz hukûmet konağı meydânında gerek memûrin-i kirâm ve gerek ahâliden büyük bir izdihâm hâzır olduğu hâlde Mamûretü'l-Azîz Süyrânî Katolik râhibi faziletli [el-Kasr?] Cebrâîl Ahmer [Dakane?] hakîkî ittihâd fikren, kalben, filen olur diye Arabca bir nutk irâde edip defaâtla alkışlanmıştır.": [untitled article], *Mürşid-i Âsûriyûn*, 3, no. 7 (Ağustos 1911), 120.

[389] Located in the *sancak* of Dersim, Çarsancak, or Perri as it was also known, was renamed Akpazar after the establishment of the Turkish Republic.

humanity and shake gently the world of our fathers and sons."[390]

"And thus, as long as we have our lion-hearted men and our minds of fire, breasts of iron and wrists of steel, Ottomanism (*Osmânlılık*) will live and be made to prosper. Long live justice, camaraderie and peace."[391]

Âşûr Yûsuf selected one frequently reoccurring term, *muhabbet* [camaraderie], to entitle the transcription printed over thirteen pages and three issues of *Mürşid-i Âsûriyûn*.[392] Indeed this friendship and cooperative effort between the different peoples of the Empire resurfaces elsewhere. Âşûr Yûsuf, for example, noted how a *Süryânî* student had taught an enthusiastic Turkish classmate

---

[390] "İşte muhabbetin, insânlığın, kardeşliğin, bu belli başlı destûrları [illegible], menfaat-i şahsiyesini, menâfi-i umûmiyeye fedâ edip fırka fırka ayrılmayarak, hep el birliğiyle, ittihâd-ı tâm ve ittifâkıyla çalışıldığı, kemâl-i ihrârâne ve fedâkârâne uğraşıldığı, bu sûretle Osmânlı toprağında bulunan milel ve akvâm hukûmet ve siyâsetinin adl ve hayrdan başka bir yol ve gâyesi olmamasına cânla, başla hep birden savaşıldığı, Türklük, Arablık, Kürdlük, Ermenîlik, Rûmluk, Yahûdîlik, Arnavudluk, Lâzlık, Ulahlık, Bulgarlık, Sırblık, Karadağlılık, Dürüzîlik, Acemlik, hulâsa aklık karalık tanışmayıp da 'vatanım rû-yı zemîn, milletim nev-i beşer' diyerek hep bir vücûd, hep bir cân oldukları zamân insânlar râhat yüzü görecek Osmânlılık, insâniyet yükselecek, ecdâdımızın heyeti ahlâfımızın himmeti dünyâlar tatlı bir sûrette titretecektir." The line "vatanım rû-yı zemîn, milletim nev-i beşer" had been popularised in a 1911 poem by Tevfîk Fikret – another individual affiliated with the *Hürriyet ve İtilâf Fırkası* – although he had borrowed the words from İbrâhîm Şinâsî, who was, in turn, translating Victor Hugo's "avoir pour patrie le monde et pour nation l'humanité."

[391] "İşte böyle arslan yürekli erlerimiz ve ateşten yapılmış dimâğlarımız pûlâddan mamûl yüreklerimiz, çelikten kavî bileklerimiz, mevcûd oldukça Osmânlılık yaşayacak ve her hâlde yaşatacaktır. Yaşasın hak ve muhabbet ve es-selâm."

[392] The complete text may be found in: "Muhabbet," *Mürşid-i Âsûriyûn*, 5, no. 4 (Mart 1913), 53-56; "Muhabbet," *Mürşid-i Âsûriyûn*, 5, no. 5 (Nîsân 1913), 73-75; and "Muhabbet," *Mürşid-i Âsûriyûn*, 5, no. 7 (Hazîrân 1913), 102-107.

at the Diyarbakır *Dârü'l-Muallimîn* [teachers' school] how to read in the Syriac alphabet after only a few months study.[393]

From *Kevkeb Mednho* and *İntibâh* we learn about Ottomanist activities in Diyarbakır. There, the Ottoman government helped establish the *Uhuvvet-i Osmânî Cemiyeti* [Ottoman Fraternal Association] to promote to the Ottoman people (*millet-i necîbe-i Osmâniye*) the idea of Ottomanism and to forge a fraternity, union and alliance between these elements (*beyne'n-anâsır*). A letter by Beşâr Hilmî to *İntibâh* described that there had been an announcement that the *Uhuvvet-i Osmânî Cemiyeti* "would be honouring our *İntibâh Cemiyeti* with its presence on 8 February 1910" at the *Meryem Ana Kilisesi* as one of its regular bi-weekly visits to local churches and organisations.[394]

A letter by Naûm Fâik also wrote of the activities of the *Uhuvvet-i Osmânî Cemiyeti*, which he described as a union of "Muslim, Arab, Armenian, *Süryânî*, *Keldânî*, *Rûm*, Catholics, Protestant and Jewish" organisations seeking to put the old calamities behind them. The six leading members included *Yüzbaşı* [lieutenant] Mazher and two Armenians. On the prescribed day, Naûm Fâik described the *Süryânî* church having been "honoured by the presence of numerous individuals from each community [*unsur*], including some 150 of our Muslim brothers."[395] Among the organisations represented at this conference were the *İttihâd ve Terakkî Cemiyeti*, the *Dashnaktsutiun*, the *Mesâîperver Cemiyeti*, the *Askerî Kulübü* and the *Keldânî Tekâmül Cemiyeti*. The assembled guests were treated to numerous speeches, songs and poetry recitals which extolled the Ottoman state and people. The conference concluded with the serving of deserts, coffee and cigarettes, after

---

[393] The story came originally from *Şifuro* but was repeated in "Süryânî lisânının kesb-i hayâtı," *Mürşid-i Âsûriyûn*, 5, no. 13 (Kânûn-ı Evvel 1913), 204: "(Şifuro)nun beyânâtına nazaran Diyârbekir Dârü'l-Muallimi'nde Süryânî bir talebe bir heveskâr Türk talebeye bir kaç ay tarafında Süryânî hurûfâtıyla okumağa öğretmiştir."

[394] "Diyâbekir'de Uhuvvet-i Osmânî Cemiyeti," *İntibâh*, 1, no. 7 (Mayıs 1910), 7.

[395] "Kilisemizde her bir unsurden bir çok devât hâzır oldukları gibi İslâm kardeşlerimizden de yüz elli kadar devât teşrîf buyurmuşlardı.": "Diyârbekir'den bir mektûb," *İntibâh*, 1, no. 7 (Mayıs 1910), 2-3.

which "the attendees dispersed with perfect happiness and spilled out with the glorious words of freedom, equaliy, fraternity again on thier lips and the desire for camaraderie and unity in their hearts."[396] In *Kevkeb Mednho*, Naûm Fâik spoke of how the *İntibâh Cemiyeti* was be working towards the same goal as these other organisations in Diyarbakır, that being "the progress of the *vatan*."[397]

Whereas the *Dashnaktsutiun* were involved in activities with the *İttihâd ve Terakkî Cemiyeti*, the April 1912 issue of *Mürşid-i Âsûriyûn* reprinted a joint declaration of cooperation between the *Hürriyet ve İtilâf Fırkası* and the *Hunchakian* party.[398] The articles of the document stated the two parties' commitment to protecting the sovereignty of the state, the constitution and the political rights of the various peoples (*milel-i muhtelife*) that compose the Ottoman

---

[396] "... huzzâr-ı kerâm kemâl-i memnûniyetle dağılıp, hürriyet, ve müsâvât, uhuvvet kelimât-ı mübeccelesi yeniden efvâh-ı âmmede devrân ve muhabbet ve ittifâk ârzûsu kalblerinde feverân ediyorlardı."

[397] "İşte Osmânlıların İttihâd ve Terakkî'si, Uhuvvet-i Osmâniye'si, Ermenîlerin Taşnaksutyun ve Hinçakyan'ı, genç Osmânlıların Mesâiper-ver'leri, Keldânîlerin Tekâmül'ü, Ermenî Katoliklerin Terakkîperver'i, Pro-testanların İlmperver'i hep rivâyât-ı muhtelifeleriyle berâber bir maksada hâdim olmaları ve bu da terakkî-yi vatan fikrinden ibâret bulunduğu çeşm-i mübâhâtla görülmektedir." See "İntibâh-ı İlmî cemiyetlerinin ic-timâ-ı umûmîsi," *Kevkeb Mednho*, 1, no. 3 (13 Ağustos 1910), 1-3.

[398] "İtilâfnâme," *Mürşid-i Âsûriyûn*, 4, no. 4 (Nîsân 1912), 61-62. The text originally appeared on 21 Şubât 1912 in the Istanbul daily *Temînât*, one of the successors to Lütfî Fikrî Bey's *Tanzîmât*. That it was immedi-ately reproduced in *Mürşid-i Âsûriyûn* strongly suggests that Âşur Yûsuf was himself a reader of Lütfî Fikrî Bey's newspapers (also see note 360 on page 130). Incidentally, it was Lütfî Bey who had been responsible for bringing the *Hunchakian* into the *Hürriyet ve İtilâf Fırkası* in the first place; shortly after the agreement was reached in Istanbul, he set out for Dersim, stopping in Beirut, Damascus, Aleppo and several other locations in greater Syria, giving speeches in support of his party. Upon arriving in Harput on 28 Şubât, however, Lütfî Bey found out the CUP had arranged to have him excluded from the Dersim elections. He made a last-minute attempt at being elected by standing in both Malatya and Mamûretü'l-Azîz, but this did not prove to be successful. See Ali Birinci, *Hürriyet ve İtilâf Fırkası: II. Meşrutiyet devrinde İttihat ve Terakki'ye karşı çı-kanlar* (Istanbul: Dergâh Yayınları, 1990), 135, 139-140, 151 and 276.

Empire. It also strongly rejected separatist tendencies (*vucûd-ı devletten ayırmak temâyülât*) or any *millet* being in a position of political inferiority to any other (*bir milletin siyâseten diğerinin mâdûnu*).

Many similar themes are present in the Zionist declarations of Max Nordau published in *Mürşid-i Âsûriyûn* a year later in 1913. Unlike other countries, especially those in Eastern Europe, the Ottoman Empire is extolled for having always treated its Jewish populations well. Zionists, according to Nordau, wished to remain Ottomans, while preserving their own national language, customs, religion and culture.[399] The Ottoman Empire's 400,000 Jews, he argued, were well prepared to help the remaining – that is to say, post-Balkan War – Ottoman territories to flourish and strengthen, since only in this way could peace in the region be ensured.[400]

In contrast to his championing of cooperative and inclusive efforts, Âşûr Yûsuf decried the rising instability in Cebel-i Tûr and the eastern provinces in general. He attributed the cause to a drive by Kurdish chiefs (*mîrler*) to obtain autonomy (*muhtâriyet*) in Diyarbakır, Bitlis and Van on the grounds that before the time of Adam there had been a Kurdish empire across the region.[401] In response to the residents of Hasankeyf writing to *Mürşid-i Âsûriyûn* speaking of sacked villages and monasteries and stating that "in these districts there is no government", he implored the Patriarchate and the Ottoman state to resolve the problem of a rise

---

[399] "... kendi millî lisân, âdet, mezheb ve terbiyemiz ile yaşamak isteriz.": "Yahûdîler ve Balkan meselesi," *Mürşid-i Âsûriyûn*, 5, no. 2 (Şubât 1913), 27-30.

[400] "Şarkta sulhun bekâsı için âhir bir şart dahi Türkiye'nin bâkî kısmını mamûr ve kuvvetli olmasıdır ... İşte bu teceddüd icrâsında Türkiye'deki 400,000 Yahûdîler büyük hidmet îfâ etmeğe hâzırdırlar."

[401] "Cebel-i Tûr ahvâli," *Mürşid-i Âsûriyûn*, 5, no. 5 (Nîsân 1913), 79: "Botan mîrlerinin efkârı yakın bir vaktte alenen zuhûr edecektir. Bu cihetten Midyât ve Cebel-i Tûr ahvâli günbegün fenâlaşıyor, mîrlerin maksadları, Van, Bitlis ve Diyârbekir vilâyetlerinin Kürdler için ilân-ı muhtâriyetidir, çünki hazret-i Adam zamânından evvel Kürdler bu vilâyetlerde bir hukûmet-i imparatoriye sürmüş imişler!!!"

in Kurdish attacks since 1908.[402] But where the government did act to protect the people, Âşûr Yûsuf would point out the community's gratitude for its intervention. When these same Kurds made off with the livestock of a mixed Muslim, Protestant and Yezidi village, the government dispatched troops, resulting in an engagement that saw some 14 rebels and one soldier killed.[403] Likewise, when four Kurds murdered a *Süryânî* man and his daughter in Cizre, the police and *jandarma* [gendarmerie] immediately arrested three of the suspects who had hidden in a mosque. Then, "the local administration, showing great perseverance, located the final Kurd in the village of Pîşâpûr three or four days later."[404] Faith was placed in the the "state's justice" that the four imprisoned murderers would be handed the punishment that they deserved.[405]

The inclusion of such articles, even when he did not write them himself, I believe to be nonetheless important as they reveal his own thoughts. I also believe there to be no irony in Âşûr Yûsuf's publishing of Rızâ Tevfîk's article or Ebû Rıdvân's *Yeni Ay Gâziler*; he was a strongly opinionated author and was not one to hold back when he disagreed with someone, even when these were important figures. He had, for instance, an ongoing dispute with Abdünnûr of Harput which resulted in the *mutrân* bringing at least two unsuccessful cases against him and his paper in the Ottoman courts.[406] He also published a reply to a letter from the *Süryânî-i*

---

[402] "Hasankeyf'ten bir feryâd," *Mürşid-i Âsûriyûn*, 5, no. 7 (Hazîrân 1913), 113-115: "bu nâhiyelerde hukûmet yoktur." Similar news appears in "Hasankeyf'ten bir haber," *Mürşid-i Âsûriyûn*, 5, no. 6 (Mayıs 1913), 91-92.

[403] "Cebel-i Tûr ahvâli," *Mürşid-i Âsûriyûn*, 5, no. 6 (Mayıs 1913), 92-94. This article notes that while the attacks on villages were Kurdish led, some *Süryânî* had formed a union with the Kurds and were also participating in the raids.

[404] Pîşâpûr is a village in present-day Iraq, near the border with Syria.

[405] "Cezîre'den bir hâdise-i dilsûz," *Mürşid-i Âsûriyûn*, 5, no. 4 (Mart 1913), 63. "Hükûmet-i mahalliye ep iyi gayret edip üç dört günden sonra kaçanı dahi Pîşâpûr'da tutar. Şimdi kâtillerin her dördü dahi habiste olup cezâ-yı sezâlarına uğrayacakları hükûmetin adâletinden memûl olunur."

[406] "Berâet," *Mürşid-i Âsûriyûn*, 3, no. 5 (Hazîrân 1911), 88. I have not been able to trace the exact nature of the court cases: "Mutrân Abdünnûr

*Kadîm keşîş* involved in a mass conversion to the Armenian Church in the village of Ağvan, calling him "ignorant, empty-headed and disobedient."[407] But perhaps the best parallel may be found in the reaction to a firebrand article by Şeyh Abdülhak Bağdâdî entitled "Islam's last word to Europe".[408] Having made the rounds in the Arabic, Ottoman Turkish and Armenian press, the article appeared in *Mürşid-i Âsûriyûn* in November of 1912 and was followed a month later by a comprehensive criticism of Abdülhak Bağdâdî's ideas, which were very much in opposition to those expressed by Mehmed Şükrî in his address at the Protestant church in Perri.[409]

I do not wish to overemphasise the Ottoman nature of Âşûr Yûsuf, Naûm Fâik or Cebbûr Boyacı; overt Ottomanist sentiments were by no means the dominant theme of *Mürşid-i Âsûriyûn, Kevkeb Mednho* or *İntibâh*. And yet they still overshadow any overt expression of Assyrian identity, and the fact that they selected these subjects for inclusion stands in stark contrast to what one would expect having read the Assyrian nationalist literature. Considering the name of Âşûr Yûsuf's publication, it is no surprise that many scholars have presumed it to be a repository of nationalist thought, but this is an assumption which can not be supported by an actual reading of *Mürşid-i Âsûriyûn*.

There is no evidence of Nestorian or Chaldeans, let alone Melkites or Maronites, being subscribers or writing letters to any publication. The audience of *Kevkeb Mednho, Mürşid-i Âsûriyûn* and

---

efendi tarafından Mürşid'in muharririne karşı açılan davâ birinci defa men-i muhâkeme olundu. Mutrânın ikinci bir mürâcaatı üzerine lüzûm-ı muhâkeme gösterildi ise de muharrir-i Mürşid muhâkemede yine müdâfaasını edip berâet olundu."

[407] "[C]âhil, boş kafâ ve serkeş bir keşîş olup ...": "İşte keşîşin yazdığı mektûb," *Mürşid-i Âsûriyûn*, 5, no. 4 (Mart 1913), 57-59. For more on this particular event, see page 202.

[408] "İslâmın Avrupa'ya son sözü," *Mürşid-i Âsûriyûn*, 4, no. 7 (Teşrîn-i Sânî 1912), 103-110.

[409] Âşûr Yûsuf's reaction is contained in "Şu iki mektûblar üzere bir mutalaa," *Mürşid-i Âsûriyûn*, 4, no. 8 (Teşrîn-i Sânî 1912), 124-125. It follows another criticism from a reader in the United States: "Şeyh Abdülhak Bağdâdî'ye açık bir mektûb," *Mürşid-i Âsûriyûn*, 4, no. 8 (Teşrîn-i Sânî 1912), 121-124.

*İntibâh* was clearly not some larger Assyrian community but rather the cross-denominational *Süryânî* one. There were no calls for a unity amongst all the Assyrian peoples, only a recognition of a common historical heritage. Âşûr Yûsuf decried many failings of the *Süryânî* community, but I have seen nothing to support the suggestion that "[t]o the dismay of men such as Ashur Yousif, Assyrian nationalism gained little ground among Jacobites and Chaldeans."[410]

From both *Mürşid-i Âsûriyûn* and *Kevkeb Mednho* we have seen that the term *Âsûrî* appeared often in letters or articles written in the United States, whereas Naûm Fâik and Âşûr Yûsuf largely eschewed it. There is evidence to suggest that it was not so much the early twentieth-century activities of Ottoman intellectuals which cemented an Assyrian identity in the *Süryânî* community. Instead, Assyrian nationalism appears to have developed most amongst the emigrants to the United States, where *Süryânî* came into closer contact with Nestorians and Chaldeans who had also settled there. Moreover, the massacres of First World War, when expectations from the Ottoman Empire were dashed once and for all, had a great impact on the *Süryânî*, turning them away from Ottomanism and towards an Assyrian identity. Naûm Fâik and İbrâhîm Yûsuf exemplify this process. I have not personally studied Naûm Fâik's later publications in great detail, but the secondary sources imply that there was a transformation in notions of *millet* and *vatan* towards concrete symbols of Assyrian nationalism.

The news of the difficulties being endured by Christians in the Ottoman Empire motivated Naûm Fâik to aid in campaigns to raise funds for the families of *Süryânî* who had been killed.[411] In 1916, *İntibâh* [Awakening] became *Bethnahrin* [Mesopotamia] (the geographic expression of the Assyrian nation), a newspaper in which details of this suffering regularly appeared. *Bethnahrin*'s Arabic-language mission statement expressed a desire for Assyrian unity which was completely absent from his pre-1914 writings:

---

[410] De Kelaita, "On the Road to Nineveh", 14.
[411] Çıkkı, *Naum Faik ve Süryani Rönesansı*, 35-36.

"Our goal is not to show how learned we are, but to serve our *vatan* ... for all brothers of the *Süryânî* to come together under a single umbrella. These brothers are Nestorians, Chaldeans, Maronites, Catholics, Protestants ... I remind these groups that their past, their race, their blood and flesh, their tongue, their *vatan* are all that of the *Süryânî* ... We must work to exalt the name of the Assyrians ... Our primary goal is to secure the rights of the Assyrians."[412]

His second endeavour in the United States, *Huyodo* [Unity], also suggested a more Assyrianist outlook, especially as it was backed by the *Assyro-Chaldean National Unity of America*. The meeting of Assyrians in the United States does appear to have forged a unity between the separate communities which is not visible in *Mürşid-i Âsûriyûn* or the Diyarbakır-based publications.

There was also the story of Senharîb Bâli's "discovery" of an Urmiye native in New Jersey, who then facilitated a larger meeting of Assyrians in the New York area.[413] At one such gathering, held on 10 June 1917 as a function of the *Assyrian Erootha Society*, "[t]he Nestorians and the Jacobites, like true and loving brethren, mingled together."[414] The *Assyrian Erootha Society* was, in fact, the İntibâh Cemiyeti in the United States, which had, at some point during the war years, dropped the Ottoman Turkish *intibâh* in favour of its Syriac equivalent and begun working towards the unity of the different communities. Senharîb Bâli's early twentieth-century newspaper *Savto d-Oromoye* [Voice of the Aramaeans] appears in his own personal notes written some decades later as *Savto d-Othoroye* [Voice of the Assyrians], while the names of others were recorded under Syriac translation of their actual Ottoman Turkish names.[415]

---

[412] Ibid., 66-68.

[413] The story appears in *Ünlü Asurlardan (Kildanilerden, Süryanilerden) Seçmeler II*, 64 and Naby, "The Assyrian diaspora," 221.

[414] "The Assyrian Erootha Society," *Assyrian Progress*, 1, no. 10 (15 June 1917), 6.

[415] A copy of these were provided to me by Jan Bet-Şawoce.

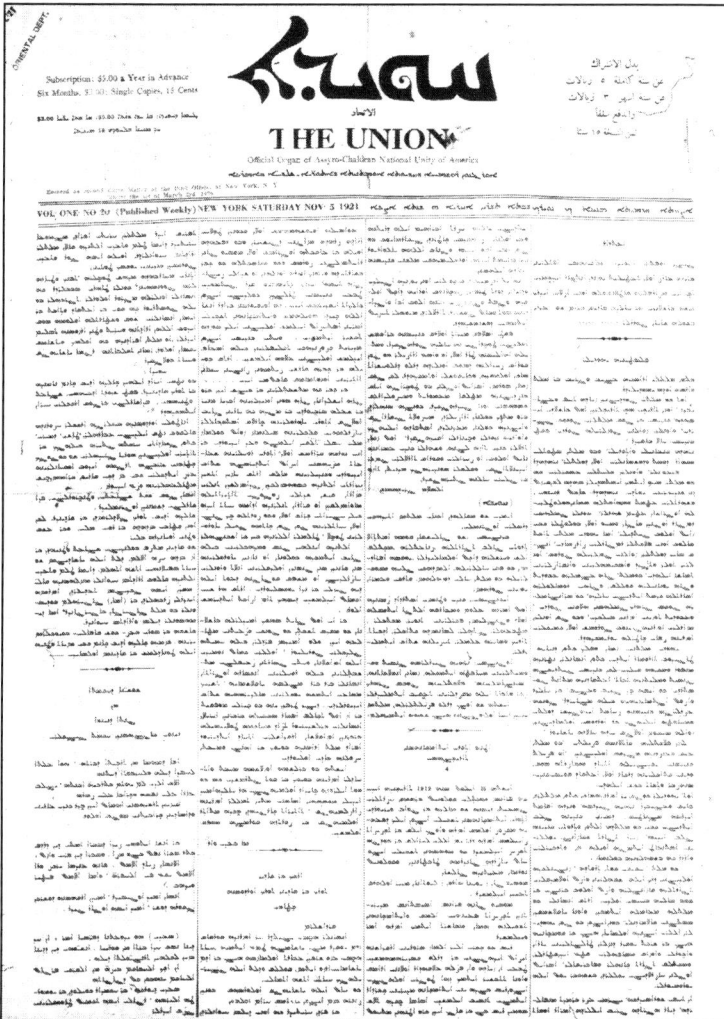

Image 8 – *Huyodo*

A similar shift in *Süryânî* perceptions may be observed in the activities of İbrâhîm Yûsuf, who despite having volunteered in the Ottoman army during the Balkan Wars to great acclaim, served in the United States military once it entered the First World War.[416] İbrâhîm Yûsuf himself wrote that the Balkan Wars marked a breaking point in the direction of the Ottoman Empire, as the government under Enver Paşa sought to reclaim lost territories and restore lost Ottoman pride.[417]

But what shows best his abandonment of the Ottoman ideal was İbrâhîm Yûsuf's participation at the Paris Peace Conference as a representative of the Assyrian delegation which asked for the emancipation of the provinces of Diyarbakır, Bitlis and Mamûretü'l-Azîz as well as the *sancak* of Urfa from Turkish rule.[418] The delegation even floated the idea of a vast independent Assyrian homeland including Diyarbakır, Mosul, Urmiye, Hakkâri and the lands between.[419] The *Süryânî* periodical *The New Assyria*, published in the United States between 1916 and 1919, had on the cover of each issue the nationalist perception of the Assyrian homeland, which was to include most of Iraq, Syria and Lebanon, in addition to parts of Turkey and Iran (see Image 9 below). While these appeals obviously came to nothing, the transformation of figures such as İbrâhîm Yûsuf over a short period of time is palpable.

---

[416] Naby, "The Assyrian diaspora," 221. He was "a World War I hero" according to Aydın, *The History of the Syriac Orthodox Church of Antioch in North America*.

[417] "Assyria and the Peace Conference," *Assyrian Progress*, 3, 29 (15 January 1919), 2-3.

[418] The request was signed by Barsûm, *mutrân* of Homs and future Patriarch of the Jacobite Church. A facsimile of the document appears in de Courtois, *The Forgotten Genocide*, 334-335.

[419] de Courtois, *The Forgotten Genocide*, 217-223.

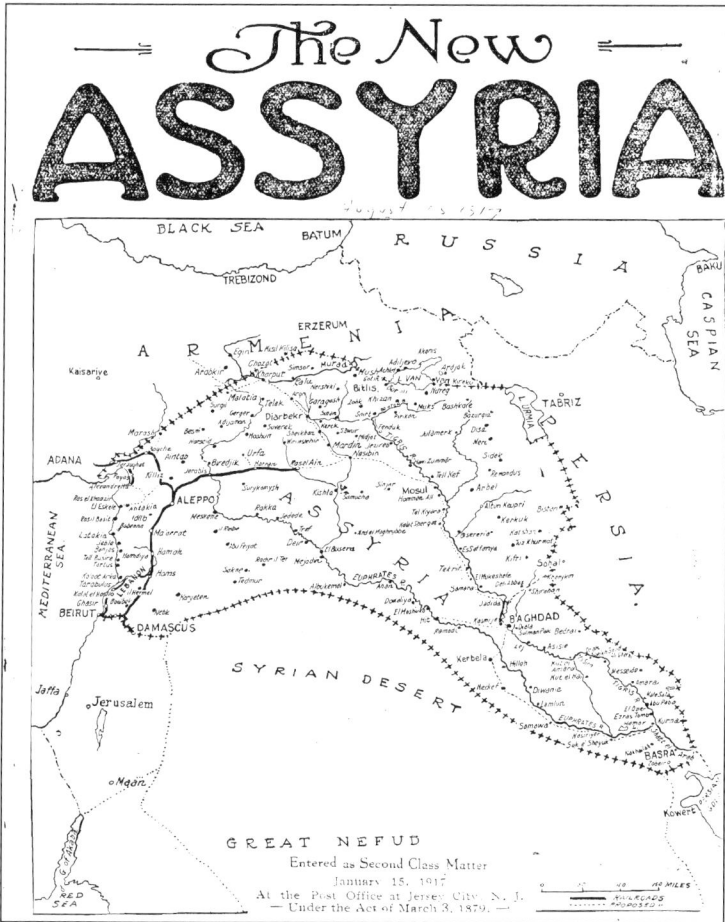

Image 9 – The cover of *The New Assyria*

Rising anti-Christian sentiments due to the Ottoman-Italian War have been cited as the reason that Naûm Fâik emigrated to the United States.[420] This is, however, not made entirely clear either in

---

[420] Çıkkı, *Naum Faik ve Süryani Rönesansı*, 27. Naûm Fâik left Diyarbakır on 22 September 1912, just prior to the outbreak of the Balkan Wars.

the latest issues of *Kevkeb Mednho* that I possess or in the issues of *İntibâh* or *Mürşid-i Âsûriyûn* from the time at which he emigrated. It is possible that economic factors, including famine, prompted Naûm Fâik to leave in search of better fortunes elsewhere; this was certainly the case with many others, *Süryânî* or not, in the Ottoman Empire at that time.[421] Indeed, *Mürşid-i Âsûriyûn* occasionally noted the diminishing stocks and rising prices of staples in Cebel-i Tûr and even recorded the increasing number of people leaving the area for Syria and Adana.[422] Whatever his own reasons for leaving, at some point between 1912 and 1916 Naûm Fâik abandoned any Ottomanist sympathies that he had and began looking to Assyrian nationalism for the future of the *Süryânî*.

We should not see the transformation of İbrâhîm Yûsuf, Naûm Fâik or other *Süryânî* figures as something exceptional, however. Similar stories of disenchantment and disillusionment may be found in the experiences of Greeks and Armenians during the same period. There have been several case studies which have examined erstwhile supporters of the CUP or Ottomanism and how they reformulated their outlook at some point between the Balkan Wars and the establishment of the Turkish Republic. Examples include the Greek deputy for Izmir, Emmanouēl Emmanouēlidēs, whose memoires would conceal his own cooperation with and support for the CUP and concentrate on his supposed "Byzantinist" leanings.[423] Nicolae Batzaria, a Vlach and early member of the CUP, similarly believed that the group's Turkish nationalist policies were a catastrophe for the Christians as it caused them to abandon Ottomanism in favour of anti-Turkish alliances.[424] Âşûr Yûsuf, on the other hand, experienced first-hand just how the hopes from 1908 that he expressed in *Mürşid-i Âsûriyûn* had failed to materialise. In this he resembles Krikor Zohrab, the Armenian deputy for Istanbul, both in their support for the Ottoman Empire and their death at its hands in 1915.[425]

---

[421] Joseph, *Muslim-Christian Relations*, 96.

[422] "Cebel-i Tûr ahvâli," *Mürşid-i Âsûriyûn*, 5, no. 5 (Nîsân 1913), 78.

[423] Kechriotis, "On the Margins of National Historiography."

[424] Karpat, "The Memoirs of N. Batzaria", 293-296.

[425] See Koptaş, *Armenian Political Thinking*.

# 4   *İNTİBÂH* OR *HÂB-I GAFLET*

If Âşûr Yûsuf, Cebbûr Boyacı and Naûm Fâik – in his Ottoman days at least – were not the Assyrian nationalists as we have been led to believe, then there must be another motivation for their prolific literary output. In Assyrian historiography it is their supposed adherence to secularism which allowed the deep theological divide between the different denominations to be bridged and a union of all Assyrians to finally occur. I argue that their real goal was to reform aspects of their community which they saw as backwards, hindering the progress of the *Süryânî* people. Moreover, I suggest that a central component of any such reform was the participation of the church. In reinforcing the Jacobite nature of the *Süryânî* people, Âşûr Yûsuf and Naûm Fâik demonstrate that there remained an uneasiness in the adoption of a shared secular national identity.

## THE ROLE OF THE CHURCH AND THE ROLE OF THE LAITY

> "Although a number of intellectuals and professionals, such as the noted and widely respected writer and poet Naum Faik, were nationalists, the movement among Jacobites and Chaldeans was extremely confined and subject to internal resistance. Among the clergy in particular, there was grave concern that nationalism would mean ruin for their possessed institutions that were geographically too close to Ottoman ... seats of power ... Another concern of the clergy was power;

secular nationalist leadership would naturally undermine the influence of the church."[426]

This appraisal is very much consistent with the emphasis on lay-religious conflict in the present-day nationalist histories. Since the Jacobite church is often found at the head of resistance to the Assyrian thesis amongst the *Süryânî*, it is presumed that *Süryânî* intellectuals challenged the authority of the church using the weapons of secularism and nationalism. For example, we read that: "For 500 years Assyrians in Iraq and Turkey lived under the Millat System of the Ottoman sultans ... The concept of "Assyrian" or "Assyrianism" was nearly non-existent and acknowledged by those who dared to link themselves to the pre-Christian periods."[427]

Eden Naby is somewhat more tempered in her language, but she has proclaimed that "... the seeds for secular identity as Assyrians had been laid in the late nineteenth century prior to their arrival in the United States through the activities of such intellectuals as Ashour Yusuf ... and Naum Faik." This statement is accurate to an extent. To them, their community was the *Süryânî* one, whether they be Jacobite, Catholic or Protestant, so in that respect they promoted secularism; but we have also seen that little or no effort was made to enjoin an Assyrian identity encompassing Nestorians and Chaldeans. More importantly, I also believe that Naby's statement must be qualified, lest one conclude that the lay figures sought to shut the religious hierarchy out of their leading position in community affairs.

First of all, of the important *Süryânî* figures that Âşûr Yûsuf held in high esteem, roughly half from the clergy and half were from the laity. To these respected members of the community, Âşûr Yûsuf would address questions, sometimes on spiritual matters and sometimes on worldly ones. Of special importance were *mutrân* Tûmâ (Diyarbakır), *mutrân* İlyâs (Mosul), *serepiskopos* Pavlûs (Istanbul) and the Protestant *üskuf* Amanûyil (Midyat). In addition, he would appeal to Cercîs Alacacı, an unnamed teacher (*muallim*) at the *Süryânî-i Kadîm* school in Urfa, *muallim* Hannâ Sırrı

---

[426] De Kelaita, "On the Road to Nineveh", 14.
[427] Bet-Alkhas, "*Omta*, NOT *Millat*!"

Çıkkı (Mardin), İbrâhîm Yûsuf (Worcester) and Antûn Ulubeğ (the United States).[428] He also tried to elicit information from a variety of institutions, such as the other *Süryânî* newspapers – in particular *İntibâh* – as well as local organisations (either a *millet meclisi* or branches of the *İntibâh Cemiyeti*) and schools.

More importantly, neither Naûm Fâik nor Âşûr Yûsuf saw himself as a political leader and nor did they envisage a secular political leadership for the *Süryânî*. Indeed in political matters, both looked to either the Patriarchate or the Patriarchal representative (*patrik vekîlî*) in the Ottoman capital to intervene on behalf of the community. This does not mean, however, that there was no criticism of religious leaders. *Mürşid-i Âsûriyûn* and *Kevkeb Mednho* each contain strong denunciations of what they saw as detrimental activities, a lack of action or ignorance on the part of local priests, bishops and even the Patriarch himself. As the clergy were the leaders of the community, Âşûr Yûsuf and Naûm Fâik held them to a high standard; infallibility was not something gained simply by entering into church service, but was rather earned through actions benefiting the *Süryânî* people.

Perhaps the strongest indictment of Abdullah Sattûf, the Jacobite Patriarch, came as a response to his long presence in India, where he attempted to assert both spiritual and temporal authority over the Indian congregation. The Patriarch's efforts culminated in the senior bishop of India, *mutrân* Gevergis, to lead a break-away faction from the parent church.[429] With the majority of the Indian congregation behind Gevergis, Abdullah resorted to excommunicating him and appointing a loyal replacement. In response, the congregation invited Abdülmesîh, who still claimed

---

[428] The only individuals who never answered Âşûr Yûsuf's requests were *mutrân* İlyâs and Antûn Ulubeğ. About the latter I have been unable to find any concrete information, although the *Süryânî* cemetery in Elâzığ contains a number of graves of contemporary Ulubeğ family members who are described as *tüccâr* [merchant]. I suspect that Antûn Ulubeğ may have been the Anthony George who had been born in Harput in 1880 and emigrated to the United States in 1896: "The Death of Anthony George," *Assyrian Progress* 2, no. 19 (15 March 1918), 10-11.

[429] Gevergis's title was *metropolit* Mar Diyannûsiyûs and he was some-times called as such in *Mürşid-i Âsûriyûn*.

to be the rightful Patriarch of the Jacobite Church, to India, where he annulled the excommunication of Gevergis and installed him as metropolitan over all of Malabar.

This Indian schism was not, in the eyes of Naûm Fâik and Âşûr Yûsuf, reason enough for the Patriarch to desert his congregation in the Ottoman Empire, leaving them "fallen, lifeless and immersed in ignorance." Âşûr Yûsuf wrote, "it would have been better [for the Patriarch] to be a missionary to his *millettaş* in Turkey than to the pagans of India."[430] Âşûr Yûsuf wished to see the return of the Patriarch revitalise what he called the "*Süryânî* mother church," but there is also an implication that he wished to see *Süryânî* from other denominations return to this same church.

It was furthermore Âşûr Yûsuf's opinion that the Patriarch's obstinacy was prolonging the dispute which had rent the Indian congregation, and indeed Jacobite church as a whole:

> "In this matter, is it the Patriarch or the Indians who are wrong? The time for this question has passed. Even if the Patriarch is right, this excommunication [of Gevergis] will be the cause of an population of 200,000 separating from the See of Antioch. In the memory of our messiah's affection [for his flock], the Patriarchal seat and the *Süryânî-i Kadîm* congregation, the Patriarch must reverse this excommunication."[431]

---

[430] "... Türkiye'de bulunan düşkün, hayâtsız ve cehâlette gark olmuş olan Süryânî ana kilisesinin ve millettaşlarının hâl-i pürmelâline atf-i nazar edip Hindistân pütperestlerine misyoner olacak yerde Türkiye'deki Süryânîlerin tecdîd-i hayât etmekleri için en evvel misyoner diye kendi millettaşlarına gelseler idi daha iyi olur idi." The quote comes from Âşûr Yûsuf's commentary on "Hindistân Süryânî hıristiyânları," *Mürşid-i Âsûriyûn*, 5, no. 7 (Haziran 1913), 111-112. He was not calling the Indian Jacobites pagans, but was referring to the missionary efforts aimed at the non-Christian populace.

[431] "Hindistân'dan yine bir feryâd," *Mürşid-i Âsûriyûn*, 5, no. 11 (Teşrîn-i Evvel 1913), 168-169: "Bu mesele patrik mi yoksa Hindliler mi haksızdır? Bu suâli edecek vakt geçmiştir. Patrik muamelesinde haklı bile olsa mâdem ki şu haram iki yüz bin nüfûsun Antâkya kürsîsinden ayrılmasına sebeb oluyor. Patrik hazretleri, mesîhin muhabbeti Antâkya kürsîsi ve

The Patriarch's duty was to defer to the good of both the *cemâat* – including the non-*Süryânî* Indians – and the *millet* rather than to rule by *fiat*. Besides arguing for the the preservation of the Antiochian See, Âşûr Yûsuf also prioritised the well-being of the *millet* over the rights of the Patriarch:

> "We love our Patriarch and if necessary we are ready to defend him against his enemies; however, when the rights of the Patriarch or the *millet* are in question, we prefer the rights of the *millet* over that of the Patriarch. First you need the *millet*, then the Patriarch. Without a *millet*, there can be no Patriarch."[432]

He echoed the same sentiments in a later article, in which he further outlined what he felt was the role of the Patriarch in the life of the community:

> "When the day came that he [Abdullah] took the seat [of Antioch], we had hopes that he would make an effort to establish new schools, stimulate education and culture and train the clergy of Turkey for the enlightening of the *millet* and in this manner the progress of the *Süryânî*

---

Süryânî-i Kadîm cemâatinin hatırı için şu haramını çözmelidir." At the end of the year, Âşûr Yûsuf reported that in both Mardin and Diyarbakır, the *millet meclisi* had petitioned Abdullah to have the excommunication overturned. "Yine Hindistân meselesi," *Mürşid-i Âsûriyûn*, 5, no. 13 (Kânûn-ı Evvel 1913), 211: "İlâve - dostlarımızın birinden aldığımız bir mektûbe nazaran Diyârbekir ve Mârdîn millet meclisleri tarafından mutrân Gevergis'in haramını çözülmesi için mürâcaatler olunmuş. Bakalım bunun netîcesi ne olacaktır. Ne mutlu sulh edicilere."

[432] "Biz patrikimizi severiz îcâb hâlde düşmânlara karşı onu müdâfaa etmeğe dahî hâzır isek de mesele patrik ile millet hukûkuna gelir ise evvel-vakt patrikin hukûkundan ziyâde millet hukûku tercîh ederiz. Evvelen millet ve sonra patrik lâzımdır. Millet olmazsa patrik hiç olmaz. Ve memûl ederiz ki mutrân İlyâs efendi dahi bunun hakikat olduğunu tasdîk buyuruyorlar." Âşûr Yûsuf wrote this in defence of his criticisms of Abdullah's activities, which in turn had been criticised by *mutrân* İlyâs: "Bir müdâfaa," *Mürşid-i Âsûriyûn*, 3, no. 3 (Mart 1911), 47-48 and "Şu müdâfaaya cevâbımız," *Mürşid-i Âsûriyûn*, 3, no. 3 (Mart 1911), 49-52.

would enter into an new age so that our Patriarch would outstrip his predecessors in glory and honour."[433]

The Indian question dominated the issues of *Mürşid-i Âsûriyûn* from late 1913 in particular, but numerous articles from earlier years and from *Kevkeb Mednho* and *İntibâh* are also present. The consensus was that the foray into India was detrimental to the community, and yet there was never any suggestion that lay figures or organisations should step in and assume the leadership position that had been left vacant by Abdullah. When, for example, the Ottoman government began offering funds for the repair of damaged Armenian churches in and around Adana (presumably as a result of the 1909 massacres), Âşûr Yûsuf placed the responsibility on *serepiskopos* Pavlûs, the *patrik vekîli* in Istanbul, to look into the possibility of *Süryânî* also benefiting from this measure.[434]

Similarly, when the government offered the opportunity for students to study free of charge at schools in Istanbul, a resident of Adana was angered that *serepiskopos* Pavlûs had informed the local community only to send children of wealthy families.[435] Naûm Fâik used this occasion to extend the criticism to the religious leadership, not the secular, for not being more aware of this opportunity for *Süryânî* youth; in particular, the Patriarch was singled out for being unaware of events in the Ottoman Empire.[436]

---

[433] "Onun kürsîye oturduğu günde memûl ediyor idik ki yeni yeni mektebler küşâd edip talîm ve terbiyeyi teşvîk ve Türkiyeli ruhbânlar yetiştirip milletin tenvîrine belz-i gayret edecek ve bu vechle Süryânîlerin terakkisine yeni bir asır başlatılacak ve patrikimiz seleflerinden fevkalâde bir sûrette şânlı ve şerifli bir patrik olacak.": "Hindistân meselerinden dolayı," *Mürşid-i Âsûriyûn*, 5, no. 12 (Teşrîn-i Sânî 1913), 182-184.

[434] "Cerîdelerden," *Mürşid-i Âsûriyûn*, 4, no. 3 (Mart 1912), 45-47.

[435] "Kevkeb Mednho cerîdesine," *Kevkeb Mednho*, 2, no. 3 (12 Ağustos 1911), 4-5. Pavlûs specifically requested that they be able to pay 10 Ottoman lira.

[436] [untitled article], *Kevkeb Mednho*, 2, no. 3 (12 Ağustos 1911), 5-6. Government funds were also available for the construction of schools in Diyarbakır, something which Âşûr Yûsuf directed the *cemâat* to take advantage of. But it is not clear that by *cemâat* and not *millet* he was instruct-

Part of the assumption on the part of the *Süryânî* intellectuals that the Patriarch must be the intermediary between the state and the people was a consequence of the Ottoman administrative system. And yet, there was no indication that they saw the laity as a substitute for the leadership provided by the Patriarchate. Indeed, for all his mistakes, Abdullah was still considered the sole figure who could right the wrongs in the community. When the Patriarch finally returned to the Ottoman Empire in late 1913, he took up residence in Jerusalem and began a treatment for a serious eye condition. Âşûr Yûsuf was exasperated: the Patriarch was so close and yet so far. Jerusalem turned out to be little better than India, and he again called for action to be taken by *serepiskopos* Pavlûs to resolve the impasse, so that Abdullah might once again take up residence in Mardin.[437] But it was to no avail and in 1915, the year of Âşûr Yûsuf's death, Abdullah too passed away in Jerusalem, blind and never having returned to the seat of the Patriarchate.

Amidst all the scathing attacks on the clergy, there were times at which Âşûr Yûsuf would praise those who were involved in community affairs. On hearing that the *mutrân* of Diyarbakır had become an instructor at the local *Süryânî* school, Âşûr Yûsuf would write, "[i]f our religious leaders everywhere showed the fervour and self-sacrifice of *mutrân* Tûmâ Efendi, the *Süryânî* community would not have fallen into such a state of ignorance."[438] Far from removing the clergy from daily life, he sought to incite them to take a much greater role in administration and education.

Surprisingly, he occasionally had kind words to say concerning *mutrân* Abdünnûr of Harput, who would find himself severely criticised on many other occasions in *Mürşid-i Âsûriyûn*. In 1913, an orphaned *Süryânî* girl who had wed an Armenian proceeded to

---

ing the local religious leaders to make the application: "Diyârbekir'de mekteb inşası," *Mürşid-i Âsûriyûn*, 5, no. 12 (Teşrîn-i Sânî 1913), 190.

[437] "Havâdis-i milliye," *Mürşid-i Âsûriyûn*, 5, no. 13 (Kânûn-ı Evvel 1913), 212.

[438] "Diyârbekir'de Süryânî mektebi," *Mürşid-i Âsûriyûn*, 5, no. 1 (Kânûn-ı Sânî 1913), 14: "Eğer her yerde dahi reis-i rûhânîlerimiz mutrân Tûmâ efendi gibi gayûr ve fedâkâr bulunmuş olsalar idi Süryânî cemâat bu derece cehâlette garak olmaz idi."

marry a Kurdish youth from a neighbouring household while her husband was away in the United States. With the Christian community much alarmed, *mutrân* Abdünnûr intervened, and although unable to persuade the girl to return to her first husband, he petitioned the government and succeeded in having her second marriage annulled.[439] About this event, Âşûr Yûsuf wrote that "Abdünnûr has performed his duty rather well."

But when it came to Abdünnûr, more often the tone was a critical one. In early 1913, rumours began spreading in Harput that Abdünnûr would lose his position as *mutrân*, Âşûr Yûsuf commented that "[t]he conflict between the Italian and Balkan governments and the Ottomans have come to an end. But the years-long conflict happening between the Harput congregation and metropolitans has not." Consequently, "[s]o now any honour and virtue of being pious, of being *Süryânî*, of the Patriarch and the Patriarchate has been spoilt. Such is the product of being without a leader."[440]

One Assyrian nationalist scholar has stated that the publications of the period "tended to be less religion-laden, and ... more the inspiration of nationalistic and creative lay persons."[441] But this is misleading; Âşûr Yûsuf published numerous articles celebrating the church, praising Christ or instructing his readers how to be better Christians.[442] Most of his poetry, whether

---

[439] "Mutrân Abdünnûr efendi borcunu pek güzel îfâ etti," *Mürşid-i Âsûriyûn*, 5, no. 5 (Nîsân 1913), 80. It is not entirely clear to what church the individuals belonged to as Abdünnûr consulted with both the Armenian *murahhasa* as well as the local Protestant *vekîl* on the matter. Abdünnûr's primary role in resolving the matter suggests that the woman was a Jacobite.

[440] "Artık rûhânîliğin de Süryânîliğin de, Patrik ve Patrikhânenin de nâmûs ve itibârı berbâd oldu. İşte idâresizliğin bir netîcesi.": "Harpût abraşiyesi ahvâli," *Mürşid-i Âsûriyûn*, 5, no. 6 (Mayıs 1913), 96.

[441] Benjamin, "Assyrian Journalism," 7-8.

[442] For example, see: "Mîlâd perhîzi," *Mürşid-i Âsûriyûn*, 4, no. 9 (Kânûn-ı Evvel 1912), 130-132; "Mesîhin şahsı," *Mürşid-i Âsûriyûn*, 5, no. 3 (Mart 1913), 38-39; "İngiliz milleti ve kitâb-ı mukkades," *Mürşid-i Âsûriyûn*, 5, no. 2 (Şubât 1913), 30-31; "Mesîhin şahsı," *Mürşid-i Âsûriyûn*, 5, no. 3

appearing in *Mürşid-i Âsûriyûn* or not, also contained overt religious imagery.[443] Moreover, his purported assistant in the publication of *Mürşid-i Âsûriyûn*, Yakûb Denho, was himself a *şemmâs* in the *Süryânî-i Kadîm* church of Harput.

Âşûr Yûsuf was not alone in attributing to the religious hierarchy a central role in the *Süryânî* life, however. Naûm Fâik felt that the Jacobite community had allowed other peoples (*unsur*) to prosper in the great cities of the world, while the *Süryânî* were relegated to desolate and mountainous places devoid of civilisation. Using Baghdad as an example of a city without a proper place of worship or a *Süryânî-i Kadîm* priest, he implored that men of religion be dispatched to ports such as Izmir, Samsun, Alexandria, Marseilles and even the great capitals of Paris, London and Rome – cities which "attract people like magnets" – so that *Süryânî* would also settle there.[444]

Naûm Fâik was himself a *şemmâs* in the Jacobite church and was addressed by letter writers as one would a man of the church: *mübârek rûhânî azîzimiz Naûm Fâik*.[445] While his was by no means a position of high authority, it was sufficient to grant one certain privileges, including exemption from military service.[446] So despite dire warnings that neither the Patriarch, nor his metropolitans and priests were the path to betterment, I still see Naûm Fâik and Âşûr

---

(Mart 1913), 38-39; "Velâdet bayramı tefekkûrleri," *Mürşid-i Âsûriyûn*, 5, no. 13 (Kânûn-ı Evvel 1913), 198-200.

[443] See Appendix C for more on this poetry as well as a sample.

[444] "Kevkeb Mednho," *Kevkeb Mednho*, 1, no. 20 (8 Nîsân 1911), 3-4. One sentence, for example, reads: "Bağdâd yalnız değil bu zamânda Beyrût, İskenderiye, Mısr, Marsilya ve daha mühim iskelelerde ve hatta Paris, Londra, Roma gibi pâyitahtlarda bile milletimiz nâmına birer kâhin ikâmet ettirmek ileri de millete fevâid-i azîme-yi câlib olacağı derkârdır."

[445] "Mübârek rûhânî azîzimiz Naûm Fâik," *Kevkeb Mednho*, 1, no. 22 (6 Mayıs 1911), 15-16.

[446] For his being a *şemmâs*, see Şimşek, *Süryaniler ve Diyarbakır*, 269. Naûm Fâik was of course far too old to be drafted once the Ottoman army began taking Christians.

Yûsuf as representing disillusionment with the religious leaders of his day rather than the institution as a whole.[447]

The laity, however, did have the right to some say in the administration of church affairs. The *millet meclisi* [council] of Harput, to which Naûm Fâik wrote his letter pleading for unity, was responsible for managing the finances of the *Süryânî-i Kadîm* community in Mamûretü'l-Azîz.[448] In its budgets, its sources of revenue included shops, foundations (*vakf*) and "church income (*kilise vâridâti*)", while it provided for the upkeep of churches and schools as well as the salaries of a priest (*keşîş*), the *mutrân* and two teachers.[449]

Other such councils definitely existed in Mardin and Diyarbakır, and presumably in each bishopric of the Jacobite church. With respect to the composition of the councils, there is unfortunately little to inform us other than a mention of Petris Efendi, a member of the *millet meclis* (presumably of Harput), who married an Armenian girl from Palu.[450] But if there were lay members like Petris, there were also spiritual leaders on the council, and it was these who dominated.

Âşûr Yûsuf was quick to point out discrepancies and omissions in the published figures, noting, for example, that the subsidies from the Ministry of Education (*Maârif*) should have

---

[447] For Naûm Fâik's most extreme attacks on the religious establishment, see Çıkkı, *Naum Faik ve Süryani Rönesansı*, 135-136: "Bu onulmaz yaramıza kimden şifa umuyoruz, patriğimizden mi? Yoksa mıtranlarımızdan mı? Yahut rahiplerimizden mi? ... Bunlar milletin yaralarını saramaz, ancak paralarını alıp soyabilirler." By comparison, the language of *Kevkeb Mednho* is quite subdued.

[448] Here the term *millet* reflects the standard Ottoman usage of religious community and not Âşûr Yûsuf's secular one.

[449] One of those receiving a wage was *muallim* Yakûb; this was presumably Yakûb Denho, who was a teacher in a *Süryânî* school in Harput according to oral testimony. The budgets for the periods 21 Kânûn-ı Evvel 1325 to 31 Kânûn-ı Evvel 1326 [*sic*] and 21 Kânûn-ı Evvel 1326 to 20 Kânûn-ı Evvel 1327 are in "Harpût millet meclisinin senevî hesâbları," *Mürşid-i Âsûriyûn*, 5, no. 1 (*Kânûn-ı Sânî* 1913), 10-13.

[450] "Münâkihât," *Mürşid-i Âsûriyûn*, 5, no. 4 (Mart 1913), 64. Palu was in the *sancak* of Ergani, in *vilâyet* of Diyarbakır, but it was closer to Harput and is, in fact, in the present-day province of Elâzığ.

been greater than was listed. He blamed Abdünnûr for having hand-picked the "contemptible group (*millet kepâzeleri*)" and then illegitimately profiting through their place on the council. According to the government, it was the community's right, and not that of the *mutrân*, to elect the council members and so he demanded the appointment of a new council composed of "sincere men."[451] I do not believe that this conflict demonstrates a cleavage in lay and religious relations; it was also not simply a personal one, although the history of tensions between Âşûr Yûsuf and Abdünnûr probably lay behind some of the former's vitriol and presumptions of the latter's guilt.[452] Instead, I see it as less of an attempt to assert lay authority, than an effort to remedy the ills of the community, ills for which Âşûr Yûsuf and Naûm Fâik held certain – but by no means all – members of the clergy responsible.

We must, however, recognise that simply by questioning the inherent right of the clergy to automatically be the community leaders was, in fact, a form of secularism. Infringing on the traditional authority of the religious establishment was part of a process in which lay members would assume a greater participation in the administration of the *millet*. The single secular institution which could have assumed the role of the Jacobite church in providing answers to the community's problems was the *İntibâh Cemiyeti* [Society of the Awakening], a somewhat nebulous organisation about which a fair amount of information exists. Founded on 1 Eylûl 1324 [14 September 1908] in Diyarbakır, the

---

[451] "Hükûmet her bir cemâatın kendi umûr-ı milliye ve dîniyesini idâreye memûr olacak meclisleri cemâatın ekseriyet arasıyla intihâb etmek hukûkunu kendilere terk etmiştir. Nizâm ve kânûn bu olduğu takdîrde mutrân efendi değil milletin illâ kendinin intihâb ettiği adamları hükûmete millet meclisi diye tavsiyeye nasıl cesâret edebilmiştir?": "Hesâbâttan dolayı îrâd olunan suâle cevâb," *Mürşid-i Âsûriyûn*, 5, no. 3 (Mart 1913), 48.

[452] For example, when Abdünnûr accused a man of entering his office and stealing a sum of money set aside for the purchase of a printing press, Âşûr Yûsuf dismissed the accusations ("İşte mutrân efendinin bu sâbıkası onun şimdiki şu iddiâsının doğruluğunu tasdîk etmekten bizi men ediyor.") citing the *mutrân*'s record of slandering and intimidating his opponents: [untitled article], *Mürşid-i Âsûriyûn*, 5, no. 11 (Teşrîn-i Evvel 1913), 179-180.

organisation was initially known as the *Süryânî-i Kadîm İntibâh-ı İlmî Cemiyeti* and stated explicitly that its mission was to serve the Jacobite community.[453] The religious designation, however, was only used by the newspapers in the first few months of its existence, with later references dropping both *Kadîm* and *İlmî* from the name.[454] Naûm Fâik, who was instrumental in its establishment, stated that to achieve its goal of edifying the community, new branches were to be opened in every province, town and village of the Ottoman Empire where *Süryânî* resided. Within six or seven weeks of its founding, there numbered some 200 members in Diyarbakır, and these in turn produced a short constitution (*nizâmnâme*) and elected twelve individuals to the society's board, including a chairman, a treasurer and a secretary.[455]

Cebbûr Boyacı published a copy of the constitution in a special supplement (*ilâvet-i İntibâh*) to the May 1910 issue of *İntibâh*.[456] The first article read:

> "This organisation's primary mission is to improve the *Süryânî-i Kadîm cemâat*'s schools; and to disseminate the knowledge and learning which serves to fortify and exalt the glorious constitution which we have attained; and to found and build boys' and girls' schools in the hopes of explaining Ottomanism [*Osmanlılık*], thereby doing justice to the Ottoman state's laws and pronouncements to which we are obedient; and to publish various newspapers and books and series which may exalt the

---

[453] See the first article of the organisation's constitution in "Süryânî-i Kadîm İntibâh-ı İlmî Cemiyeti'ne mahsûs umûmî nizâmnâmedir," *İntibâh*, 1, no. 7 (Mayıs 1910), supplement.

[454] In 1910 it was often called the *İntibâh-ı İlmî Cemiyeti*. I have also found occasional references to it as the *İntibâh Şirketi* or *Cemiyetü'l-İntibâh*.

[455] This information is contained within Naûm Fâik's letter to the Harput *millet meclisi*: Çıkkı, *Naum Faik ve Süryani Rönesansı*, 133-136. There is a small transcription error in "... şu cemiyet namına on iki zat aza intibah edilerek bunlardan biri reis, diğeri sandûk ve diğeri katip tayin edilmiş." Instead of "intibah", it should be "intihâb".

[456] "Süryânî-i Kadîm İntibâh-ı İlmî Cemiyeti'ne mahsûs umûmî nizâmnâmedir," *İntibâh*, 1, no. 7 (Mayıs 1910).

sacred Ottoman constitution in the Syriac language, the tongue of the *Süryânî-i Kadîm cemâat*, which seeks to advance the loyalty and honesty of feelings for the Ottoman *millet* and *vatan*; and to establish a secondary school; and [this mission] comprises of performing every sort of agreeable service benefitting the *vatan* and *millet* and expending effort and exertion with the aim of increasing the glory of learning."[457]

The second article outlined the desire for the creation of mixed spiritual and lay councils for the administration of the *cemâat* and the writing of a constitution (*nizâmnâme*) as was the case for the other communities in the Empire. The third article proposed the establishment of a library containing books in "Turkish, Syriac, Arabic and other languages". The fourth and final article of the first section stipulated the examination of the accounts of the church and *Süryânî* organisations at the end of each year. The second chapter covered in more detail the regular operations and administration of the organisation.

At its first general conference, the organisation was attended by elected representatives from the branches in Mardin, Midyat, Vîrânşehir, Siirt, Siverek and Mosul. Naûm Fâik expressed that the delegates from the branch in the United States were prevented from attending, despite the desire for them to do so, due to the long distance involved.[458] The conference, held in Diyarbakır on 22

---

[457] "İşbu cemiyetin yekâne maksadı Süryânî-i Kadîm cemâatimizin mektebleri terakkîsine ve nâil olduğumuz meşrûtiyet-i muazzezenin taziz ve tahkîmine hâdim olan ulûm ve maârifin tamîmine, ve devlet-i Osmâniye'nin kavânîn ve evâmirine inkıyâd, ve onlara bihakkın Osmânlılığı tefhîm etmek zımnında zükûr ve inâs mekteblerinin tesîs ve küşâdına, ve vatan ve millet-i Osmâniye hissin sadâkat ve istikâmeti sebkat eden Süryânî-i Kadîm cemâatimizin lisânı olup Süryânîce lugâtıyla da meşrûtiyet-i mukaddese-i Osmâniyeyi tebcîl için bir tâkım kitâblarla risâil-i mevkûta ve cerîdeler neşrine ve ilerde âlî bir mektebin küşâdına matûf olup vatan ve millete nâfi her nev hidemât-ı makbûleyi îfâ ile ilâ-yı şân-ı maârif zımnında bedel-i gayret sarf-ı himmet etmekten ibârettir."

[458] "İntibâh cemiyetlerinin ictimâ-i umûmîsi," *Kevkeb Mednho*, 1, no. 4 (27 Ağustos 1910), 6: "Amerika'da kâin İntibâh cemiyetimizden de bir iki zâtın bu ictimâde bulunmalarını pek ârzû ediyor isek de ancak bade-

Ağustos 1326 [4 September 1910], consisted of musical performances, speeches and other ceremonies attended by dignitaries from the community and the government. The *İntibâh* delegates furthermore announced 20 "decisions" addressing both how the association was to be run and what its initiatives should be.[459]

A large part of *İntibâh*'s programme was education, and several of the 20 points were centred around the maintenance of existing schools and the establishment of new ones, including an institute of higher education (*âlî mekteb*)[460] in a city to be determined later. Although it was pursuing the secular goal of educating the *Süryânî* youth, *İntibâh* still maintained strong ties with many members the Jacobite clergy. In fact, at the 1910 conference, at least two of the delegates from the six represented cities were priests (*râhib* Efrâm from Mosul and *kas* Yûsuf from Siverek) while *mutrân* İlyâs and *keşîş kas* Mûsî were amongst those who presented speeches. In later years, members of the clergy continued to be members of the society; although not originally elected the representative, the head of the Vîrânşehir church (*el-râî kenîsetü'l-Süryân*) Abdülmesîh wrote a letter to *Mürşid-i Âsûriyûn* in 1911 on behalf of the local *İntibâh* branch.[461]

Along with the involvement of Church members in *İntibâh*, there was also the involvement of *İntibâh* in the Church. The plans outlined in 1910 included the decisions to move control of the incomes of churches, monasteries and religious schools into the hands of the *heyet-i umûmî*, the central committee of *İntibâh*. In addition, the association decided to undertake the construction of

---

mesâfe bu ârzûmuza mâni oluyor." Note that this sentence implies that there was only a single branch in the United States; this was presumably located in New Jersey. Also missing at the conference were delegates from Harput, Hısn-ı Mansûr and Urfa.

[459] For a complete list, see "İctimâ-ı umûmî karârları," *Kevkeb Mednho*, 1, no. 6 (24 Eylûl 1910), 2-5.

[460] This was expressed in decision number 12.

[461] "Mürşid-i Âsûriyûn'un suâline cevâb," *Mürşid-i Âsûriyûn*, 5, no. 7 (Hazîrân 1913), 100-102.

a seminary at *Deyrü'z-Zaferân*.[462] It is, consequently, no surprise that I have thus far been unable to find any evidence that Catholics or Protests involved themselves with *İntibâh*.

Although Diyarbakır was chosen as the headquarters for *İntibâh*, the feeling from reading articles in *Mürşid-i Âsûriyûn*, *İntibâh* and *Kevkeb Mednho* is that in the end it was distributed, with the branches in each locality acting more or less independently.[463] And Âşûr Yûsuf was critical of precisely this, stating that for *İntibâh* to be a success, it needed greater centralisation like similar organisations of the Armenians and Jews.[464] Unfortunately, despite the auspicious beginnings that Naûm Fâik described, there is little information available on its actual activities. In some respects, we know more about what *İntibâh* was *not* doing than about what it was from criticisms of its inactivities in *Kevkeb Mednho* and *Mürşid-i Âsûriyûn*. For example, Naûm Fâik expressed his hopes that *İntibâh* would do something about the large number of widows and orphans in and around Adana.[465]

On the positive side, we have seen that *İntibâh* in the United States was somehow involved in the publishing of Senharîb Bâlî's newspaper, *Savto d-Oromoye*. Indeed, *İntibâh* had been active in the United States from the very beginning. With its headquarters in Paterson, by the end of 1909, it had some 28 members and made an appeal in the newspaper *İntibâh* for all those "who go by the *Süryânî* name" to contact Naûm Palak.[466] The most concrete example of an *İntibâh* initiative in the Ottoman Empire was the conference held by Urfa's *Süryânî* in January of 1911, during which

---

[462] "İctimâ-ı umûmî karârları," *Kevkeb Mednho*, 1, no. 6 (24 Eylûl 1910), 2-5.

[463] See "İntibâh-ı İlmî cemiyetlerinin ictima-ı umûmîsi," *Kevkeb Mednho*, 1, no. 3 (13 Ağustos 1910), 1-3 for the selection of Diyarbakır as the *merkez-i umûmî* [central office].

[464] "Süryânî İntibâh cemiyetlerine teklîfimiz," *Mürşid-i Âsûriyûn*, 5, no. 3 (Mart 1913), 34.

[465] "Urfa'da konferans," *Kevkeb Mednho*, 1, no. 16 (11 Şubât 1911), 8: "Keşke umûm İntibâh cemiyetleri şu bîkes ve bîçârelere dahi bir tedbîr düşünseler idi."

[466] This was not Naûm Fâik. "Amerika'da İntibâh Cemiyeti," *İntibâh*, 1, no. 2 (Kânûn-ı Evvel 1909), 4.

lay and religious figures announced the establishment of the local branch and set their targets for serving the community. The discussions largely surrounded education and the attendees came away with "hope that in the coming year our schools will see a great improvement through the efforts of the *İntibâh Cemiyeti.*"[467]

*İntibâh* was actually pre-dated by two other associations, one in the Ottoman Empire and one in the United States. The *Kadîm Süryânî Kardeşler Şirketi*, established in 1879, was a charitable organisation responsible for opening a school in Diyarbakır.[468] The school did not survive into the twentieth century and there is no indication that the *Kadîm Süryânî Kardeşler Şirketi* did either. On the other hand, the *Terakkiyât-ı Mekteb-i Süryânî Cemiyeti* [Association for the Progress of *Süryânî* Schools], formed before the turn of the century, still exists to this day and has engaged in activities well beyond the confines of the locale in which it was founded.

The original Ottoman Turkish name is today masked behind the initials T.M.S., which are usually said to mean simply "Taw Mim Semkat", the names of the three Syriac letters in question. Cebbûr Boyacı, who would later publish *İntibâh*, was instrumental in bringing about the organisation of T.M.S. in Sterling, New Jersey in December 1899. Starting with six individuals, by 1910, the organisation had established three other branches – West Hoboken, College Point and Paterson – and had a total of 104 members. The original goal of T.M.S. was to finance a *Süryânî* school on the premises of the *Meryem Ana Kilisesi* in Diyarbakır, but it also undertook to provide the families of members who had fallen ill or had died with emergency funds.[469] This organisation was also responsible for building the original T.M.S. school and orphanage in Adana following the end of World War I. This institution later

---

[467] "Urfa'da konferans," *Kevkeb Mednho*, 1, no. 16 (11 Şubât 1911), 8: "Bu yeni teşkîl olunan İntibâh cemiyeti gayretiyle gelecek sene mekteblerimizin daha terakkî edeceği umîd olunuyor."

[468] For more on the organisation and school, see page 173 above.

[469] "Terakkiyât-ı Mekteb-i Süryâniye Şirketi," *İntibâh*, 1, no. 2 (Kânûn-ı Evvel 1909), 3-4 and "Terakkiyât-ı Mekteb-i Süryânî Cemiyeti," *İntibâh*, 1, no. 5 (Mart 1910), 8. The second article is a report of two conferences held by the organisation in West Hoboken and College Point on 30 January and 20 February 1910 respectively.

moved to Beirut after French forces evacuated Adana in 1921, and it continues to operate there today.[470] The initials T.M.S. continued to have significance to the community and they appear again on Naûm Fâik's gravestone.[471]

There are also a handful of other organisations about which less information has reached us today. For example there was the *Mar Efrîm Şirketi* or *Cemiyeti*, named after St Ephrem, an early Christian scholar from Nusaybin. This was an association established by natives of Harput residing in Worcester. Bearing the name of a saint, the society was presumably sympathetic towards the views of the Jacobite Church, by whom St Ephrem is particularly revered. Nevertheless, one of the activities we know of the *Mar Efrîm Şirketi* to be engaged in was the collection of funds for the donation of newspaper subscriptions to those who could not afford them.[472]

In addition, there were also: the *Mart Şimûnî Şirketi* in Harput; the *Cemiyetü'l-İttihâdü'l-Kavmü's-Süryânü'l-Kadîm* in Hama; the *Süryânî Gençler Şirketi* in Boston; the *Süryânî Kadınlar Cemiyeti* and *Süryânî Talûn Cemiyeti* in Worcester; the *Terakkiyât-ı Edebiyât Cemiyeti* in Fitchburg; the *Terakkîperver Cemiyeti* in Providence; and the *Süryânî Yakûbî Nisâ Teâvün Cemiyeti* and the *Himâye-i Eytâm Cemiyeti* in West Hoboken. And finally, in 1909 a group of twelve *Süryânî* in College Point, New York, established the *Kütübhâne-i Süryânî-i Kadîm Cemiyeti* [Association of the *Süryânî-i Kadîm* Library] and quickly build up a membership of some 40 individuals under the directorship of Hûsrev Malûl [K. Malool].[473]

---

[470] For a more complete history, visit the school's website at http://www.tmsschool.net in addition to Aydın, *The History of the Syrian Orthodox Church of Antioch in North America* and Kiraz, "Suryoye and Suryoyutho."

[471] See Şimşek, *Süryaniler ve Diyarbakır*, 272 for a photograph.

[472] "Hediyeler," *Mürşid-i Âsûriyûn*, 5, no. 6 (Mayıs 1913), 88-90. We also know that the *Mar Efrîm Cemiyeti* sold prints of a palace in Nineveh once inhabited by Assyrian kings: "Satılık sûretler," *İntibâh*, 1, no. 5 (Mart 1910), 8.

[473] "College Point'de Kütübhâne-i Süryânî-i Kadîm Cemiyeti," *İntibâh*, 1, no. 2 (Kânûn-ı Evvel 1909), 4. Several other articles about the same group appeared in subsequent years.

The large number of organisations in the United States should not come as a great surprise as it was there that the layity was forced to take on the administration of the community as it existed without a religious establishment. For this reason, Cebbûr Boyacı appears to have been less concerned with strife between the clergy and laity, although even the disputes between Abdünnûr and the Harput congregation did make the pages of *İntibâh* in letters from his readership. Perhaps Cebbûr Boyacı's most overt criticism of the clergy came when he suggested that the *Süryânî* of Gerger and Venk, whose only contact with the Church came during the yearly collection of taxes, give priests on such rounds neither money nor a bed to sleep in. Instead, he argued, they should record their names and send them to the *İntibâh Cemiyeti* so as to save themselves from the destitution brough on by the Church's greed.[474]

This being said, *İntibâh* and the other newspapers were also critical of the *Süryânî* organisation when they failed to fulfil the expectations of the community. Âşûr Yûsuf, for example, typically measured *Süryânî* successes and failures against those of the Armenians, and in assessing the *İntibâh Cemiyeti*, he used the specific examples of those Armenians resident in Africa. A small community established in Ethiopia, for example, had quickly organised itself, built a school and had requested a priest from the Patriarchate.[475] Meanwhile, Armenians in Egypt had established a charitable organisation, the *Ermenî Hayrhâh Şirketi İttihâdı* [Union of Armenian Charitable Organisations], which had subsequently expanded to have 100 branches and some 7,000 members in the Ottoman Empire, Europe, the United States and the Caucasus. Amongst other activities, the organisation was building schools,

---

[474] "... şimdiye kadar oraları ziyâret eden rûhânîler insân değil imişler. Binâen aleyh bu cemâate tavsiye ederiz ki o (Lavilo) gibi rûhânîler tekrâr kendilerini ziyâret ederlerse onlar para değil ancak yatacak yer bile ver-meyip tekrâr geriye göndersinler. Ve ismlerini İntibâh Cemiyetine yazdırıp merkezi-i umûmî ile muhâbere etsinler inşallah bundan sonra kendiler de herkes gibi artık bu sefâletten kurtulurlar.": "Gerger cemâati hakkında," *İntibâh*, 2, no. 3 (Kânûn-ı Sânî 1911), 8.

[475] [untitled article], *Mürşid-i Asûriyûn*, 4, no. 4 (Nîsân 1912), 64.

with a particular focus on areas where Armenians spoke Kurdish and Arabic.[476]

In these reports, two of Âşûr Yûsuf's prime concerns reveal themselves: education and language. Making the comparison with the relative Armenian and *Süryânî* efforts at establishing charitable organisations, Âşûr Yûsuf wrote:

> "We had at one time found solace in the news that *İntibâh* societies were being organised within the *Süryânî* community. And yet, we have yet to receive any information concerning their efforts or initiatives. Perhaps they have wilted like a flower without ever having bloomed? Or perhaps we simply have no news of their activities? ... If these *İntibâh* societies, which we had invited to perform a great and beneficial service for our *millet*, have been abandoned so quickly, then we are truly grieved and saddened. For we had hoped that they would be the salvation from the ignorance in our *millet*."[477]

To motivate them to provide details on their activities, Âşûr Yûsuf announced he would be sending copies of *Mürşid-i Âsûriyûn* to each *İntibâh* branch free of charge, snidely adding, "Fear not! Newspapers, even if they do you no benefit, will do you no harm either."[478]

In these as well as in his articles on the mistakes of the Mardin *İntibâh Cemiyeti*, it is interesting to note that Âşûr Yûsuf

---

[476] "Ermenî hayrhâh şirketi ittihâdı ve Süryânî İntibâh cemiyetleri," *Mürşid-i Âsûriyûn*, 5, no. 1 (Kânûn-ı Sânî 1913), 8-9.

[477] "Süryânîler miyânesinde dahi öte beri de İntibâh şirketleri teşkîl olundğuna bir vakt haberler alıp tesselî bulmakta idik. Lâkin şimdiye kadar bunların ne gibi teşebbüsâtlarda bulunduklarına ne iş gördüklerine de hiç bir malûmât alamadık. Bilmiyoruz bir çiçek gibi açılmazdan soldular mı? Yoksa biz onların faâliyetinden habersiz mi bulunuyoruz? ... Milletimiz için pek büyük ve hayrlı bir hidmet îfâ etmeğe davet olunan şu İntibâh cemiyetleri eğer şu kadar çabuk yüz üstüne bırakıldı ise bundan dolayı pek meyûs ve mukedder olacağız. Zîrâ milletimizin cehâletten halâsını onlardan umîd etmekte idik."

[478] "Korkmayınız, cerîdeler size hayr etmez ise zarar hiç bir vakt vermez."

made no distinction between the secular or religious when it came to ascribing blame.[479] Just as there was much criticism of the clergy for their incompetence and dishonesty, the laity did not escape the wrath of Âşûr Yûsuf's pen. Indeed, when we understand why the men of religion were being targeted, then the fact that secular organisations were also reproached for not demonstrating any ability at solving the same problems should come as no surprise. What may seem like contradictions in attacks on religion and the religious establishment should, I argue, be understood rather as displeasure at the degradation of the offices under certain corrupt or incompetent individuals. Âşûr Yûsuf and Naûm Fâik wished to see the church reformed so that it could play a leading role in the community for the benefit of all *Süryânî*. The need was not the elimination of religious leadership but rather the eradication of those unworthy of their posts, as was succinctly expressed in *Mürşid-i Âsûriyûn*:

> "At no time do we wish for out religious leaders to have their rights taken away, and it is our hope and desire that they remain in their exalted position and that their influence and authority will be used in a manner becoming to them so as to attain the affection and respect of the *cemâat*. But to achieve this there is one condition. That condition is that these men of religion show that they are deserving of their exalted position and their holy duty."[480]

---

[479] Concerning the activities in Mardin, see "Mârdîn İntibâh cemiyetinin hatâları," *Mürşid-i Âsûriyûn*, 3, no. 6 (Temmûz 1911), 90-95 and "Mârdîn İntibâh cemiyetinin hatâları," *Mürşid-i Âsûriyûn*, 3, no. 7 (Ağustos 1911), 118-120.

[480] "Biz hiç bir vakt rüesâ-yı rûhânîlerimizin hukûkunun gasb olunmasınız istemiyoruz ve her ân emel ve ârzûmuz budur ki onlar âlî bir mevkide bulunup kendi nüfûz ve tesîrleri ile kendilere yakışır bir sûrette cemâatın muhabbet ve ihtirâmına nâil olsunlar. Lakin buna mazhar olmak için bir şart vardır. O şart dahi rûhânîlerimizin kendi âlî mevkilerinde ve mükaddes vazîfelerine liyâkat göstermeleridir.": "Mârdîn İntibâh cemiyetinin hatâları," *Mürşid-i Âsûriyûn*, 3, no. 6 (Temmûz 1911), 90-95.

## EDUCATION AND PROGRESS

An essential step in "waking the *Süryânî* from their slumber" was providing them with a proper education, through both formal schooling as well as moral and religious instruction. There were *Süryânî* schools well before the twentieth century; Naûm Fâik, it may be remembered, taught at a number of schools around the Ottoman Empire before resettling in Diyarbakır and founding *Kevkeb Mednho*. His own education, however, was at perhaps the exceptional *Süryânî* school since it did not follow the well-established model of religious education in churches and monasteries aimed at training future priests.[481]

Encouraged by the *Tanzîmât*, leading *Süryânî* of Diyarbakır created the *Kadîm Süryânî Kardeşler Şirketi*, which then established a school in 1879. Education was mostly conducted in Ottoman Turkish and Syriac with additional lessons in Arabic, Farsi, English, science, mathematics, Christian theology and church music. Even though all the students were male, they were not all Jacobites but also came from the Catholic, Chaldean and even Armenian communities. Adverse economic conditions forced the school to close its doors in 1889, but not before producing several notable graduates, including future priests and the two high-ranking members of the Ottoman Ministry of Justice.[482]

In the same year, a second *Süryânî* school also opened in Diyarbakır; after receiving its government licence in 1891, it survived into the twentieth century. Ottoman *sâlnâme* from the ministry of education (*maârif*) indicate that the *Süryânî-i Kadîm Mektebi* had the rank of a *rüşdiye* [middle] school with a total of 85 students in 1316 [1898/1899], 61 in 1317 [1899/1900] and 51 in 1319 [1901/1902].[483] The situation evidently improved considerably over the next decade, as *Mürşid-i Âsûriyûn* reported no less than 150 boys and 100 girls studying at the school by beginning of 1913, and by the end of the same year, a new building was

---

[481] Atiya, *A History of Eastern Christianity*, 212.

[482] Şimşek, *Süryaniler ve Diyarbakır*, 172-182 and Çıkkı, *Naum Faik ve Süryani Rönesansı*, 50-53.

[483] Şimşek, *Süryaniler ve Diyarbakır*, 174-175.

under construction.[484] It was at this school that Naûm Fâik worked as an instructor before his emigration to the United States in 1912. In total, there were approximately six teachers for the boys, including one appointee from the ministry of education, and two for the girls. Modern *Süryânî* education may have begun in Diyarbakır, but by the twentieth century, there were numerous others in existence.

| Location | Notes |
| --- | --- |
| Adana | 60-70 boys and 15-20 girls |
| Diyarbakır | 250 boys and girls educated in four classes at the level of *firdevs*, *ibtidâî* and *sıbyân*; attached to the *Meryem Ana Kilisesi* |
| Harput | *Mart Şimûnî* girls' school with 60 students |
| Harput | boys' school closed by 1911 |
| Meyyâfârkî n | 45 regular students with a *Keldânî* teacher approved by the Patriarchate |
| Urfa | boys and girls educated at the level of *sıbyân*, *ibtidâî* and *rüşdiye* on the grounds of the *Mar Petrûs Pavlûs Kilisesi*; the programme was approved by the Ministry of Education |
| Urfa | boys' *ibtidâî* not attached to a church |
| Urfa | girls' *sıbyân* not attached to a church |
| Urfa | German Protestant school for *Süryânî*; graduates continued their education at the Central Turkey College in Antep |

Table 2 – Schools reported in *Mürşid-i Âsûriyûn*
and *Kevkeb Mednho*

Both Naûm Fâik and Âşûr Yûsuf took a keen interest in the state of all the *Süryânî* schools around the Ottoman Empire. The latter must have requested specific information from each, as he

---

[484] "Diyârbekir'de Süryânî mektebi," *Mürşid-i Âsûriyûn*, 5, no. 1 (Kânûn-ı Sânî 1913), 13-14 and "Diyârbekir'de mekteb inşası," *Mürşid-i Âsûriyûn*, 5, no. 12 (Teşrîn-i Sânî 1913), 190.

published letters containing detailed information on students numbers, the teachers, class schedules and the languages of instruction. Âşûr Yûsuf then wrote his opinion of each aspect of these schools; although he could be critical, the tone was never hostile and he usually praised any initiative irrespective of its shortcomings.

Interestingly, I have found only a single offhand reference to a branch of the *İntibâh Cemiyeti* in Harput, but Âşûr Yûsuf published information regarding a women's organisation, the *Mart Şimûnî Şirketi*, which had established a school in response to the inadequacies of the Euphrates College for girls.[485] Founded in 1909 by Hanım Barsûm and *muallime* Meryem Donabed, the *Mart Şimûnî* school grew so that the teachers, five female and one male, were providing education in Ottoman Turkish, Syriac, Armenian and English for some 60 girls by 1912. Composed entirely of women, the board was headed by Serpuhi Taşo, which raises the possibility that the school was cross-confessional since many of the Taşo family were Catholic. Besides tuition fees, funds came from government subsidies, American missionaries and private donations.[486]

Âşûr Yûsuf appears to have been much more pleased with the conditions at *Mart Şimûnî* than with the opportunities available to boys in Harput since the closing of the only boys' school for *Süryânî* in the city.[487] The boys of Mamûretü'l-Azîz could, of

---

[485] Naûm Fâik wrote of the establishment of a branch in Harput in "İntibâh-ı İlmî cemiyetlerinin ictima-ı umûmîsi," *Kevkeb Mednho*, 1, no. 3 (13 Ağustos 1910), 2.

[486] "Harpût'da Süryânî Kadınların Mart Şimûnî Şirketi," *Mürşid-i Âsûriyûn*, 4, no. 2 (Şubât 1912), 28-32 and "Harpût Mart Şimûnî kızlar mektebinin senevî raporu," *Mürşid-i Âsûriyûn*, 5, no. 4 (Mart 1913), 59-62.

[487] The lack of a boys' school was noted in "1912 senesi," *Mürşid-i Âsûriyûn*, 5, no. 1 (Kânûn-ı Sânî 1913), 16. By 1911, the former school building had already fallen into a state of disrepair, but the government had granted permission (*ruhsat*) to build a new one: "Kolera," *Mürşid-i Âsûriyûn*, 3, no. 8 (Eylûl 1911), 134 and [untitled article], *Mürşid-i Âsûriyûn*, 3, no. 8 (Eylûl 1911), 136.

course, still study at the Euphrates College, at the Protestant and Catholic schools or in government institutions.[488]

Âşûr Yûsuf did not dwell specifically on girls' education or the rights of women, but nor did he differentiate between boys and girls when discussing the need to improve opportunities for the *Süryânî* youth. As we have seen above, he did publish lengthy reports on the activities of women's organisations in the Ottoman Empire and the United States. More interesting, however, are a series of articles from *Mürşid-i Âsûriyûn* concerning hardships under which Chinese women live.[489] For example, Âşûr Yûsuf published an article entitled "*Malûmât-ı müfîde* [beneficial information]" describing the reform program announced by "the new China (*Çin-i cedîd*)", meaning the Republic of China established following the 1911 Xinhai Revolution. Among the initiatives were a declaration of the equality of men and women and a banning of practices such as the binding of young girls' feet.[490] Another piece of *malûmât-ı müfîde* according to Âşûr Yûsuf was that Muslim girls were now allowed to study at the American Girls' College in Istanbul, something forbidden by Abdülhamîd but not by the new government.[491]

Âşûr Yûsuf was not alone in promoting the education of *Süryânî* girls; one of the 20 decisions of the 1910 congress of the

---

[488] Very few *Süryânî* actually studied at Euphrates College, however. The graduating class of June 1912 comprised 25 girls and 22 boys, of which only two – one boy and one girl – were *Süryânî*. At the same time, two more boys graduated from the Protestant school and one from a vocational program. These, and progressions at *Mart Şimûnî*, were all recorded in "Sene hitâmı mekteb zînetleri," *Mürşid-i Âsûriyûn*, 5, no. 7 (Hazîrân 1913), 116. Sunguroğlu also mentioned a *Süryânî* primary school with 40 or 50 students, but it is not clear whether this was the school which Âşûr Yûsuf said to be closed: *Harput Yollarında*, vol. 2, 84.

[489] "Misyonerlik âleminden," *Mürşid-i Âsûriyûn*, 4, no. 11 (Kânûn-ı Evvel 1912), 175-176 and "Misyonerlik âleminden," *Mürşid-i Âsûriyûn*, 4, no. 12 (Kânûn-ı Evvel 1912), 185-189. Both are subtitled, "Çin'de tâife-i Nîsânın mevkii."

[490] "Malûmât-ı müfîde," *Mürşid-i Âsûriyûn*, 5, no. 6 (Mayıs 1913), 94.

[491] "Malûmât-ı müfîde," *Mürşid-i Âsûriyûn*, 5, no. 7 (Hazîrân 1913), 112.

*İntibâh Cemiyeti* was the establishment of girls' schools in each city with a branch of the organisation.[492] Despite this attention, there were no women to which Âşûr Yûsuf or Naûm Fâik addressed questions, and outside the aforementioned instances, female *Süryânî* rarely appeared in the pages of either *Mürşid-i Âsûriyûn* or *Kevkeb Mednho*, and when they did, it was usually in the listings of marriages or deaths.

It was not only in the schools of the *Süryânî-i Kadîm* or the Catholic and Protestant missionaries that the *Süryânî* youth received their education, however.[493] The government-run schools also provided education to Ottoman citizens at a variety of levels. *Süryânî* could be found studying at the *Mekteb-i Sultânî* [imperial college] in Beirut and the *Dârü'l-Muallimîn* [teachers' school] in Harput.[494] The most striking case that I have encountered in the press was that of the *Dârü'l-Muallimîn* in Diyarbakır, which in its initial year had no less than six *Süryânî* students.[495] The institution, established in Eylûl 1325 [September 1909],[496] saw three of these successfully pass their year-end examinations and three forced to repeat. Remarkably, the school's two top students, İlyâs Yesû from Mardin and Saîd Feyzî, were in fact, both *Süryânî*.[497]

---

[492] "İctimâ-ı umûmî karârları," *Kevkeb Mednho*, 1, no. 6 (24 Eylûl 1910), 4. Specifically, see decision 16.

[493] Other missionary schools were also attended by *Süryânî*. In 1910, Tarsus American College had at least one *Süryânî* student, Lûkâ Beşîr, who was probably a native of Diyarbakır: [untitled article], *Kevkeb Mednho*, 1, no. 4 (27 Ağustos 1910), 8. Another, again from Diyarbakır, was studying at the American College in Beirut: "Hâşiye," *İntibâh*, 5, no. 7 (Hazîrân 1914), 2.

[494] See "Beyrût'te Mekteb-i Sultânî müntehî sınıf talebesinden Nikola Abdünnûr efendiye," and "Harpût Dârü'l-muallimîn talebesinden Hısn-ı Mansûrlu Salîbâ efendiye," *Kevkeb Mednho*, 2, no. 11 (27 Kânûn-ı Sânî 1912), 8.

[495] "Dârü'l-muallimîn talebeleri," *Kevkeb Mednho*, 1, no. 3 (13 Ağustos 1910), 5-6.

[496] Naûm Fâik actually wrote "Geçen Eylûl 1326 târîhinde Diyâr-bekir'de Dârü'l-muallimîn mektebi küşâd olunup ..." but, writing in Ağustos 1326 [August 1910], it is clear that he meant 1325.

[497] Naûm Nişmî was eleventh, Lütfî Çulcu was seventeenth, Naûm Behdu was eighteenth and Lütfî Asfer was twentieth. There is no indica-

Formal schooling was not the sole area in which Âşûr Yûsuf and Naûm Fâik believed that the community could address the lack of education. The family and the church were guides, and the breakdown of each was seen as the cause of a lack of cultivation and refinement (*talîm ve terbiye*) in the *Süryânî* youth. In fact, the refrain of *talîm* and *terbiye* was a frequent rallying call in the newspapers for parents to take responsibility for the education of their children, especially those who intended on sending their young to the United States to work.[498] According to one transplanted *Süryânî*, the lure of quick profits in the United States had caused parents to forgo educating their young:

> "Is so much ignorance and blindness possible? A *millet* with no schools can have no proper guide. And a *millet* with no guide is condemned to disperse like a flock with no shepherd. By looking on schools with contempt, we have ruined our homes, blinded our families and we shall never wake from this ignorance (*hâb-ı gaflet*)."[499]

Âşûr Yûsuf blamed this lust for money to be one of the roots of the community's problems, both for the laity and for the clergy. He felt Abdünnûr to be particularly avaricious, and we have already seen that a financial dispute over a loan to the Patriarch had deteriorated into a court case involving high-ranking church figures in Jerusalem.[500] But this greed extended right down to the lowest

---

tion as to the total number of students; however, if we consider that the seventeenth-place student did not score high enough to pass, there were probably not many more than twenty or thirty students in total, meaning that the *Süryânî* contingent of six was a relatively large one.

[498] See, for example, "Muvaffakiyetsizliğin sebebleri," *Mürşid-i Âsûriyûn*, 4, no. 7 (Teşrîn-i Sânî 1912), 98-102.

[499] "Türkiye'deki milletdaşlarımıza bir kaç söz," *Mürşid-i Âsûriyûn*, 4, no. 8 (Teşrîn-i Sânî 1912), 125-128. The letter, signed by S. S. Perçi, reads, "Hiç bu derece cehâlet ve körlük olur mu? Mektebi olmayan millet iyi kılâvûzlara mâlik olamaz. İyi kılâvûza mâlik olmayan milletler dahi çobansız sürü gibi dağılıp kayıp olmağa mahkûmdurlar. Biz mektebe talîm ve terbiyeye hor baka baka evimizi yıktık ocağımızı kör ettik ve yine de şu hâb-ı gafletten aslâ ayılmıyoruz."

[500] See page 98.

levels of the clergy, with a letter-writer from the United States calling them "thieves with crosses (*haçlı hırsızlar*)".[501] It was in the clergy's profit to keep the community "asleep" as was argued in an interview in *Mürşid-i Âsûriyûn*:

> "Question: You say that the *Süryânî* are in a deep sleep of ignorance (*derin hâb-ı gaflet*). I wonder what the Patriarchate is doing about this?
>
> Answer: The Patriarchate is rocking the community's cradle and singing it lullabies.
>
> Qu: And what are the religious leaders doing?
>
> An: If some from within this sleeping community should awake, [the religious leaders] drug them with opiates."[502]

Âşûr Yûsuf felt that certain elements from within the religious establishment were actively attempting to prevent the founding of *Süryânî* schools for their own profit. He furthermore dismissed a call from one of his readers to forgive the clergy's own ignorance, responding "is the *millet* supposed to educate them or will they instruct the *millet* and be its guide (*mürşid*)?"[503] Just as a *millet* without schools was considered to be a flock without a shepherd, so was one without upright religious leaders. He appealed to the Patriarch "not to leave the diocese of Harput without a shepherd" by repeating the mistake that was Abdünnûr when it came to selecting the *mutrân*'s successor.[504]

---

[501] "Amerika'dan diğer bir mektûb," *Mürşid-i Âsûriyûn*, 4, no. 10 (Kânûn-ı Evvel 1912), 159-160. This letter writer was, as indicated on page 108, probably İbrâhîm Yûsuf.

[502] The interview "with a reporter" again feels contrived and full of loaded questions. I suspect again that Âşûr Yûsuf wrote this article in its entirety. "Muhabirimizi isticvâb," *Mürşid-i Âsûriyûn*, 3, no. 9 (Teşrîn-i Evvel 1911), 151-152.

[503] "Acaba millet mi bunları terbiye edecek yoksa bunlar mı milleti terbiye edip onlara mürşid olacaktır?": "Mürşid'in cevâbı," *Mürşid-i Âsûriyûn*, 4, no. 9 (Kânûn-ı Evvel 1912), 143.

[504] "Memûl ederiz ki patrik hazretleri Harpût abraşiyesi çobansız bırakmayıp, göndereceği çobanı intihâb eder iken diğer bir liyâkatsızı

As mentioned earlier, *Mürşid-i Âsûriyûn* and *Kevkeb Mednho* carried very few stories concerning current events, unless they directly involved *Süryânî*; political events – say, the *Bâb-ı Âlî* coup or the outbreak of the Balkan Wars – went unmentioned as news stories except in *İntibâh*. There was evidently an assumption that the readership in the Ottoman Empire would already have received word of such events when they read articles concerning them.[505] *İntibâh* evidently served as a medium for the communication of recent events in the Ottoman Empire and abroad, often by means of translated articles from the *New York Times*, to a population in the United States which would have been more isolated from the normal sources of such information. Nevertheless, it can be surmised that the *Süryânî* newspapers of the pre-war era were not political but cultural endeavours.[506]

Unlike current events, however, reports about scientific discoveries or other worldly knowledge do make an occasional appearance. Âşûr Yûsuf printed news of several archaeological finds in Mesopotamia as well as the discovery of papyri in Egypt which included several letters in the prophet Muhammad's own handwriting.[507] He was keenly interested in the "truly astonishing advances in medicine" and wrote of a French doctor who was able

---

göndermekten sakınacaktır.": "Mutrân Abdünnûr efendinin Harpût'tan infikâki," *Mürşid-i Âsûriyûn*, 5, no. 10 (Eylûl 1913), 163-164.

[505] For example, in the first issue after the outbreak of the first Balkan War, Âşûr Yûsuf printed an article describing the duties of Ottoman citizens during the conflict without having ever announced that there was a war. See "Şimdiki vazîfemiz," *Mürşid-i Âsûriyûn*, 4, no. 8 (Teşrîn-i Sânî 1912), 114-118.

[506] In calling *Mürşid-i Âsûriyûn* and *Kevkeb Mednho* newspapers, I am reflecting the vocabulary of Âşûr Yûsuf and Naûm Fâik. Both men referred to their publications as *gazete* or *cerîde*, Ottoman Turkish words of Italian and Arabic origin respectively meaning "newspaper". Cebbûr Boyacı did likewise, calling *İntibâh* "The Assyrian's [*sic*] monthly newspaper". However, in many ways these could more accurately be described as journals both for their frequency of issuance and their content.

[507] "Yeni bir keşf," *Mürşid-i Âsûriyûn*, 4, no. 12 (Kânûn-ı Evvel 1912), 192.

to restore the dead to life.[508] A reoccurring section in *Mürşid-i Âsûriyûn* were articles from missionaries who wrote curious tales from their experiences in various parts of Asia such as China and Japan.

Health was another area of in which there was considerable concern. A particularly severe outbreak of cholera "brought by a traveller" to Mamûretü'l-Azîz appeared in a number of issues from 1911 and Naûm Fâik reported on a violent case of yellow fever in Urfa.[509] But *Mürşid-i Âsûriyûn* and *Kevkeb Mednho* could also be didactic, with articles imploring readers to kill mosquitoes as a means of disease-prevention or giving advice on keeping crops and livestock healthy.[510] *İntibâh* also recorded widespread instances of disease in New York and Istanbul.

I see these, and other articles, as a demonstration of the belief that the *Süryânî* intellectuals had, in the press, the power to edify their community. They despaired at the sorry state of both the religious and lay leadership but their faith in printing was unshaken – if only the people would make use of the service they provided. Naûm Fâik, Cebbûr Boyacı and Âşûr Yûsuf went to pains to show that the printing of their newspapers was a purely altruistic, and not a commercial, venture. The calls for schools and education were more frequent, but those for printing presses were more impassioned. Naûm Fâik wrote:

---

[508] "Şu son vaktlerde âlem-i tabâbette hakîkaten mûcib-i hayret olan yeni terakkîler zuhûra gelmektedirler ... Şöyle ki ölmüş zan olunanların iâde-i hayât edip kıyâm etmelerini mümkün kılar." This article also contains news of a French archaeological discovery at the site of Babylon. "Câlib-i dikkat haberler," *Mürşid-i Âsûriyûn*, 5, no. 10 (Eylûl 1913), 157-158.

[509] For example, there was "Kolera," *Mürşid-i Âsûriyûn*, 3, no. 7 (Ağustos 1911), 109 and "Kolera," *Mürşid-i Âsûriyûn*, 3, no. 8 (Eylûl 1911), 134. For Urfa, see "Urfa'da şiddet-i bürûdet," *Kevkeb Mednho*, 1, no. 16 (11 Şubât 1911), 8.

[510] On preventing the spread of disease, see "Adâ-yı insân," *Kevkeb Mednho*, 1, no. 19 (25 Mart 1911), 5-6 and "Sinekleri öldürünüz," *Mürşid-i Âsûriyûn*, 5, no. 8 (Temmûz 1913), 120-123. I have mentioned the articles pertaining to farming on page 104, footnote 271.

"What brings us to good ends and to sublime heights is the press, what puts to rest this destitution of ours is the press, what truly says that we are *Süryânî* is once more the press, what will secure our future is, by God, the press, the press, the press."[511]

For his part, Âşûr Yûsuf was quite generous in sending free copies to members of the community, though he often complained about the financial hardships that he was enduring in the publishing of *Mürşid-i Âsûriyûn*. He also had much praise for the establishment of other *Süryânî* newspapers. Announcing *el-Hikmet* and *Savto d-Oromoye*, he advised his own readership to subscribe and offered his congratulations and wishes for their future success.[512] Perhaps his greatest preoccupation, however, was with the printing the Syriac alphabet using cast type, and he requested the opinions of the community on whether such a purchase should be made. Hannâ Sırrı Çıkkı responded from Mardin with an endorsement: "newspapers interpret the ideas of the *millet*, a *millet* without the printing [of newspapers] resembles a heart with no soul."[513] The encouragement that Âşûr Yûsuf received from his readership helped reinforce his determination to continue publishing *Mürşid-i Âsûriyûn*, despite having occasionally expressed his doubts about the value of doing so.

Ultimately, I hope to have drawn attention to the individuals themselves: Naûm Fâik, who would announce the fact that he was a teacher on the masthead of each issue of *Kevkeb Mednho*, and Âşûr Yûsuf, an instructor at the Euphrates College. Both men repeatedly stressed the importance of education in the betterment

---

[511] "Cerîdeler âlem'nde cerîdelerimiz, ve zavâlli nâşirleri," *Kevkeb Mednho*, 1, no. 19 (25 Mart 1911), 3: "Bizi hüsn-i hitâme, taâli-i şân ve nâme îsâl eden ancak matbûâttır, bu mahrûmiyetimize hâtime veren matbûâttır, hakkımızda hakîkaten Süryânî var imiş derdiren şey de yine matbûâttır, istikbâlimizi temîn eyleyen billâh matbûâttır, matbûâttır, matbûâttır."

[512] "Süryânîler için iki yeni cerîde dahâ," *Mürşid-i Âsûriyûn*, 5, no. 9 (Ağustos 1913), 148.

[513] "Mürşid-i Âsûriyûn'un suâline cevâb," *Mürşid-i Âsûriyûn*, 5, no. 3 (Mart 1913), 41-42: "Cerîdeler milletin tercümân-ı efkârıdır, neşriyâtı olmayan bir millet rûhsuz bir kalbe benzer."

of the *Süryânî* community. In the United States, Cebbûr Boyacı gave detailed reports on the activities of the *Terakkiyât-ı Mekteb-i Süryâniye Cemiyeti* and the *Kütübhâne-i Süryânî-i Kadîm Cemiyeti*, two local organisations dedicated to the expansion of learning and knowledge. I argue that, broadly speaking, education was the single point at which we see the convergence of all of the other areas of their programme for reform. It was both a prerequisite and a consequence of an enlightened and engaged clergy. It was the motivation for the press. It was also the means for unity of all *Süryânî*, as only through a modern education system could a common bond between them – the Syriac language – be reforged.

## LANGUAGE

Despite not knowing the tongue himself, Âşûr Yûsuf took more than a passing interest in the Syriac language. His concern was centred around the reintroduction of the tongue into the community following centuries of inroads by Arabic, Turkish, Armenian and Kurdish. But although the programme would certainly begin in the schools, this revival would not be simply a question of teaching Syriac to the *Süryânî* youth; Âşûr Yûsuf also had ideas of reforming language more akin to those present in the Greek, Armenian and other communities.

Naûm Fâik saw one of *Kevkeb Mednho*'s goals to be "the teaching of the knowledge and virtues we have gained from the Ottomans to the coming generations using the language of our forefathers."[514] But Naûm Fâik's words ring hollow when we consider how much Syriac he actually used: in the 75 articles from the first eight issues of *Kevkeb Mednho* that I surveyed, only 5 were written in Syriac, while 23 were in Arabic and 47 in Ottoman Turkish. The reality was that Syriac could not be the only – or even the primary – medium for communicating with his readership, which for the most part had little knowledge of its spoken, let alone its written, form.

Naûm Fâik actually seems to have been somewhat less sure about the possibility of using Syriac as a spoken tongue and for

---

[514] Çıkkı, *Naum Faik ve Süryani Rönesansı*, 58-59.

this Âşûr Yûsuf criticised him. The latter pointed to the Jewish immigrants to Palestine and how they were in the process of reviving Hebrew, "a neighbour of Syriac", after two thousand years of disuse. Drawing on the Jewish experience and quoting Napoleon's saying that "impossible is a word to be found only in the dictionary of fools", he outlined a plan for restoring the Syriac language to life (*kesb-i hayât*). This included printing books – especially bibles – in Syriac, creating language societies and, of course, it should be the language of instruction at schools.[515]

Consequently, Âşûr Yûsuf was critical of the *Süryânî* schools in which Syriac was not part of the programme of instruction. It was, for example, the sole problem he found with the school in Diyarbakır; and he used the opportunity to expound the reasons for the language's instruction:

> "The first is because we are *Süryânî*. The second is to bring to light the pearls [of wisdom] in the buried treasures of the *Süryânî* language. The third is that for our commercial activities (*ticâret*) and many more such reasons we need to teach Syriac to the children of our *millet*."[516]

Being *Süryânî* and the rediscovery of an ancient past were again cited as rational when he chastised the *Süryânî* Protestant school in Urfa for teaching German but not Syriac:

> "If the Germans wish to encourage the German language, then why should they not want the *Süryânî* to teach their own language? If German will be needed for the Baghdad [rail] line, then the Syriac language will also be needed to read the ancient works in Aramaic that are being discovered from Urfa to Baghdad. And why should

---

[515] "Süryânî lisânının kesb-i hayâtı," *Mürşid-i Âsûriyûn*, 5, no. 13 (Kânûn-ı Evvel 1913), 200-206.

[516] "Diyârbekir'de Süryânî mektebi," *Mürşid-i Âsûriyûn*, 5, no. 1 (Kânûn-ı Sânî 1913), 13-14: "Birinci Süryânî olduğumuz için, ikinci Süryânî lisânında defn olunan altın inci defineleri meydâna çıkarmak için. Üçüncü ticâretimiz için ve daha sâir nice nice sebebler için lisân-ı Süryâniyi millet evlâdına talîm etmeliyiz."

the *Süryânî* youth be barred from performing this service and trade? Even if we had no other reason, we must learn Syriac because we are *Süryânî*."[517]

Âşûr Yûsuf furthermore argued that his plan should be suggested to the Maronites, the Indian *Süryânî* and the Catholic *Süryânî*.[518] This mention of the Maronites hints that the Syriac language – which the Maronites still used as a liturgical tongue – was a critical aspect of the *Süryânî* identity. But then why were the Chaldeans and Nestorians excluded? Geographically, they lived in much closer proximity to the core *Süryânî* areas than did the Maronites. And they too used Syriac as a liturgical language, and moreover, in many areas they used its modern dialects colloquially.[519]

I argue that Âşûr Yûsuf maintained an "Antiochian" outlook based on religious rite and liturgical language for what constituted his community. The rite of the *Süryânî* was different from that of the Copts, with whom they were theologically very close, and that of the Nestorians, with whom they shared a similar liturgical language but who were theologically distant.[520] Language as an, or even the, identifying characteristic is, of course, not unique to the *Süryânî* of the late nineteenth and early twentieth centuries. But

---

[517] "Diğer Süryânî Protestan mektebleri," *Mürşid-i Âsûriyûn*, 5, no. 12 (Teşrîn-i Sânî 1913), 192-193: "Eğer Almanlar Alman lisânını teşvîk etmek istiyorlar ise Süryânîler kendi lisânlarını talîm etmeği niçin istemesinler. Eğer Bağdâd hattı geçmesi için Almanca lâzım olacak ise Urfa'dan Bağdâd'a kadar keşf edilen Ârâmî lisânıyla yazılân asâr-ı atîka okumak için dahi Süryânî lisânı lâzım olacak ve bu hidmetten, bu ticâretten Süryânî evlâdı niçin mahrûm edilsin. Süryânîce öğrenmeğe için başka hiç bir sebebimiz yok ise Süryânî olduğumuz için Süryânîceyi öğrenmeğe mecbûruz."

[518] "Bu plan üzere hareket etmeğe Hindistân Süryânîlerine, Mârûnîlere, Süryânî Katoliklere de de tavsiye etmeli."

[519] As mentioned in the introduction, the alphabet and pronunciation of their liturgical language were slightly different from those of the *Süryânî*.

[520] Fortescue gives detailed information on the rite of the Jacobites in *The Lesser Eastern Churches*, 343-352. He "noticed that the Jacobite rite is almost the only thing of importance about them."

there is an interesting interplay between language and confession to be observed:

> "One of the chief characteristics of the Churches [of the Middle East], which expresses their individual identities and testifies their rich history, is their rite. A Church's rite consists of the form of its official prayer, publicly expressed in the liturgy. This includes above all the prayers, the formularies and the structure of the Mass, the divine office, and other liturgical celebrations. Other expressions of the rite are the cycle of feasts in the liturgical calendar, religious vestments and objects used in worship, and more generally the spiritual and literary tradition of the Churches and the communities. The rite is thus not only the form of the liturgy, but also the religious 'environment' in which a community lives and worships. It is therefore a fundamental aspect of the community's collective identity, to which individual believers adhere. The role of providing an identity is particularly important in an area which contains many different churches, like the Middle East."[521]

Syriac, being the liturgical language, was a very public expression of the Antiochian connection between the *Süryânî* and the Maronites. On the other hand, the Melkites – both Orthodox and Catholic – gradually adopted the mainstream Byzantine rite and the Greek tongue for liturgical purposes in the centuries after the Council of Chalcedon. The Arabic-speaking Maronites, for all their differences, retained the Antiochian rite and the Syriac language for their church rituals, and consequently are considered to have some sort of kinship to the *Süryânî*, whereas the Melkites are not. The first steps to breach the divide between the different Assyrian groups lies in the establishment of a secular national identity, but even the Nestorians and Chaldeans, despite their linguistic proximity, were considered to be speakers of *Keldânîce*

---

[521] Andrea Pacini, *Christian Communities in the Arab Middle East*, 305.

[Chaldean] – not *Süryânîce* [Syriac] – and consequently receive only a hesitant reception from Âşûr Yûsuf and Naûm Fâik.[522]

Returning to Âşûr Yûsuf's plans for Syriac, we encounter some intriguing ides about the modern language and alphabet. Continuing his reports on the revolution in China, he noticed that the Chinese were abandoning their ancient writing system in favour of a new, 40-letter alphabet composed of Latin, Greek and Russian letters. This started Âşûr Yûsuf thinking:

> "Do you know that the *Süryânî* alphabet also requires reform (*ıslâhât*)? It has a great fault, since one can have great difficulties in reading a word written with *Süryânî* letters. If it were up to me, I would do away completely with the vowel points (*hareke*) ... and in their place I would add a new set of letters, and this would not be such a hard thing."[523]

Replacing the vowel points, or diacritics, would be a radical change for any Semitic writing system, and this suggestion, therefore, probably stems from the impracticality of using such alphabets (Arabic or Syriac) to write Turkish as well as his own ignorance of the Syriac tongue. Âşûr Yûsuf was, however, very much supportive of the simplification of language in general.

---

[522] For *Keldânîce*, refer to page 120. While the "Aramaean language" was mentioned in *Mürşid-i Âsûriyûn* on several occasions, I have encountered a single instance of the newspapers referring to an "Assyrian language": "Âsûrî lisânımızın tamîmi," *İntibâh*, 5, no. 6 (Mayıs 1914), 2-3. The author, Naûm Fâik, only used *Âsûrî lisânı* in the title and the first sentence, revering to *Süryânîce* in the remainder of the article.

[523] "Bunu yazar iken senelerden beri beni düşündüren Süryânî hurûfâtı hatırıma vârid olunuyor. Bilir misiniz ki Süryânî hurûfâtına dahi ıslâhâtı muhtâctır. Büyük bir kusûr vardır. Zîrâ Süryânî hurûfâtı ile yazılar bir lugât doğru okumak için bir adam epiyi müşkilât uğruyor. Bana kalırsa (Abrohom Odom) gibi bir tâkım harekeleri külliyen def edip onların yerine bir tâkım yeni harfler ihtirâ üzerine zam ve ilâve ederim ve bu iş de pek müşkül bir şey değildir. Hususen ki biz bundan böyle bize mahsûs yeni bir edebiyâta âşnâ muallimleri ve rûhânîleri cerîdelerimizde yazıp bu hususta beyân-ı efkâr etmeğe davet ederiz.": "Çin hurûfâtında ıslâhât," *Mürşid-i Âsûriyûn*, 5, no. 12 (Teşrîn-i Sânî 1913), 195-196.

In one case, he tried to dissuade *Süryânî* poets and writers from employing excessively elegant language which not everyone would be able to understand. "Our goal", he wrote, "is not to show our skill with language but rather to be beneficial to others." Moreover, he wholeheartedly agreed with the current trend to move away from the complexities of often present in Ottoman Turkish, contrasting it with the notion of a simpler Turkish language:

> "Firstly, even if men of letters desired to express themselves with a language difficult to understand so as to show their accomplishments of learning, today they are mostly working to transform the Ottoman language into a more basic Turkish, and this is really is for the best.[524]

Âşûr Yûsuf's awareness of the Young Turks' desire to employ a more understandable language manifests itself in his own publication, which, as I have already mentioned, employs a fairly simple language – especially in comparison with the more literary Naûm Fâik.[525] He may have also followed the efforts of some intellectuals to regularise the spelling of Ottoman Turkish or even to replace the Arabic alphabet with the Latin one – something first

---

[524] "Medîhalar mecmuası," *Mürşid-i Âsûriyûn*, 5, no. 8 (Temmûz 1913), 128: "Lisân - medîhalardan bazıları bana geliyor ki cemâatımızın güç ile anlayacağı bir lisânında yazılmıştır. Evvelce edebler lisânında kendi ma-hâret-i marifetlerini göstermek için oldukça anlaşılması güç olan bir lisân-ında ifâde-i merâm etmek emelinde idiler ise de hâl-i hâzırda husûsıyla lisân-ı Osmâniyeyi oldukça basît bir Türkçeye tahavvül etmeye çalışılıyor, ve hem en doğrusu da budur. Zîrâ yazmaktan maksad mahâret göstermek olmayıp ancak daha ziyâde başkalara fâideli olmaktır. Öyle ise kendi millet-ine ve husûsıyla câhil bir millet ve cemâate bir şey anlatıp fâideli olmak emelinde bulunan bir adam, kimler için yazdığını hesâba alıp lisânını onların bilgisine uydurmalıdır."

[525] Âşûr Yûsuf's advocacy of simple language did not extend to being sympathetic to those whose education precluded them from using language well. On one occasion he printed a letter, transcribing the text letter-for-letter to show the numerous mistakes in the original and, consequently, to highlight the ignorance of its author. See Appendix A for some examples.

alluded to by Abdullah Cevdet, another member of the *Hürriyet ve İtilâf Fırkası*, the founder of a private school in Mamûretü'l-Azîz and the publisher of *İctihâd*, a newspaper from which at least one article appeared in *Mürşid-i Âsûriyûn*.[526]

At the same time, Âşûr Yûsuf must surely have been familiar with the disputes and conflicts which surrounded the use of the vernacular Armenian over the classical. He himself showed an appreciation of the colloquial Syriac spoken in Cebel-i Tûr. He argued that these "mountain *Süryânî*" had lost everything except their language and even this was being subsumed by Arabic and Kurdish rather than being conserved and encouraged to grow.[527] By comparison, the Armenians had, with the help of foreign charities, been successful in spreading the Armenian language through the distribution of bibles. The first order of business, he concluded, was for the Patriarchate to protect and nourish the language of the *Süryânî* in Cebel-i Tûr, halting the spread of Arabic and Kurdish. Part of this drive was to include a selecting (*temyîz*) and purification (*tashîh*) of the Cebel-i Tûr Syriac, but it is not clear if he was referring to the many foreign elements in the vernacular or if it was to be "corrected" into the literary language.[528]

---

[526] Abdullah Cevdet established the school jointly with İshâk Sükûtî: Hanioğlu, *The Young Turks in Opposition*, 204. For more on Abdullah Cevdet, see page 56, note 142. Note that both men were closely involved in the establishment of the *İttihâd ve Terakkî Cemiyeti*. Another major contributor to this process of linguistic simplification was the Albanian author and lexicographer Şemseddîn Sâmî, whose *Kamûs-ı Türkî* [Dictionary of Turkish], provided the impetus for much of the reform.

[527] "Bundan da geçelim, Tûr Dağı'nda evvel dağlı Süryânîler her şeyi gâib etmişler ise de şimdiye kadar Süryânî lisânını muhâfaza edip o lisânında tekellüm etmektedirler. Bu dağlı Süryânîler Süryânî lisânın bekâsına ve tamîmine mâye hâlinde besleyip muhâfaza etmek için onlar miyânesinde âlî mektebler şöyle dursun, âdî mektebler olsun açacak yerde, onlarda dahi Süryânîcenin aheste aheste unutulup onun yerine Arabca ve Kürdcenin tamîmine meydân veriliyor." See "Süryânî lisânının kesb-i hayâtı," *Mürşid-i Âsûriyûn*, 5, no. 13 (Kânûn-ı Evvel 1913), 206.

[528] "Cebel-i Tûr'da şimdiye kadar istimâl olunan Süryânîceyi Patrikhânemiz husûsî bir sûrette kayırıp beslesin. Onların lisânını temyîz ve tashîh etmek için evvel cemâate Süryânî lisânında tab edilmiş kitâb-ı mukaddes ve kitâb-ı mukaddesin cüzlerini verip okumağa mecbûr etsin ...

I suspect that he was willing to accept the spoken vernacular as being just as good as the literary Syriac of the church and *Kevkeb Mednho*. Evidence for this exists in a pair of articles written by *üskuf* Amanûyil in Midyat on *Tûrânî* [Ṭuroyo] or "the new Syriac (*lisân-ı Süryânî-i cedîd*)" used in Cebel-i Tûr and the *kazâ* of Nusaybin. The language, according to the Protestant *üskuf*, "had mixed and adapted with Arabic, Kurdish, Turkish, Farsi and other languages and so over time had lost the natural fluidity, ease and soundness of its mother tongue."[529] Despite describing it as lacking in proverbs and sayings, Amanûyil had collected a number of examples which had emerged in the vulgar tongue over the years. And since the colloquial tongue did "not obey any of the rules of writing or composition for the Syriac alphabet," he prefaced the proverbs with his rules of orthography so that the spoken language could finally be written.[530] Âşûr Yûsuf expressed his gratitude for Amanûyil's work and requested more such "valuable" proverbs to publish in *Mürşid-i Âsûriyûn*.[531]

After some abortive efforts by missionaries in the late nineteenth century, efforts to promoted the use of Ṭuroyo as a

---

Evvel dağlılara Arabî ve Kürdîyi men edip yalnız Süryânî lisânıyla vaz ve nesîhat etmeli, mekteblerine her bir ders Süryânî lisânıyla tedrîs etmeli." Ibid., 205.

[529] "Bugün Midyât dağında yani Cebel-i Tûr'la Nusaybîn kazâsında Hristyânlar beyninde müstamel bulunan lisâna lisân-ı Süryânî-i cedîd ve bazen dahî lisân-ı Tûrânî denilir. İşbu lisânın aslî lisân-ı Süryânî olmağıyla berâber Arabca, Kürdce, Türkçe ve Farsça lisânlarıyla ve daha başka lisânlarla ihtilât ve imtizâcı sebebiyle alâ temâdî-i zamân eski mâder lisânımızın cezâlet sühûlet ve selâmet-i tabîiyesini gâib ederek kabâil gayr-ı mütemeddine lisânları gibi bir âdî lisân hâline varmıştır."

[530] "Lisân-ı Süryânî-i cedîd yazılacak olsa kitâbet ve kırâatçe eski Süryânîcenin bütün kâidelerine uymuyacağından kitâbet ve kırâati husûsunda burada bir kaç mülâhaza takdîm eyledikten sonra işbu lisân-ı cedîdde müstamel bulunan bazı meseller kurrâûn-ı kirâmın çeşm-i itibârlarına arz edeceğim." The introduction comes from "Midyât Süryânîcesinin bazı meselleri," *Mürşid-i Âsûriyûn*, 3, no. 10 (Teşrîn-i Sânî 1911), 161-163. More proverbs are in "Midyât Süryânîcesinin bazı meselleri," *Mürşid-i Âsûriyûn*, 4, no. 1 (Kânûn-ı Sânî 1912), 13-15.

[531] "Beyne'n-nâs mesel makâmında tedâvül olunur," *Mürşid-i Âsûriyûn*, 3, no. 10 (Teşrîn-i Sânî 1911), 164.

written language would only restart amongst the emigrant communities of Europe during the 1980s. A project supported by the Swedish government caused a rift, with Assyrian nationalist organisations opposing it on the grounds that it was divisive for Assyrian identity.[532] As mentioned in the Introduction, in Cebel-i Tûr there was a diglossia, the phenomenon whereby a high and low language co-exist, between literary Syriac, which was written, and Ṭūroyo, which was spoken.

Diglossia and its existence in the Ottoman Empire has been subject to a study by Johann Strauss.[533] We have already seen that the question of language polarised the Armenian and Greek communities during the nineteenth century. But the *Süryânî* diglossic situation was confined to the limited area that was Cebel-i Tûr.[534] The normal resolution of a diglossia occurs with either the convergence of the two languages or the elimination of one variety. Gabriele Yonan, formulates this same resolution as a necessary step in the creation of a national movement.[535] She argues that in Persia, the spoken vernacular won out but failed to spread to the Ottoman Empire, where it was incomprehensible to the *Süryânî* living there. Is has further been argued that instead, Naûm Fâik and Âşûr Yûsuf sought the reintroduction of classical Syriac as a means of unifying all groups under a single Assyrian banner. But with so few

---

[532] BarAbrahem, "The Question of Assyrian Journalism Revisited," 3. An example of the arguments made in favour of Ṭūroyo may be found in an interview with Assad Sauma Assad in which he states that the written tongue is dead while the spoken one lives on. He also pushes for a reform of the methods of writing vowels with the Syriac alphabet: "Süryanice Ölüm Döşeğinde Yatan Bir Hastaya Benziyor," *Heto* 6, no. 10-11 (Ocak, 2004), 6-8.

[533] Strauss, "Diglossie dans le domaine ottoman". Strauss's exploration of diglossia focuses on the Armenian and Greek cases in particular, but also touches on the Ottoman Turkish, Arabic and Judeo-Spanish cases. It does not, however, deal with the case of the *Süryânî*.

[534] There was also Mlaḥsô, but its range was extremely limited, even in comparison to Ṭūroyo.

[535] Yonan, "Asurlar'da Gazetecilik," *Hujådå* 11, no. 5 (Maj 1988), 17-18. This is also described in BarAbrahem, "The Question of Assyrian Journalism Revisited," 3-4.

*Süryânî* using either Syriac in the first place, Yonan's notion of diglossia hardly seems applicable here.

If the creation of a "national language" is a fundamental part of a national movement, then we must make note of the fact that Âşûr Yûsuf's ideas on the need for the revival of Syriac were very poorly formulated. Critically, he did not even include the Nestorians and Chaldeans in his vision; we need only look at the name of the language he was promoting, *lisân-ı Süryânî* (the language of the *Süryânî*) or *Süryânîce*, to see that this was not part of some nationalist Assyrian project. Indeed, in his plan for the language, he sought aid from fellow Antiochian-rite Christians, the Maronites, and, most remarkably, the distant Indian Jacobites, whom he did not even consider to be from the same *millet*.

Sadly Naûm Fâik's reaction, which was printed in *İntibâh*, has not survived in particularly good copy, making its contents extremely difficult to read; he appears to be supportive of many of Âşûr Yûsuf's ideas, encouraging, for example, *el-Hikmet* to switch from Arabic to Syriac letters and praising *üskuf* Amanûyil for his work, but disappointed that efforts thus far had met with little success.[536] Whatever doubts he may have had, Naûm Fâik was still part of the attempt to halt the decline of Syriac. This is illustrated in a May 1914 statement in *İntibâh*, which by then had Naûm Fâik as a regular contributor, that "seeing as our newspaper is a *Süryânî* newspaper, to grace the beginning of each issue with a Syriac-language article is a requirement."[537]

As mentioned above, Âşûr Yûsuf encouraged the *Süryânî* to at least make the fairly minor concession of writing Arabic and Ottoman Turkish in the Syriac alphabet.[538] There would not have been any *Süryânî* literate in either of the two languages who could not have read them in Arabic letters, so the decision to employ the

---

[536] "Âsûrî lisânımızın tamîmi," *İntibâh*, 5, no. 6 (Mayıs 1914), 2-3.

[537] "Cerîdemiz mâdâmki Süryânî cerîdesidir, her nüshanın sadrında bir Süryânîce makâle ile tezyîn eylemek hem şarttır ...": [untitled article], *İntibâh*, 5, no. 6 (Mayıs 1914), 1. Only three more issues of *İntibâh* would be printed and in all but one of these, the first article was in Syriac.

[538] "Süryânî lisânının kesb-i hayâtı," *Mürşid-i Âsûriyûn*, 5, no. 13 (Kânûn-ı Evvel 1913), 204-205.

Syriac alphabet in *Mürşid-i Âsûriyûn*, *İntibâh* and *Kevkeb Mednho* must be recognised for what it was: part of the effort to strengthen a *Süryânî* identity. Cebbûr Boyacı must have realised that the decision had negative implications for the size of his readership, and set out the rules in an issue of *İntibâh* for "those desiring to read Turkish with Syriac letters".[539]

Interestingly, Âşûr Yûsuf wrote that learned (*kafâlı*) *Süryânî* saw Armenian as a foreign (*garîb*) language but did not hold similar views about Arabic or Ottoman Turkish.[540] Unfortunately, we have no information as to why this should have been the case. One hypothesis would be that Armenian – the liturgical language of the Armenian church – would have been more overtly "foreign" than Arabic and Ottoman Turkish, which did not yet have (to the *Süryânî* at least) any such connotations. Indeed, if there was a diglossia within the *Süryânî* community, one could argue that in many places it was more between Armenian as a spoken tongue and Ottoman Turkish as the written. In any case, there was no conflict parallel to those that existed in the Armenian and Greek communities over language reform.[541]

---

[539] "Süryânî hurûfâtıyla Türkçe okumak ârzû edenlere," *İntibâh*, 2, no. 1 (Teşrîn-i Evvel 1910), 4.

[540] "Süryânî lisânının kesb-i hayâtı," *Mürşid-i Âsûriyûn*, 5, no. 13 (Kânûn-ı Evvel 1913), 203: "Görüyor musunuz bu devrin kafâlıları, Ermenîce garîb bir lisân imiş de, Türkçe ya Arabca garîb değil imiş."

[541] Regrettably, I do not possess the issues in which the reaction to Âşûr Yûsuf's alphabet reform would have been published so it is impossible to gauge how it was received.

# 5 *SÜRYÂNÎ* IDENTITY: A REPRISE

## A DROP IN A SEA

In speaking of the Urmiye community, Eden Naby may have inadvertently come to a correct conclusion with respect to the Ottoman Empire, despite her assertion that the *millet* in question was that of the Assyrian nation. It would appear that the Persian communities were pursuing, like those in the Ottoman Empire, a distinctly local project to unify the disparate groups formerly of a single church. I argue that this was not a unification (*ittihâd*) defined simply on ethnicity and geography but rather on common ecclesiastical heritage. There were, first of all, numerous locations in which *Süryânî* settlement intersected with areas inhabited by Chaldeans or Nestorians. Secondly, as the wide distribution of *Mürşid-i Âsûriyûn* and *Kevkeb Mednho* demonstrates, newspapers knew no geographic or political borders and yet they were consumed uniquely by *Süryânî-i Kadîm*, *Süryânî Katolik* and *Süryânî Protestan* members of a common *millet*.

Moreover, Âşûr Yûsuf, Naûm Fâik and Cebbûr Boyacı predicated this unification on progress (*terakkî*) and an "awakening (*intibâh*) from the sleep of ignorance (*hâb-ı gaflet*)". Instigating this itself depended on reforming several facets of *Süryânî* life, from education to language. It also necessitated a restructuring of relations between the laity and the religious hierarchy, but far from secularising the *Süryânî millet*, the intellectuals saw greater participation of the Jacobite Patriarch, the metropolitans and the local clergy as integral to reforming the community.

But what was the objective of the *Süryânî* "reunification"? It was certainly not political independence or autonomy from the Ottoman Empire. Instead, I believe there to be evidence to support the conclusion that the intellectuals' views were still coloured by a desire for a different sort of independence, that of the *Süryânî* from the Armenian *millet*. To justify the separation of the *Süryânî* from the Armenians required a history which had heretofore not been subject of much thought. These arguments are perhaps more speculative than those that I have been making, but there is nevertheless some evidence to support them.

We may begin by looking at a debate which emerged in the United States during 1909 over whether Turks, Armenians, Syrians (probably meaning Christians from Syria and Lebanon and not specifically *Süryânî*) and Arabs were to be considered of the white race, and thus automatically entitled to American citizenship. The United States government, perhaps influenced by appeals from the Ottoman ambassador in Washington, would eventually decree that these individuals were, in fact, white, something which came as a great relief to the thousands of immigrants already living there.

All this was reported by *İntibâh*; Cebbûr Boyacı supplemented the discussion with a few lines from an article on the same topic which appeared in the Armenian publication *Goçnag* in late 1909. In it, the author Kebâbyan described Turks as being of Mongol stock, though much mixed with other white races. The Assyrians, on the other hand, he described as speaking Arabic and being partly *Muhammedî* [Mohammedan] and partly Christian, and to this he added that "If they are [considered] white, then their stock is of particular uncertainty."[542] This article elicited an angry reaction from Abdülazîz Huri which was duly printed in *İntibâh*. Rejecting that the Assyrians were "partly of the Mongol tribes and party of uncertain origins," Abdülazîz used extensive quotations from the Old Testament to show the ancient provenance of the Assyrians.[543] *İntibâh* also printed an Ottoman Turkish translation of an English-language article by Saîd Dertli on the history of *Âsûristân*, in which the author drew on numerous nineteenth century works on ancient

---

[542] "Hürr-i beyâz kimseler," *İntibâh*, 1, no. 2 (Kânûn-ı Evvel 1909), 2-3. Kebâbyan wrote, "Âsûrîlere gelince bunların bir kısmı Muhammedî bir kısmı Hıristiyândırlar ve Arabca tekellüm ederler. Bunlar da beyâz iseler de cinsiyetleri husûsî nâ malûmdur."

[543] "Bir kaç söz," *İntibâh*, 1, no. 4 (Şubât 1910), 1.

Mesopotamia to detail the accomplishments of the Assyrian peoples.[544]

Claiming an Assyrian past that would make the *Süryânî* a "more ancient" people than the Armenians was possible, but this was secondary in importance to the Antiochian past which makes the *Süryânî* older Christians than the Armenians.[545] We must recognise that the first tentative step towards the establishment of a separate *millet* for the *Süryânî* was the formal renaming of the church to *Süryânî-i Kadîm*, thus emphasising the ancient nature of its adherents. Even the Catholics and Protestants could claim the same heritage by emphasising their rite or their use of Syriac as a liturgical or a spoken language.

It may have only been an indirect concern to Âşûr Yûsuf, but he was certainly well aware of the fact that the *Süryânî* of Harput – and indeed the rest of the Ottoman Empire – always came second to Armenians when it came to the administration of either the Protestant or Catholic *millet*. When the Protestant *millet meclisi* in Mamûretü'l-Azîz sent a lengthy report of their conference to *Mürşid-i Âsûriyûn*, Âşûr Yûsuf observed that:

> "The Protestant congregation has been present in this country of ours for 50 or 60 years. To manage the schools and the church, each year a synod, or a council, is convened and new regulations are enacted and new plans are thought up, but the *Süryânî*, who have centuries of laws and arrangements [of their own], are never able to benefit from these."[546]

---

[544] "Âsûristân'a dâir mücemmel târîh," *İntibâh*, 4, no. 3 (Kânûn-ı Sânî 1913), 4-5 and "Âsûristân'a dâir mücemmel târîh," *İntibâh*, 4, no. 5 (Mart 1913), 5-6.

[545] It must be remembered that Armenians claim to have been the first people to accept Christianity at a state level.

[546] See "Protestan ittihâd meclisleri," *Mürşid-i Âsûriyûn*, 4, no. 6 (Eylûl 1912), 83-86, and "Mutâlaalarımız," *Mürşid-i Âsûriyûn*, 4, no. 6 (Eylûl 1912), 87-88. In the latter, we read: "Evvelen Protestan cemâati şu memleketimizde ısbât-ı vücûd etmesi henüz elli ya altmış sene oldu. Onlar kilise ve mekteb umûrlarını idâre etmek için her sene sinotos yâhûd ittihâd meclisi teşkîl ve yeni yeni nizâmlar vaz etmek ve yeni yeni tedbîrler düşün-

Of course, by the twentieth century, the *Süryânî-i Kadîm* had their own *millet* and there was no question of the Ottoman state revoking this right. But the old hierarchy in which the Armenians dominated still coloured relations between the two communities. The nineteenth century had seen the emergence of conflicts between Armenian and *Süryânî* churches over the ownership of properties. For example, one confrontation came about as Catholic Armenians attempted to bring *Süryânî* into its own orbit during the mid-1830s. In this case, the appropriation of Jacobite properties including churches and monasteries was prevented by an appeal to the Porte and its subsequent intervention.[547]

Problems were naturally exacerbated by the moves to establish a *Süryânî millet* independent of the Armenians. The culmination of this tension came during the 1895 and 1896 massacres of Armenians in the eastern provinces of the Empire. The experience of the *Süryânî* was a rather different one: to a degree, the killing passed them by with less effect on life or property. While this is interesting in itself, more telling for their blunt language are the comments of Patriarch Abdülmesîh in 1896: "the Armenians have for some time past endeavoured to Armenianise our language and religion, ... Letters from our spiritual chiefs at Ourfa and Bitlis, amongst other places ... have reached us which prove that the Armenians have slain and plundered many of our community." Abdülmesîh continues by thanking the Ottoman government for having protected the *Süryânî* during the attacks.[548] The sincerity of the *Süryânî* Patriarch's statements was called into question by local consular officials, but the existence of friction is clear.

Even into the twentieth century, conflicts over church properties were as yet unresolved: a dispute over a church in the *kazâ* of Lice, for example, was still in the Ottoman courts in 1911. Meanwhile, *mutrân* Tûmâ was accused of allowing Armenians to make use of the *Erbaín Kilisesi* in Mardin on the premise that there

---

mekte iken Süryânî milleti asrlardan beri nizâmât ve tertîbâta mâlik iken evvel nizâmât ve tertîbâttan aslâ istifâde edemiyor."

[547] *Osmanlı Belgeleri'nde Diyarbakır Tarihi*, 60-67.
[548] Quoted in Joseph, *Muslim-Christian Relations*, 92-93.

"was no difference" between the two communities.[549] Naûm Fâik reacted harshly, stating that in the past, seeing the *Süryânî* and Armenians as one and the same "ruined our *millet*, our kind (*cinsiyet*) and our language and allowed [the Armenians] to occupy our churches, monasteries and religious foundations, making us their subordinates, and to conceal what was rightfully ours."[550] He further reiterated the common refrain of "a great sleep of ignorance (*azîm hâb-ı gaflet*)", here referring to the clergy for not asserting themselves against Armenian pre-eminence during "the era of awakening (*devr-i intibâh*)". The constant criticism of the *Süryânî-i Kadîm* clergy was, I believe, rooted in the desire to reclaim what the *Süryânî* intellectuals saw as rightfully belonging to their community.

Âşûr Yûsuf made his own case for this in his articles evaluating a book by Yervant Der Minasyan about the connections between the Armenian and *Süryânî* churches. Originally appearing in German in 1904, the book was published four years later in Armenian at Echmiadzin, where Der Minasyan served as a priest. Its contents included the work of *Süryânî* historians which had themselves been translated into Armenian. Over two issues of *Mürşid-i Âsûriyûn*, Âşûr Yûsuf gave a comprehensive summary of the first chapter of the book, asking his readership for comments

---

[549] "Devr-i intibâhta bir azîm gaflet," *Kevkeb Mednho*, 1, no. 22 (6 Mayıs 1911), 1-3: "Sâniyen mutrân Tûmâ efendi, bizimle Ermenîler farkı-mız yok fikr-i sakîmine zâhib olup muvakkaten îfâ-yı ibâdet etmek üzere Erbaîn Kilisesi'nde kendilere bir mahal-i tahsîs etmiş ..." A visitor from Harput also noticed that the Armenian language was being used in the same church: "Kevkeb Mednho gazete-i muteberesi sâhib-i imtiyâzına," *Kevkeb Mednho*, 1, no. 24 (3 Hazîrân 1911), 5-6. The *Erbaîn Kilisesi*, today better known by the Turkish *Kırklar Kilisesi*, is the largest church in the city of Mardin.

[550] "Vaktıyla yani merhûm patrik Petrûs'tan evvel Ermenîler dahi farkımız yok diye milletimizi, cinsiyetimizi, isânımızı mahv etmek ve Süryânîlerin bütün kilise ve manastır ve evkâflarını zabt etmek niyet-i tagallübkârânesiyle bizi kendilerine yamak ettirmiş ve hukûk-ı sarîhamızı ketm ile kolumuzu kanadımızı kırmış oldukarı hâlâ hatırlardadır."

and corrections.[551] In Der Minasyan's book, the spread of Christianity to Edessa [Urfa] received particular attention. According to it, by the year 200, the imperial family (*âile-i pâdişâhî*) had converted Christianity along with most of the populace.[552] One of the two figures cited as being behind the spread of the religion in Urfa was Tatian of Assyria (*Âsûryâlı Tatiyanus*), whose Syriac-language synthesis of the four gospels was widely used in the *Süryânî* and Armenian churches.[553] Through such great scholars and missionary efforts, it was argued that:

> "... the *Süryânî* performed a great service in the development of the Armenian church. On many occasions, [*Süryânî*] even held the seat of the Armenian Catholicos. Is this not proof enough? Long before, that is to say before Gregory, the missionary to and illuminator of the Armenians, received instruction from the Greeks and succeeded in having the Armenians kings recognise Christianity as the official religion, *Süryânî* priests had settled in Armenia."[554]

---

[551] "Ermenî kilisesinin Süryânî kiliseleriyle olan alâkaları," *Mürşid-i Âsûriyûn*, 4, no. 11 (Kânûn-ı Evvel 1912), 162-168 and "Ermenî kilisesinin Süryânî kiliseleri ile olan alâkaları," *Mürşid-i Âsûriyûn*, 5, no. 1 (Kânûn-ı Sânî 1913), 2-8. Following the second article, Âşûr Yûsuf wrote that the series would continue, but nothing further appeared in 1913.

[552] "... 190den evvel Urfa'da Hıristiyanlık büyük bir nisbetle intişâr etmiş idi. Şöyle ki 200 târîhlerinde âile-i pâdişâhî dahi Hıristiyanlığı kabûl etmiş idi."

[553] Not surprisingly, the fact that Tatian described himself as "of Assyria" has been seized upon by both the defenders and opponents of the Assyrian thesis as proof of their respective positions.

[554] "Biz göreceğiz ki Süryânîler Ermenîlerin hayât-ı kiliseviyesinde ne azîm hidmet îfâ etmişlerdir ... Çok defa onlar Ermernîlerin katolıkos kürsîsinde bile oturmuşlardır. Şu açık ısbât değil mi ki? Pek evvelce yani Ermenîlerin hakikî resûlü ve münevviri bulunan Gregoryus Yûnânlarda talîm almış olarak Hıristiyanlığı Ermenî pâdişâhlığının resmî mezhebi diye tanıtmağa muvaffak olduğu târîhten dahi evvel Süryânî ruhbânları Ermenistân'da yerleşmişler idi." St Gregory the Illuminator is revered by Armenians for having brought about their conversion from pagan beliefs in the early fourth century.

To further show evidence of the impact of the *Süryânî*, Der Minasyan listed several Armenian church terms and the seven days of the week along with their Syriac glosses. The object was to show the Syriac origins of these words, the significance of which Âṣûr Yûsuf recognised.[555] More historical discussions follow, including one in which the Syriac influence on the development of the Armenian alphabet is stressed. Emphasising the *Süryânî* origins of fundamental aspects of Armenian identity is clearly something that intellectuals engaging in a rediscovery of ancient history would find attractive considering the realities of the early twentieth century. Naûm Fâik was not oblivious to this past age in which *Süryânî* schools were renowned "in the east and the west and in the four corners of the world."[556]

A similar strategy had, in fact, been employed by the *Süryânî-i Kadîm* hierarchy in the late nineteenth century in its conflict with the Armenians. In correspondence with the government, it was emphasised that the *Süryânî* were the ancient people of Babylon and that they were speakers of Aramaic. Moreover, the letter asserted that the Armenian Patriarch in Istanbul was but a bishop (*piskopos*) while the *Süryânî-i Kadîm* Patriarch was, like the Orthodox Patriarch and the Pope, a truly universal leader (*reis-i umûmî*).[557] This should best be understood again as a an emphasis on the primacy of the Antiochian past over the Christianity of the Armenians, which did not derive from one of the original Patriarchates.

For all this, the Armenian Church remained a threat to the *Süryânî-i Kadîm* into the twentieth century. For example, based on the number of reports in *Mürşid-i Âsûriyûn* of an Armenian and a *Süryânî* marrying, such occurrences must have been fairly common. The woman in such mixed marriages could be from either community, but presumably converted to her husband's confession unless, of course, they were already both Protestant. But even more

---

[555] One example was, for instance, ܟ̈ܗܢܐ in Syriac and ܩܫܝܫܐ (** քահանա**) in Armenian, both meaning "priest" (cf. Arabic كاهن and Ottoman Turkish *kâhin*).

[556] Çıkkı, *Naum Faik ve Süryani Rönesansı*, 135.

[557] Details on this letter appear in Özcoşar, *Bir Yüzyıl Bir Sancak Bir Cemaat*, 64-65.

remarkable is to see how Zeytûn, the *Süryânî-i Kadîm keşîş* of
Ağvan, telegraphed the Harput *millet meclisi*, stating that he and his
entire congregation had "become Armenians (*Ermenî olduk*)" due
to a dispute with *mutrân* Abdünnûr.[558] As it turned out, the *keşîş*,
and not Abdünnûr, was to blame as he had contravened church
rules in conducting a marriage between two relatives and was
attempting to escape censure or even excommunication.[559] In any
case, the *Süryânî-i Kadîm* community had by then taken the
announcement quite seriously, and Âşûr Yûsuf expressed his
sorrow upon hearing the news but not surprise at the conversion
or the accusations levelled against Abdünnûr. The apparent fluidity
between the two groups suggests that there would have been every
reason for Âşûr Yûsuf and Naûm Fâik to help buttress the *Süryânî*
against being subsumed by the numerically superior Armenians
whether through marriage or conversion. Naûm Fâik summed up
these very sentiments using the imagery of a *Süryânî* drop in an
Armenian sea:

> "Enough of this ignorance (*hâb-ı gaflet*), enough of this
> languor and idleness! Tomorrow our language will be
> completely lost, our *millet* will have disappeared, our
> churches will have closed, our name will have been
> erased from the pages of history, and as time goes on,
> we are being reduced to nothing but a cup of water in a
> sea, and in this way, with this neglect, all [we have] will
> dry up and be gone. What a shame."[560]

---

[558] "Mûcib-i teessüf bir telgraf," *Mürşid-i Âsûriyûn*, 4, no. 12 (Kânûn-ı
Evvel 1912), 190-191.

[559] This came out in full a few months later: "Mutrân Abdünnûr
efendinin haklı muâmelesi," *Mürşid-i Âsûriyûn*, 5, no. 4 (Mart 1913), 57-59.
Âşûr Yûsuf published the letter of resignation that Zeytûn sent to Abdünnûr in Harput. I have reproduced parts of this letter in Appendix A.

[560] "Artık yeter bu hâb-ı gaflet, artık kâfidir bu fütûr ve atâlet, yarın
lisânımız bütün bütün gâib olur, milletimiz nâbedîd olur, kiliselerimiz ka-
panır, nâmımız sahâif-i târîhten silinir, zâten kala kala denizden bir sâkiye
nisbetinde kalmışız, o da bu gidişle, bu kaydsızlığıyla kuruyup biter. Yazık-
tır.": "Cerîdeler âlem'nde cerîdelerimiz, ve zavâlli nâşirleri," *Kevkeb Mednho*,
1, no. 19 (25 Mart 1911), 3.

Politically too, the Armenians were in a position of dominance. With the exception of Mosul, Armenians were demographically dominant in every *vilâyet* inhabited by large numbers of *Süryânî* – Diyarbakır, Mamûretü'l-Azîz, Bitlis, Aleppo and Adana.[561] And this was reflected in the existence of local Armenian deputies in the Ottoman parliament and significant presence in the Ottoman administration.[562] Consequently, the *Süryânî* could not, with their memories of the Armenian control over their *millet* and religious hierarchy, accept any Armenian independence movement. I believe that a strong Ottoman Empire must have seemed as the best hope for the retention of independence from the pressures that the Armenian churches may have brought upon those of the *Süryânî*.

Working together with the Nestorians, Chaldeans and Maronites, Âşûr Yûsuf thought that the *Süryânî* could create a bulwark against the Armenians. This he expressed in what was probably the most overtly political article to appear in *Mürşid-i Âsûriyûn*. Stating that it was "a fundamental right of the *Süryânî millet* to send a representative to the Ottoman parliament", he called on his community to "lay claim to [its] rights."[563] Âşûr Yûsuf noted that the Armenians were not satisfied with ten members of parliament and were arguing for twenty seats based on their population of two million in the Empire. He retorted:

> "And the Maronites, the Protestant and Catholic *Süryânî*, the Chaldeans and the Nestorians, are they less than two million? And why shouldn't the patriarch, the *millet meclisi*, the *İntibâh Cemiyeti* of each [community] work together with one another in consultation so as to claim their rights to each send members to the parliament. Let us

---

[561] In Diyarbakır, it was only the *sancak* of Mardin in which the *Süryânî* population would have exceeded that of the Armenians.

[562] Bitlis, Aleppo and Adana all had Armenian deputies elected to the Ottoman parliament: Kansu, *The Revolution of 1908 in Turkey*, 280-287. For Armenians in the administration, see Krikorian, *Armenians in the Service of the Ottoman Empire*.

[563] "Hukûkumuza sâhib olalım," *Mürşid-i Âsûriyûn*, 4, no. 2 (Şubât 1912), 18-20.

have what is rightfully ours. It is the right of our *millet* to have representation in proportion to our numbers ... We must work in unison to claim them."[564]

Âşûr Yûsuf was not showing ignorance at the Ottoman electoral system, which did not officially assign seats to different groups based on their state-wide population. Instead, with representatives being elected from each district, it would have been obvious to Âşûr Yûsuf that no *Süryânî* – unlike the Chaldeans, who managed to secure the election of Dâvud Yûsufânî in Mosul – was likely to become a deputy when they were a demographic minority in every *vilâyet* in which they lived. However, the reality was that the Greek and Armenian communities assured themselves of CUP support for a certain number of candidates through negotiations prior to the actual elections. The *Süryânî*, however, with small numbers well away from the Ottoman capital, stood little chance of similarly influencing the CUP on their own. The Chaldeans already had a representative in Yûsufânî, but perhaps Âşûr Yûsuf felt that they would still be open to collaborating with the *Süryânî* and other unrepresented groups.

Consequently, being overshadowed by the Armenians in almost every constituency ensured that the only means of success would be to negotiate from a position of maximum strength – that is to say as a single block with the Chaldeans, Nestorians and Maronites. Indeed, Âşûr Yûsuf expressed these thoughts as a reaction to having read that Piyer Taşo was throwing his lot in with the Armenian community and was calling for an Armenian

---

[564] "Ermenîler on mebûsla iktifâ etmeyip Türkiye'de iki milyon Ermenî var diye mebûsânda yiğirmi mebûs bulundurmak iddiâsındadırlar. İşbu iki milyonda Ermenî Prosestan ve Katolikler dahi madûddurlar. Ya Mârûnî, Protestan ve Katolik Süryânîler, Keldânîler ve Nestûrîler iki milyondan az mıdırlar? Bunların patrikleri, millet meclisleri ve İntibâh cemiyetleri niçin yekdiğerleri ile bil-istişâre ve bil-ittifâk mebûsânda mebûslar bulundurmak için haklarını iddiâ etmesinler. Hukûkumuza sâhib olalım. Milletimizin adedine nisbeten mebûslar intihâb edip mebûsâne göndermek hakkımızdır. Ve bu hukûkumuz pâyîmâl oluyor. Hakkımızı bil-ittifâk iddiâ etmeliyiz."

representative from the *vilâyet* of Mamûretü'l-Azîz.[565] Interestingly, despite appealing for cooperation with the Chaldeans and Nestorians, he never once used the term "Assyrian" as a rational for his argument and he did not refer to any shared identity. His only consideration, it would seem, was securing representation through a joint effort and at the expense of the Armenians.

Âşûr Yûsuf's expressed concerns should not be understood as being anti-Armenian on a personal level, however. At the Euphrates College, almost all of his colleagues would have been Armenian. In *Mürşid-i Âsûriyûn*, he republished numerous articles written by Armenians and translated by his own hand, and printed congratulations which were as heartfelt when there was a mixed marriage as when there was a purely *Süryânî* one. Arşaluys Oğgasyan, Âşûr Yûsuf's wife, was of course herself an Armenian. It was, furthermore, inevitable that some *Süryânî* emigrants would marry outside their community when living in a country where the options within their own millet would have been so limited. The extent to which Ottoman Christians in the United States accepted this fact may be demonstrated in the marriage of two natives of Diyarbakır – the Süryânî Abdülazîz Çilingir and the Greek Sofiya – in an Armenian church in West Hoboken.[566]

If we recognise that the Armenians presented a danger to *Süryânî* religious and cultural institutions, we must also note that there was a very real threat to their personal safety in the form of the Kurds. If the neighbour of a *Süryânî* was not an Armenian, it would in most instances have been a Kurd. As we have seen, *Mürşid-i Âsûriyûn* carried numerous articles about the simmering rebellion by Kurdish chiefs in Cebel-i Tûr and in the countryside around Hasankeyf. Âşûr Yûsuf's informants told him that the Kurdish aim was to secure autonomy in the region.[567] Kurds were

---

[565] "Millettaşlarımızdan doktor Piyer efendi Taşo, vilâyetimizde bu defa bir Ermenî mebûsu intihâb olunup göndcrilmesine dâir Harpût'ta neşr olunan Ermeniyü'l-ibâre (Yeprad) nâm gazetede bir bend yazıp evvelbâbda bir faâliyet göstermektedir."

[566] [untitled article], *İntibâh*, 5, no. 8 (Temmûz 1914), 6.

[567] See page 143. The area was also heavily inhabited by Arabs, but the *Süryânî* do not appear to have perceived them as a threat.

portrayed as having a negative impact on the lives of the *Süryânî*, whether through perpetrating individual crimes or threatening the security of the region as a whole. The prospect of greater freedom for the Kurdish tribes at the expense of the Ottoman state would not have been something that the *Süryânî* relished.

Âşûr Yûsuf, Cebbûr Boyacı and Naûm Fâik saw no need for any union which involved the Nestorians or Chaldeans; recognising that the *Süryânî* were the descendants of the ancient Assyrians was sufficient to appropriate historical dominance over the Armenians. Since the first objective was to put distance between the Armenian and Jacobite churches, the Nestorians and Chaldeans, who in any case were theologically very distant, could only be useful to a limited extent. Secondly, Âşûr Yûsuf was content with cooperating politically with Maronites, Chaldeans and Nestorians to limit Armenian entry into the parliament at the expense of the *Süryânî*. But any ethnically-based union would risk a comparable situation in which the *Süryânî* would be subsumed into yet another demographically dominant group – only this time the Chaldeans.

It is, moreover, no surprise that Âşûr Yûsuf enjoined his readers – especially those in the United States – to educate themselves so that they may be well-placed to help strengthen their *vatan* and, indeed, assume a leading role in its advancement. Indeed, while Assyrian nationalists have understood calls for "union" to imply a union of the *Süryânî* with the Chaldeans and Nestorians, this was not the case; it was rather a union of Ottomans which Âşûr Yûsuf, Naûm Fâik, Cebbûr Boyacı and others meant. Hard on the heels of the Balkan Wars, the *Süryânî* felt that they stood only to lose from the Ottoman Empire disintegrating into nation states; the prospect of an upsurge in Armenian, Kurdish or perhaps even Arab calls for independence would have seemed nothing short of terrifying. It would have been difficult for the *Süryânî* to predict that the actual threat, even in the eastern provinces of the Ottoman Empire, would in fact come in the form of Turkish nationalism and with the excuse of a World War.

## THE *SÜRYÂNÎ* OTTOMANS

This work began by questioning the meaning behind Naûm Fâik's words when, writing to the *Süryânî* of Harput, he wrote "*terakkî istersek ittihâd etmeliyiz* [if we desire progress, then we must unite]." I offered three possibilities: *Süryânî-i Kadîm*, Assyrian and Ottoman –

identities based on religion, ethnicity and citizenship respectively. And yet, I believe a fourth answer – *Süryânî* – to be the one correct answer, something made clear by Naûm Fâik, Âşûr Yûsuf and Cebbûr Boyacı with the use of language on the one hand and the issues they held to be important on the other.

I have been careful to reiterate that each of these individuals believed they were the descendants of the ancient Assyrians – of this there can be no question. It is my contention, however, that it is not accurate to describe Âşûr Yûsuf, Cebbûr Boyacı and Naûm Fâik – at least in his pre-1912 incarnation – as nationalists; simply describing oneself as an "Assyrian" is not sufficient to earn such a mantle. There is no evidence that they saw themselves as part of a greater, contemporary Assyrian community, even if an ethnic bond was claimed. They had no exposure to the Urmiye press, in which Assyrian nationalism flourished, and could not have understood its language even if they had. They were, for example, far more concerned with the distant Jacobite Indians than their purported Assyrian kinsmen, the Chaldeans and Nestorians. Naûm Fâik, Âşûr Yûsuf and Cebbûr Boyacı did not even have a word to describe the commonality between the Jacobites, the Nestorians and all the derivative churches; they used *vatan*, *millet* and *cemâat* to refer to their Ottoman, *Süryânî* and *Süryânî-i Kadîm* identities respectively but no parallel existed for their Assyrian one.

Indeed, there is evidence to suggest that these men saw their Ottoman nationality as superseding their Assyrian identity in importance. There is, of course, nothing preventing one from being Ottoman and, say, Assyrian or *Süryânî* at the same time. Âşûr Yûsuf and Naûm Fâik show how multiple identities co-existed within the their community of the twentieth century; that these were not necessarily mutually exclusive or competing identities is also demonstrated by parallel conditions existing in the Armenian, Greek and Jewish communities. How the fates of the different identities ebbed and flowed during the years from 1908 and onwards reveals much about the *Süryânî* perception of contemporary events. Naûm Fâik would become the Assyrian nationalist portrayed in the historiography after he arrived in the United States and especially after he began to receive word of the massacres endured by the Christians remaining in the Ottoman Empire during the First World War.

But they still saw their future as being in the Ottoman Empire as Ottoman subjects until at least 1912 in Naûm Fâik's case and 1914 in Âşûr Yûsuf's. Why then did Naûm Fâik abandon the Ottoman Empire whereas Âşûr Yûsuf did not? It is unfortunately a question for which we can not provide an exact answer. It could be simply that Diyarbakır and Harput were different places and that the Christian disillusionment with the CUP beginning in 1912 had not fully descended on the inhabitants of the latter city. According to the local American consul, for example, the *vâli* of Mamûretü'l-Azîz, Alî Nusret Paşa, was responsible for preventing outsiders from provoking an outbreak of violence in 1909 comparable to what occurred in Adana.[568] There appears to have been a great belief in the Ottoman government and the constitutional rule in Harput, whereas Diyarbakır has described by some as being a hostile environment for Christians in light of the Ottoman wars in Libya and the Balkans.[569] There is unfortunately only circumstantial evidence that points to Âşûr Yûsuf being a supporter of the *Hürriyet ve İtilâf Fırkası*, but the fact remains that he was familiar with a number of its leading figures. Mamûretü'l-Azîz had a branch of the opposition party; Diyarbakır, however, did not.[570] At the same time, Cebbûr Boyacı was still printing Ottomanist articles right up until the outbreak of World War I; clearly, whatever reason may have prompted his own departure from Diyarbakır around the turn of the century, he too still saw an Ottoman future for his *millet* until the very end.

In many ways, the *Süryânî* experience of the second constitutional period most closely resembles that of the Jewish *millet*. Both communities saw the Ottoman Empire as the safest guarantor of their survival in the face of independence movements

---

[568] Barbara Merguerian, "The View from the United States Consulate," in *Armenian Tsopk/Kharpert*, 297-298. In this case, however, the perpetrators were to be Kurdish.

[569] Çıkkı, *Naum Faik ve Süryani Rönesansı*, 26-27 and Üngör, *'A Reign of Terror': CUP Rule in Diyarbekir Province*, 26-32.

[570] See Birinci, *Hürriyet ve İtilâf Fırkası*, 274 for the list of branches printed in *İfhâm*, another newspaper belonging to Lütfî Fikrî Bey, himself a deputy for the *vilâyet* of Mamûretü'l-Azîz (see note 360 on page 130).

around them: Greek and Bulgarian for the Jews, Armenian and Kurdish for the *Süryânî*.[571] Neither had a specific homeland which could lend a spatial dimension to their own demands for autonomy or independence: the Ottoman Jews had yet to become receptive to Zionism whereas the *Süryânî* were yet to see Mesopotamia – *Beyne'n-nehreyn* or *Bethnahrin* – as their national homeland. In other ways, their separation from the Armenian *millet* and the tensions which followed mirrors the experience of the Bulgarians as they sought to establish a separate church free from Greek control.

With the inaccessibility of their writings, it is not surprising that Naûm Fâik and Âşûr Yûsuf have been elevated since their deaths into nationalist heroes of the Assyrian people:

> "Ashur Yusuf the founder of modern Assyrian nationalism, was the first Assyrian martyr, because he was the first person that was executed by the Ottomans for his Assyrian national believes [*sic*] (and not for being a Christian)."[572]

Partially this is a consequence of the insistence of the Assyrian nationalist scholarship to translate *Süryânî* and its cognates as "Assyrian" and the resultant loss in linguistic nuances.[573] This choice immediately reduces the value of many secondary sources since it forces the reader to question each instance of the word "Assyrian".[574] Naûm Fâik and Âşûr Yûsuf – two self-proclaimed Assyrians – were far more careful in distinguishing the two

---

[571] The Kurdish demands for autonomy of the period are best not described as a national movement.

[572] Hanna Hajjar, "Is the Term 'Assyrian' Becoming a Synonym for 'Nestorian'?" *Zinda* 5, no. 12 (10 May 1999).

[573] For example, instead of rather than the "Syriac Orthodox Church", Naby opts for the "Assyrian Orthodox Church" in "The Assyrian Diaspora," 221. The Church itself rejects this appellation which futhermore has no precedent prior to the twentieth century.

[574] The same issue may well apply to Aramaean nationalists, though I have not personally made many such observations. In this work I have presented a scheme to deal with the terminology problem. It suffers from certain drawbacks, and my reliance on Ottoman terminology will not be suitable for studies of all locations or time periods.

different groups than many of their present-day followers, and it does them no service to obscure the meaning of their writings.

The historiography of Assyrian nationalism would not be the only one to emphasise secular origins of the movement under the pressures of a tyrannical Ottoman Empire.[575] But in my formulation, I have first of all attempted to dispel some of the myths pertaining to the "secular nature" of Âşûr Yûsuf and Naûm Fâik. Secondly, I have tried to look beyond the "oppressive nature" of Ottoman rule. I have said that it is not important whether the Young Turks were true adherents to Ottomanism or not, as long as the non-Muslims believed them.

What if Naûm Fâik, Cebbûr Boyacı and Âşûr Yûsuf were also merely paying lip service to Ottomanism? Or perhaps they were not free to express their true sentiments despite the fact that the CUP had repealed much of the system of censorship present during the reign of Abdülhamîd? Both scenarios are possible, but there is no evidence that this was in fact the case. Indeed, were they suffering under censorship or some other hardships then how did Âşûr Yûsuf publish the joint declaration of the *Hunchakian* and the CUP's main opponent, the *Hürriyet ve İtilâf Fırkası*? Why else would he choose to disseminate the speech of Mehmed Şükrî Bey? And why would he print a lengthy poem by *serepiskopos* Pavlûs on the 1909 counter-revolution and the ascent of the new sultan when it was written in Syriac, a language certain not to be known outside the *Süryânî* community?[576] I can only answer this question with my

---

[575] For example, this was the case in the early studies of Arab nationalism: Hasan Kayalı, *Arabs and Young Turks: Ottomanism, Arabism, and Islamism in the Ottoman Empire, 1908-1918* (Berkeley: University of California Press, 1997), 6-7. The brutality of Ottoman Turkish rule has been a central theme in much of the Armenian, Greek and Balkan historiography.

[576] The contents are described in the poem's preface ("Birincisi Dersaâdet'te vâki olan kıtâllerle yeni pâdişâhın üzerine."): *Mürşid-i Âsûriyûn*, 3, no. 1 (Kânûn-ı Sânî 1911), 4. A short excerpt, kindly translated for me by Johny Messo, better illustrates the recurrent Ottomanist theme:

"On 11 July 1908, the Ottomans became brothers ... They all combined in unity, they walked amongst one another in love and in the true path of justice. And when the worlds' kings heard of

opinion that Âşûr Yûsuf and Naûm Fâik were very much sincere in their belief in Ottomanism. Cebbûr Boyacı would, of course, not have been operating under any pressure which might have existed in the Ottoman Empire, and yet he continued to extol the freedoms of the era and the munificence of the constitution.

It is a sad irony that in Rızâ Tevfik's article enjoining cooperation between Christians and Muslims of the Ottoman Empire, we read that "if, God forbid, [my words are] not heeded, it will mean trouble for Anatolia. The face of injustice and murder will be everywhere."[577] Originally printed in *İkdâm* and then republished in *Mürşid-i Âsûriyûn*, the article correctly foresaw just what would happen during World War I. Scholars are right to investigate how the Ottoman lands were thrust into such a time of injustice and murder, and how what would become Turkey lost all but a small part of its *Süryânî* population – and indeed its Christian population as a whole. The problem is that currently, Syriac history is written as if it can not be done without discussions of genocide, whereas it has not accepted the reality that no discussion of

---

this, they were struck by the marvellousness of the brotherhood of the Ottomans which suddenly brought peace. Everyone blessed this state of affairs, in which brotherhood had come into being between Muslims and Christians. But after a short while, Satan entered into humankind and many were killed by treacherous men ... [But] the army took courage and endeavoured to find the evil ones that had caused the revolt. They surrounded the royal city [Istanbul] so that they could punish the murderers in front of the world ... The head of the forces from Salonika ordered his men to fight the Sultan ... They forcefully toppled the disgraced Hamîd from his throne and made his brother, Mehmed, the new Sultan. Then, the wars came to an end and it suddenly became calm."

The fact that the same Pavlûs wrote another poem in commemoration of Abdülhamîd's birthday in 1902 detracts only a little from my argument; the important point is that Âsûr Yûsuf saw fit to publish it, not that religious figures close to the Porte sought favour through flattery. A copy of the latter poem was provided to me by Jan Beṭ-Şawoce.

[577] "Eğer bu noktada maâzallah bir münâsebetsizlik olursa Anadolu'nun hâli müşkül olur. Zulmlar, cinâyetler her yerde baş gösterir. Ve önüne geçmek haklıyı ve haksızı seçmek güç olur.": "Şimdiki vazîfemiz," *Mürşid-i Âsûriyûn*, 4, no. 8 (Teşrîn-i Sânî 1912), 118.

genocide should be written without looking at the entirety of Ottoman *Süryânî* history. Or to phrase it another way, genocide is presented as a consequence of the national movement, whereas I would argue that Assyrian nationalism amongst the *Süryânî* derives primarily from their experience of the First World War.

And it is precisely this which I hope to have emphasised in this work. It is incorrect to describe a nationalist movement – *Süryânî* or Assyrian – in the Ottoman Empire prior to 1914, after which there *would* finally be a politicisation of Assyrian identity. At the same time, it would be doing figures such as Âşûr Yûsuf, Naûm Fâik Palak, Cebbûr Boyacı, Beşâr Hilmî, Piyer Taşo, Cercîs Alacacı or İbrâhîm Yûsuf a great disservice to claim that their belief in Ottomanism that I have described here was in some way traitorous to their people. As with those beliefs, *Mürşid-i Âsûriyûn*, *İntibâh* and *Kevkeb Mednho* were very much the product of the second Ottoman constitutional period, infused with the specific hopes and fears of the *Süryânî* people. And even if for only a brief moment, it was the hopes that did truly dominate, as Naûm Fâik[578] would express them in 1909:

> *Ey Süryânîler dünyâ nûr ile dolu*
> *Hâb-ı gaflet intibâh ile sonu geldi*
> *Şems-i hürriyet bizlere ikbâl ile doğdu*
> *Hâb-ı gaflet intibâh ile sonu geldi*

---

[578] This is the first stanza from a poem in the same collection discussed in Appendix B. It is dated to 12 Eylûl 1909. This same poem was also recited by *Süryânî* students during the meeting of the *Uhuvvet-i Osmânî Cemiyeti* [Ottoman Fraternal Association] at the *Meryem Ana Kilisesi* in 1910. See "Diyârbekir'den bir mektûb," *İntibâh*, 1, no. 7 (Mayıs 1910), 3 for Naûm Fâik's own account of this occasion.

# APPENDIX A: ORTHOGRAPHY

I would like to include a few linguistic notes outlining the orthographic principles which guided the writing of Ottoman Turkish using the Syriac alphabet (*Süryânî hurûfâtıyla Türkçe*). These have never, as far as I can tell, been published, and as such, future research into the newspapers examined here may benefit from this short description.[579]

There are three variants of the 22-letter Syriac alphabet, differentiated only by slight modifications in letters and diacritics: classical, Eastern and Western. Presently, the classical form of the Syriac alphabet, *Eṣṭrangela*,[580] is used primarily for religious purposes. From this derived the two modern versions, *Madnḥaya* [Eastern] and *Serṭa* [line] in the West. The scriptural division follows the theological, and hence the terms applied to the religious communities (Jacobite, Nestorian and Chaldean) are sometimes employed with reference to the scripts as well. As all of the journals used in this study were published within the *Süryânî* community, it is the *Serṭa* script which I will expound upon here.

The Syriac alphabet is a Semitic *ebced* [abjad] like Arabic and Hebrew. As with other such systems, writing occurs from right to left, with long vowels represented by consonants and short vowels by superposing diacritical marks. While in the East, vowels are indi-

---

[579] A paper presented by Wolfhart Heinrichs entitled "Turkish Karshuni" did touch on the subject, but the paper was never published and I was unable to obtain a copy. Besides personal observations, I consulted two sources: Alphonse Mingana, "Garshūni or Karshūni?" *Journal of the Royal Asiatic Society* (1928): 891-893 and G. Troupeau, "Karshūnī," *Encyclopaedia of Islam*, new edition (Leiden, Brill, 1960).

[580] The name derives from the Greek στρογγυλη (*strongylê*), "rounded".

213

cated by points, in the Western script, diacritics take the form of miniature Greek letters placed above or below the preceding letter. Unlike published Arabic and Ottoman Turkish, diacritical marks were used widely in the text of *Kevkeb Mednho*, though normally only for the Syriac language portions, not for the Arabic or Ottoman Turkish. *Mürşid-i Âsûriyûn* would, however, use diacritics to clarify the pronunciation of proper nouns or names from European or Indian languages. *İntibâh* did likewise but it used the normal Arabic *hareke* rather than the Syriac diacritics.

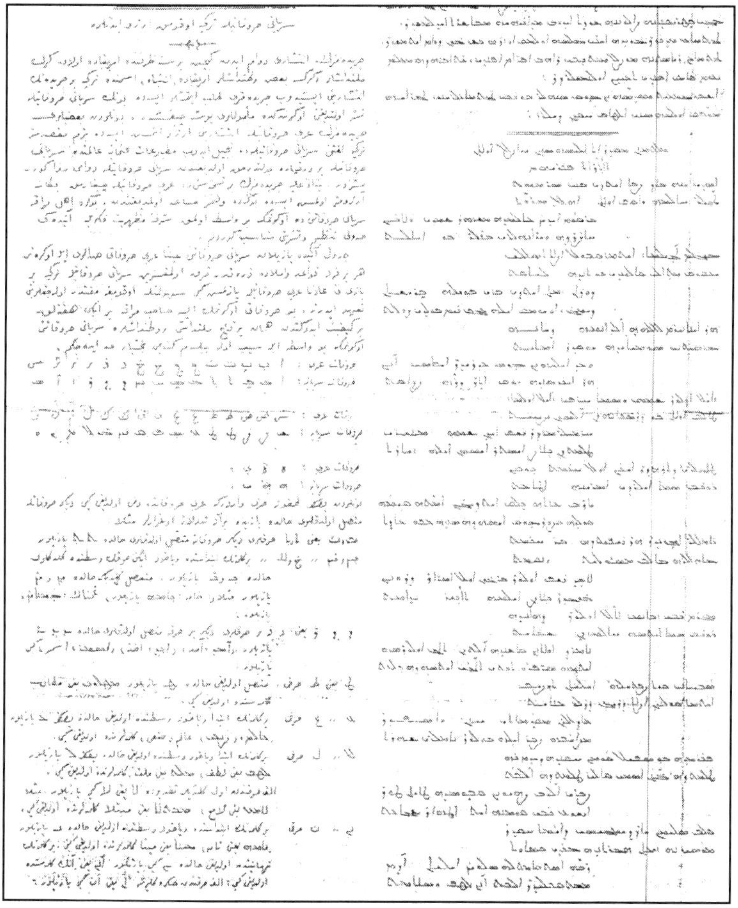

Image 10 – *İntibâh*'s guide to Ottoman in Syriac letters

Like Arabic, the *Serṭa* variant of the Syriac script is written so that the letters are connected to both their preceding and following letters. As a result, there are four separate forms for most letters: isolated, initial, medial and final. Of the 22 letters, eight are never attached to a following letter and consequently only have two forms: isolated and final.

The practice of writing Arabic using Syriac characters was established long before the emergence of printing. The term *Gerṣûnî*, while originally restricted to Arabic, has come to refer to any language which is written in the Syriac alphabet.[581] Besides Arabic and Ottoman Turkish, there are examples of Farsi, Kurdish, Armenian and Malayalam (the vernacular of the Syriac Christians in India) being thus employed. Early Nestorian missionary activities in China also produced the Mongolian script, which although written vertically, is a descendant of the Syriac alphabet.

To represent Arabic's twenty-eight consonants, six Syriac letters are used dually to represent the extra sounds. In most cases, a single point placed above or below the standard letter suffices to indicate the alternate form. An exception is the letter ܓ which is used for both the Arabic *gayn* (غ) and *cîm* (ج), neither of which have equivalents in the Syriac language. In this case, the former takes a point below while the latter is modified with a slash through the centre.

A number of Arabic orthographic practices have also carried over into *Gerṣûnî*. Notably, the following were all used as in Arabic: *med*, placed over the Syriac letter ܐ to give آ; *hemze* (ء), either alone or over ܘ to give ؤ; *tenvîn*, again placed over ܐ to give ً; and an approximation of the Arabic ة by pointing the corresponding Syriac letter to give ܗ̈. These appeared more consistently than normally appears in Ottoman Turkish with the exception of *med*, which appears much less frequently, even in words of Turkish origin. Another feature is the use of hyphenation – a practice normally forbidden with the Arabic and Syriac alphabets – rather than the insertion of a *keşîde* or *tatvîl* for the justification of text.

---

[581] *Gerṣûnî* is often rendered *Karshûnî* in Arabic since that language does not have an equivalent to the Syriac letter ܓ and consequently substitutes the letter ܟ in its place.

The traditional *Gerşûnî* system was further supplemented to accommodate words of Farsi and Turkish origin. The letter ﺳ has the same value as in Syriac (a sound which does not exist in Arabic). Although, as mentioned above, it is pointed below to represent ﻍ, it also frequently takes a point above to clearly mark it as ﻚ. Furthermore, *ç* is represented by three points below a ﺳ with a slash.[582] One simplification is that the Ottoman *sağır kef* or *kef-i nûnî* (ﮒ) was always written as if it were a normal ﻥ. When ﺑ occurs twice sequentially, single dots are usually placed under each letter � to clearly distinguish it from a single ﺳ, which it would otherwise closely resemble.

The level of Ottoman Turkish was generally very good – Cebbûr Boyacı's being the weakest of the three – although there are occasional errors or inconsistencies in orthography. The title page of *Mürşid-i Âsûriyûn* always contains a misspelling of *muharrir* (the final vowel is made long) and uses the Turkish plural *-ler* on the Arabic plural for *mahal*, giving a doubly pluralised *mahâller*. But such irregularities are extremely rare. For one, Âşûr Yûsuf and Naûm Fâik had the luxury of being able to correct their orthographic errors prior to printing, something not always possible when typesetting. It is not unusual to see a word crossed out and a correction inserted above, or for a forgotten letter or word to be added after the fact.

Traditionally, Syriac does not employ digits to indicate numbers, but rather counts using the numerical value of the letters of the alphabet (ܐ equals 1, ܒ equals 2 and so on as in the Arabic system). In the *Süryânî* press, these were employed only to enumerate the number of the article in *Mürşid-i Âsûriyûn* and the pages in *Kevkeb Mednho*. All other figures were, without exception, written using the normal numerals found in Arabic.

---

[582] This gives the base form of ﺳ four different values depending on the pointing: *c, ç, g* and *ğ*. As in Ottoman Turkish, *g* and *ğ* may also represent the two phonetic values of the letter *ğ* in modern Turkish, brining the total to six. On the other hand, *k* is a distinct letter, eliminating the confusion between ﻚ and ﻙ which sometimes occurs in Ottoman Turkish.

## THE CASE OF ZEYTÛN *KEŞÎŞ*

Naûm Fâik, Âşûr Yûsuf and Cebbûr Boyacı were proficient in the Ottoman Turkish language, but not all *Süryânî* shared their abilities. In particular, there is the example of the letter of apology from Zeytûn, the *keşîş* of Ağvan, which was printed in *Mürşid-i Âsûriyûn* and was reproduced in its original orthography.[583] Zeytûn's Ottoman Turkish spelling may be of some interest as it shows both a Syriac influence and the reliance on simplified phonetic transcription, especially for the spelling of Arabic words. The poor quality of Zeytûn's Turkish suggests that the *Süryânî* of Ağvan did not normally use the language, although it is also worth noting that it was still the preferred medium amongst the religious hierarchy in Harput.

As an example of Zeytûn's non-standard orthography, the *mutrân* Abdünnûr (properly عبدالنور) has his name spelt phonetically, عبدونور. Similarly, the Arabic portion of the word *hidmetkâr* (خدمتكار) is spelt more or less as it is pronounced in Turkish, *hizmet*, and with the Farsi suffix misspelt (خزمتكر). These and many more such examples may be seen in the quoted text below. More interesting is the way in which he addressed Abdünnûr: *rütbetlû kudşetlû vâli-i nimet efendim hazretleri*. The spelling of the first two words رتبتلوا and قدشتلوا (by which I believe he meant *kudsiyetli*) shows a probable influence from Syriac. For example, the final *elif* to represent the vowel sound *u* may be an analogy with the Western Syriac practice of pronouncing a final ܐ as *o*. Moreover, the second title is built on the Arabic root *q-d-s* (قدس) with meanings such as "holy" or "bless", but here we encounter the Syriac cognate, *q-d-ş* (ܩܕܫ), instead.

Similar confusion between letters occurred even in Turkish words, however. Zeytûn wrote *simdi, is* and *düsünmek* rather than *şimdi, iş* and *düşünmek* for example. Elsewhere there is the predictable mixing of letters which are pronounced identically by Turkish-speakers. So the letter ص is usually substituted by س in words of Turkish and Arabic origin, while the letters ذ, ز, ظ and ض (all pronounced *z* in Turkish) are often confused. He also frequently used

---

583 "Mutrân Abdünnûr efendinin haklı muâmelesi," *Mürşid-i Âsûriyûn*, 5, no. 4 (Mart 1913), 57-59.

the Arabic consonant *ʿayn* (ع) to represent the sounds *a* or *â*, even in words of Turkish or Farsi origin.

A short passage, while interesting for its content, also illustrates some of the peculiarities of Zeytûn's Turkish (note also the use of Armenian in the first line):

"Xarpût viliyet (ویلیت) azîz muṭrân Abdûnûr efendi Surp Xaç'ın hûzüründe (هوزرنده) yüz ve göz süreraq (سورهراق) ellarinigi (اللارنگی) ayaqlarınıgı (عیقلرنگی) öperim daḥa (دهحه) qul [diyülmam?] (دیولمام) xizmetker maqamında (معقمنده) bani (بانی) qabûl edasin (ایداسن) güçüqtan günah (گنه) buyuqtan af (عف) edasın ... keşîşlıq vâcîfesini (واجیفسنی = vaẓîfesini) îcre (ایجره) ettim (اتدم) hiç zetinizin (زتنزن) emrini tanımadım zetinizin ḥaqqında çok isler yaptım hem her yere tilqraf (تیلقراف) verdim. Muṭrân Cercîs efendidan keşîşlıq emrnamasını (امرنعمعسنی) aldım bade iki gün sonra (سونره) bir rûye (رویه) gördüm çoq qorqu cektim ben düsünüp fikr ettim bu isler zetinizin hâqqında (هاقنده) ilerü gelmesidir efendim rîcâ edarım heppi (هیپی) yapduqlarımı (بیدوقلریمی) îtîrâf (عیتیراف) sene (سنه) oluyorum efendim bene bereketnama îrsâl eyle ... Ne yapayım burası Kürd (کورد) yeridir qorqumdan yaptım ne edayım simdi bu nikâdan eger bir para almışsam ben sana boclu [بوجلو = borclu] qalım efendim rîcâ edarım bene bereketnama îrsâl eyle efendim."

# APPENDIX B: POETRY OF NAÛM FÂIK

The following poems come from a school notebook which belonged to Yaacoub Hajjar (Yakûb Haccâr), born in Urfa and educated at the T.M.S. School in Beirut. The handwriting is not clear in all places and the occasional word has been erased, but for the most part they are legible. In total there are eight untitled poems over 15 pages. I have transliterated two here.

A number of the poems in the Hajjar collection also appear in the 1917 mimeographed book by Naûm Fâik entitled *Süryânî Millete Mahsûs İntibâh Neşîdeleri yâhûd Millî ve Vatanî Terennümler* [Verses of the Awakening or, National and Patriotic Songs Belonging to the *Süryânî*]. In addition to Ottoman Turkish-language poems, the book also contains examples in Syriac and Arabic.

Pages 10-11

(1) Haydi kardeşler yekdil olalım
İttifâk ittihâd edelim
Hasedi nifâkı tebîd edelim
Gayret ve himmeti takîb edelim
Tarîkı bu [nikâyete?] gidelim

(2) Genç Âsûrîler ister misiniz
Terakkî etmek hür olunuz
Bedeni cân ile fedâ ediniz
Uyumuş bayılmış gaflette kalmış
Milleti gayrete ihvân çekiniz

(3) Biz genç arslanız koyunu kurttan
Pek şeciâne kurtarırız
Müstebid fikrlileri ezeriz
İntibâh nâmıyla hep gâfilleri
Kaldırıp necâte gideriz

(4) İşte kardeşler cesâret ile
Meydâna çıkın şân devridir.
Silâhlarımızı takmak günüdür
Hürriyet uhuvvet düşmânlarını
Merdâne kahr etmek vaktidir

(5) Artık gidelim ziyâya doğru
Nûr-ı hürriyet pek parlıyor
Ne için duralım vakt geçiyor
Muazzez vatanı hem kayıralım
İstibdâd elinden [illegible]

(6) Gelin gâfiller hep birleşelim
Biz olmalıyız cehd edenler
İntibâh etmekle rifat bulanlar
Yaşasın yaşasın binler yaşasın
Vatanı milleti sevenler

Naûm Fâik
1 Eyyâr sene 1909

Page 14

(1)  Ey annemiz şânlı vatan
     Ey [müderris?] Âsûrîler
     Verdin bize sen ...
     Millet bütün kurban sana
     Şânlı vatan binler yaşa

(2)  Allah sana olsun muîn
     Batsın yere hâin i laîn
     İkbâl evvel râbbim muîn
     Millet bütün kurban sana
     Şânlı vatan binler yaşa

Naûm Fâik
27 Âb 1909

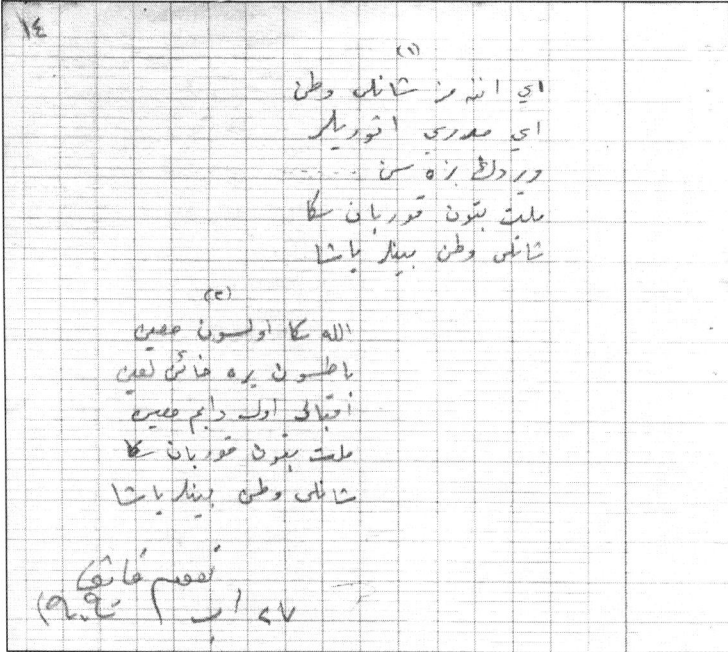

# APPENDIX C: POETRY OF ÂŞÛR YÛSUF

A number of Âşûr Yûsuf's poems have been preserved in the Süryânî community of Elâzığ. İshak Tanoğlu provided me with four examples, two of which also appeared in *Mürşid-i Âsûriyûn*. One of these, reproduced below, actually appeared twice in two slightly different forms, firstly in December of 1911 and then again in December of 1913, although it was originally penned on 20 December 1887. A celebration of Christ, the poem is today recited as a church hymn in Elâzığ in the form that it took in 1913.[584]

1911 version

(1)    Gece zulmünde nûr lemeân etti
       Semâdan melek nüzûl eyledi ...
       Sürûr-ı azîm tebşîr olundu
       Çûn ekvâma bir halâskâr doğdu.

(2)    Allah'a hamdler en yücelerde
       Sulh u selâmet rû-yı zemînde
       İnsânlarda var hem hüsn ü rızâ
       Semâvî cünûd okudu senâ.

(3)    Ey zulmette oturan insân
       Bugün azîm nûr oldu ihsân
       Mahv oldu zulmet müjdeler sana
       Tarîk-i hayât çıktı meydana
Mürşid

---

[584] *Mürşid-i Âsûriyûn*, 3, no. 12 (Kânûn-ı Evvel 1911), 195 and "Mesîh efendimizin doğumu," *Mürşid-i Âsûriyûn*, 5, no. 13 (Kânûn-ı Evvel 1913), 198.

To the poems found in *Mürşid-i Âsûriyûn* we may also add those which appear in the Armenian-language booklet about Âşûr Yûsuf published in Boston in 1919.[585] These were all written in the Ottoman Turkish language but, in this case, were printed in the Armenian alphabet.[586] The first two (*Ey kalb-i mecrûh* and *Ben de bir vakt*) may be found on page 1, facing Âşûr Yûsuf's photograph, while on page 2 there are a further two examples (*Ah nerede istirâhat* and *Var mı aceb?*). All but the last of these are known in Elâzığ.

Ey Kalb-i Mecrûh
(1)	Ey kalb-i mecrûh hâzırım ben şimdi gel bana
	Yârene dermân tatlı melhem vereyim sana
(2)	Ey kalb-i meyûs hâzırım ben şimdi gel bana
	Kalbine ferâh hem tesellî vereyim sana
(3)	Ey susamış cân hâzırım ben şimdi gel bana
	Bende bulunur âb-ı hayât vereyim sana
(4)	Ey aç olan cân hâzırım ben şimdi gel bana
	Hayât etmeği al meccânen vereyim sana
(5)	Ey karanlıkta oturan kavm şimdi gel bana
	Cân gözlerini açarak nûr vereyim sana
(6)	Ey bîtâb yorgun sefil mağdûr şimdi gel bana
	Halâs meserret dâim râhat vereyim sana
Âşûr S. Yûsuf

---

[585] Assyrian	Five	Association,	*Uunpıng	Uuqıqulquu	Ruhyhpuu*, 1-2.
[586] I would like to express my gratitude to Sevan Gökçe for the help in transliterating.

Ben de Bir Vakt

(1) Ben de bir vakt şebâb idim
   Hüsn ü kuvvete mâlik

(2) Servet ü nimetle mümtâz
   Kılmıştı beni hâlik[587]

(3) Kalbime hoş olanı ben
   Aslâ diriğ etmedim

(4) Safahâtle geçti ömrüm
   Mahşeri zikretmedim

(5) Âh cân u cismim oldu harâb
   Düştüm ben âh u zâra

(6) Ağlarım âh geçti fursat
   Dönmez gayri ne çâre

Âşûr S. Yûsuf

----

[587] In the original *hâlih* is written instead of *hâlik*; this transcription error was probably due to the fact that the letters share the same basic form in the Syriac alphabet (ܚ) distinguished only by a single diacritic point.

# APPENDIX D: PHOTOGRAPHS

The remains of the Palak household may be found near the *Meryem Ana Kilisesi* in the Lâlâ Bey neighbourhood. As with Diyarbakır's Christian cemetery and Armenian church, it is in a poor state of repair.

Image 11 – Palak family house in Diyarbakır

The gravestones of many of the important Harput families encountered in the pages of *Mürşid-i Âsûriyûn* may be found in the small graveyard which adjoins the modern *Süryânî-i Kadîm* church in Elâzığ. Amongst the notable names are members of the Taşo and Ulubeğ families. On the gravestone of *şemmâs* Yakûb Denho [Tanoğlu], there is an epitaph written in Ottoman Turkish using the classical Syriac alphabet.

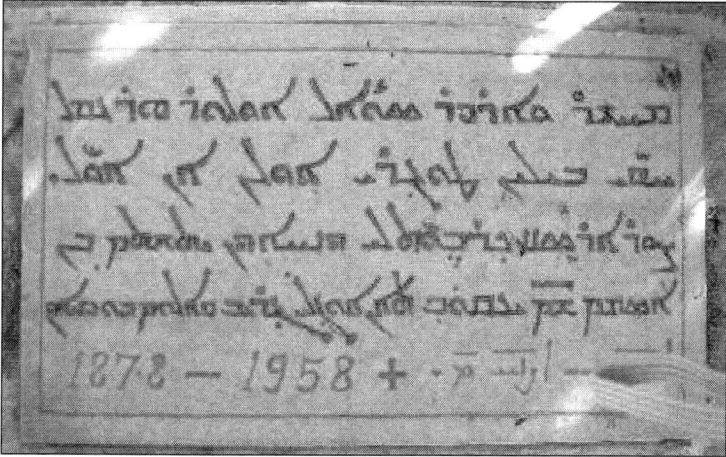

Image 12 – Gravestone of Yakûb Denho

Image 13 – Euphrates College in 1912

# BIBLIOGRAPHY

## Newspapers

*İntibâh*, birinci sene, 1-12; ikinci sene, 1-12; üçüncü sene, 1-12; dördüncü sene, 1-12; beşinci sene, 1-9.

*Kevkeb Mednho*, birinci sene, 1-26; ikinci sene, 1-14.

*Mürşid i Âsûriyûn*, cild-i sâlis, 1-12; cild-i râbi. 1-12; cild-i hâmis, 1-13.

## Secondary Sources

Ahmad, Feroz. "Unionist Relations with the Greek, Armenian, and Jewish Communities of the Ottoman Empire, 1908-1914." In *Christians and Jews in the Ottoman Empire: the Functioning of a Plural Society*, edited by Benjamin Braude and Bernard Lewis. New York: Holmes & Meier Publishers, 1982.

Akçam, Taner. *A Shameful Act: The Armenian Genocide and the Question of Turkish Responsibility*. Translated by Paul Bessemer. New York: Metropolitan Books, 2006.

Akgül, Suat. *Musul sorunu ve Nasturi isyanı*. Ankara: Berikan, 2001.

Aktürk, Şener. "Perspectives on Assyrian Nationalism," *Hemispheres: Tufts University Journal of International Affairs* (2002).

Akyüz, Gabriyel. *Tüm Yönleriyle Süryaniler*. Mardin: Kırklar Kilisesi, 2005.

Alichoran, Joseph. "Assyro-Chaldeans in the 20th Century: from Genocide to Diaspora." *Journal of the Assyrian Academic Society* 8, no. 2 (November, 1994): 45-79.

Anagnostopoulou, Sia. "The Terms *Millet*, *Génos*, *Ethnos*, *Oikoumenikótita*, *Alytrotismos* in Greek Historiography," in *The Passage from the Ottoman Empire to the Nation-States*. Istanbul: Isis Press, 2004.

————. "Tanzimat ve Rum Milletinin Kurumsal Çerçevesi: Patrikhane, Cemaat Kurumları, Eğitim," in *19. Yüzyıl İstanbul'unda Gayrimüslimler*, edited by Pinelopi Stathis, translated by

Foti Benlisoy and Stefo Benlisoy. Istanbul: Tarih Vakfı Yurt Yayınları, 1999.

Aras, Ramazan. *Migration and Memory: Assyrian Identity in Mardin Kerboran/Dargeçit*. Master's thesis, Boğaziçi University, 2005.

Artinian, Vartan. *The Armenian Constitutional System in the Ottoman Empire, 1839-1863: A Study of its Historical Development*. Istanbul, undated.

Assyrian Five Association. Ասորւոց Անզուգական Թահկիրան [Unique Vanguard of the Assyrians]. Boston: Assyrian Star Press, 1919.

Atiya, Aziz S. *A History of Eastern Christianity*. London: Methuen, 1968.

Atkinson, Tracy. *The German, the Turk and the Devil Made a Triple Alliance: Harpoot Diaries, 1908-1917*. Princeton: Gomidas Institute, 2000.

Aydın, Edip. *The History of the Syrian Orthodox Church of Antioch in North America: Challenges and Opportunities*. (Master's thesis, St. Vladimir Orthodox Seminary, 2000).

BarAbrahem, Abdulmesih. "The 'Question of Assyrian Journalism' Revisited." *Journal of the Assyrian Academic Society* 9, no. 1 (April, 1995): 3-7.

Baum, Wilhelm and Dietmar W. Winkler. *The Church of the East*. Translated by Miranda G. Henry. London: Routledge-Curzon, 2003.

Bayzan, Ali Rıza. *Misyonerin soykırım oyunu: Ermeni-Rum/Pontus ve Süryani/Keldani gailesi'nin oluşumunda misyoner örgütlerin rolü üzerine*. Istanbul: IQ Kültür Sanat Yayıncılık, 2006.

Benjamin, Yoab. "Assyrian Journalism: A 140-Year Experience." *Journal of the Assyrian Academic Society* 7, no. 2 (November, 1993): 1-28.

Beşiryan, Aylin. *Hopes of Secularization in the Ottoman Empire: The Armenian National Constitution and the Armenian Newspaper, Masis, 1856-1863*. Master's thesis, Boğaziçi University, 2007.

Birinci, Ali. *Hürriyet ve İtilâf Fırkası: II. Meşrutiyet devrinde İttihat ve Terakki'ye karşı çıkanlar*. Istanbul: Dergâh Yayınları, 1990.

Bet-Alkhas, Wilfred. "Omta, NOT Millat!" *Zinda* 14, no. 5 (23 May 2008).

Boura, Catherine. "The Greek Millet in Turkish Politics: Greeks in the Ottoman Parliament (1908-1918)." In *Ottoman Greeks in the*

*Age of Nationalism*, edited by Dimitri Gondicas and Charles Issawi. Princeton: Darwin Press, 1999.

Bozkurt, Gülnihâl. *Gayrimüslim Osmanlı Vatandaşlarının Hukukî Durumu (1839-1914)*. Ankara: Türk Tarih Kurumu, 1989.

Braude, Benjamin. "Foundation Myths of the Millet System." In *Christians and Jews in the Ottoman Empire: the Functioning of a Plural Society*, edited by Benjamin Braude and Bernard Lewis. New York: Holmes & Meier Publishers, 1982.

Browne, Edward Granville. *The Press and Poetry of Modern Persia: partly based on the manuscript work of Mírzá Muḥammad 'Alí Khán "Tarbiyat" of Tabríz*. Cambridge: University Press, 1914.

Bryce, James and Arnold Toynbee. *The Treatment of Armenians in the Ottoman Empire, 1915-16: documents presented to Viscount Grey of Fallodon, Secretary of state for foreign affairs*. London: Sir Joseph Causton and Sons, 1916.

Carney, Scott. "A Handwritten Daily Paper in India Faces the Digital Future," *Wired* (July 7, 2007).

Cole, Juan R. I. "Printing and Urban Islam in the Mediterranean World, 1890-1920." In *Modernity and Culture: from the Mediterranean to the Indian Ocean*, edited by Leila Fawaz and C. A. Baily. New York: Columbia University Press, 2002.

Corbon, Jean. "The Churches of the Middle East: Their Origins and Identity, from their Roots in the Past to their Openness to the Present." In *Christian Communities in the Arab Middle East: The Challenge of the Future*, edited by Andrea Pacini. Oxford: Clarendon, 1998.

Çıkkı, Murat Fuat. *Naum Faik ve Süryani Rönesansı*. Translated by Mehmet Şimşek. Istanbul: Belge Uluslararası Yayıncılık, 2004.

de Courtois, Sébastien. *The Forgotten Genocide: Eastern Christians, the Last Arameans*. Translated by Vincent Aurora. Piscataway, NJ: Gorgias Press, 2004.

De Kelaita [d-Qelayta], Robert William. "On the Road to Nineveh: A Brief History of Assyrian Nationalism." *Journal of the Assyrian Academic Society* 8, no.1 (April, 1994): 6-30.

————. "The Origins and Development of Assyrian Nationalism" (unpublished paper).

Denny, Frederick. "Some Religio-Communal Terms and Concepts in the Qur'ān." *Numen* 24, fasc. 1 (April, 1977): 26-59.

Duman, Hasan. *Başlangıcından Harf Devrimine Kadar Osmanlı-Türk Süreli Yayınlar ve Gazeteler Bibliyografyası ve Toplu Katalogu, 1828-*

*1928*. Ankara: Enformasyon ve Dokümantasyon Hizmetleri Vakfı, 2000.

Eren, İsmail. "La presse turque en Yougoslavie (1866-1986)." In *Presse turque et presse de Turquie*, edited by N. Clayer, A. Popovic and T. Zarcone. Istanbul: Isis Press, 1992.

Findley, Carter V. "The Acid Test of Ottomanism: The Acceptance of Non-Muslims in the Late Ottoman Bureaucracy." In *Christians and Jews in the Ottoman Empire: the Functioning of a Plural Society*, edited by Benjamin Braude and Bernard Lewis. New York: Holmes & Meier Publishers, 1982.

Fortescue, Adrian. *The Lesser Eastern Churches*. London: The Catholic Truth Society, 1913.

——————. *The Uniate Eastern Churches: the Byzantine Rite in Italy, Sicily, Syria and Egypt*. New York: Benziger Brothers, 1923.

Frazee, Charles. *Catholics and Sultans: the Church and the Ottoman Empire, 1453-1923*. London: Cambridge University Press, 1983.

Frye, Richard N. "Assyria and Syria: Synonyms." *Journal of Near Eastern Studies* 51, no. 4 (November, 1992): 281-285.

——————. "Reply to John Joseph." *Journal of the Assyrian Academic Society* 8, no. 1 (April, 1999): 69-70.

Gaunt, David. *Massacres, Resistance, Protectors: Muslim-Christian Relations in Eastern Anatolia During World War I*. Piscataway, NJ: Gorgias Press, 2006.

Gazel, Ahmet Ali. *Osmanlı Meclis-i Mebusanı'nda Parlamenter Denetim (1908-1912)*. Konya: Çizgi Kitabevi, 2007.

Gebru, Mebratu Kiros. *Miaphysite Christology: A Study of the Ethiopian Tewahedo Christological Tradition on the Nature of Christ*. Master's thesis, Toronto School of Theology, 2005.

Georgelin, Hervé. "Boycottage des non-musulmans à Smyrne et dans le *vilayet* d'Aydın d'après les archives diplomatiques." *Revue du Monde Arménien Moderne et Contemporain* no. 4 (1998), 7-22.

Gewargis, Odisho Malko. "We Are Assyrians." *Journal of the Assyrian Academic Society* 16, no. 1 (April, 2002): 77-95.

Greene, Joseph K. *Leavening the Levant*. Boston: Pilgrim Press, 1916.

Güneş, İhsan. *Türk Parlamento Tarihi*, vol. 2. Ankara: Türkiye Büyük Millet Meclisi Vakfı, 1997.

Hajjar, Hanna. "Is the Term 'Assyrian' Becoming a Synonym for 'Nestorian'?" *Zinda* 5, no. 12 (10 May 1999).

Hanioğlu, M. Şükrü. "Garbcılar: Their Attitudes toward Religion and Their Impact on the Official Ideology of the Turkish Republic." *Studia Islamica* no. 86 (1997), 133-158.

——. *The Young Turks in Opposition.* New York: Oxford University Press, 1995.

Ishaq, Yusuf M. *Definition of the Latin Alphabet and The English Glossary Used in the Primer Toxu Qorena.* Örebro: Statens Institut För Läromedel, undated.

Ishaya, Arian. "Ethnicity, Class, and Politics: Assyrians in the History of Azerbayjan, 1800-1918." *Journal of the Assyrian Academic Society* 4, no. 2 (November, 1990): 3-17.

Jastrow, Otto. "The Turoyo Language Today." *Journal of the Assyrian Academic Society* 1 (1986): 7-16.

Jeffrey, Robin. "The Three Stages of Print: testing ideas of 'Public Sphere,' 'Print-Capitalism' and 'Public Action' in Kerala, India." In *Asia Examined: Proceedings of the 15th Biennial Conference of the ASAA, 2004, Canberra, Australia,* edited by Robert Cribb. Canberra: Asian Studies Association of Australia, 2004.

Joseph, John. "Assyria and Syria: Synonyms?" *Journal of the Assyrian Academic Society* 11, no. 2 (November, 1997): 37-43.

——. *Muslim-Christian Relations and Inter-Christian Rivalries in the Middle East: the Case of the Jacobites in the Age of Transition.* Albany: State University of New York Press, 1983.

——. *The Nestorians and their Muslim Neighbors: A Study of Western Influence on their Relations.* Princeton: Princeton University Press, 1961.

Laing-Marshall, Andrea Irene. *Modern Assyrian Identity and the Church of the East: an Exploration of their Relationship and the Rise of Assyrian Nationalism, from the World Wars to 1980.* Master's thesis, Toronto School of Theology, 2001.

Lewis, Bernard. *The Emergence of Modern Turkey,* 3rd edition, New York: Oxford University Press, 2002.

Kansu, Aykut. *The Revolution of 1908 in Turkey.* Leiden: Brill, 1997.

——. *Politics in Post-Revolutionary Turkey, 1908-1913.* Leiden: Brill, 2000.

Karmi, Ilan. *The Jewish Community of Istanbul in the Nineteenth Century: Social, Legal and Administrative Transformations.* Istanbul: Isis Press, 1996.

Karpat, Kemal H. *Ottoman Population 1830-1914: Demographic and Social Characteristics.* Madison: University of Wisconsin Press, 1985.

—————. "The Memoirs of N. Batzaria: The Young Turks and Nationalism." *International Journal of Middle East Studies*, 6, no. 3 (July, 1975): 276-299.

Kayalı, Hasan. *Arabs and Young Turks: Ottomanism, Arabism, and Islamism in the Ottoman Empire, 1908-1918.* Berkeley: University of California Press, 1997.

Kechriotis, Vangelis. "Greek-Orthodox, Ottoman Greeks or just Greeks? Theories of Coexistence in the Aftermath of the Young Turk Revolution." *Études balkaniques*, 1 (2005): 51-72.

—————. "On the Margins of National Historiography: the Greek *İttihatçı* Emmanouil Emmanouilidis: Opportunists or Ottoman patriot?" Forthcoming paper.

Kılıçdağı, Ohannes. *The Bourgeois Transformation and Ottomanism among Anatolian Armenians after the 1908 Revolution.* Master's thesis, Boğaziçi University, 2005.

Kırmızı, Abdülhamit, "Son Dönem Osmanlı Bürokrasisinde Akraba Ermeniler." *Ermeni Araştırmaları* no. 8 (Winter, 2003): 137-152.

Kiraz, George A. "Suryoye and Suryoyutho: Syrian Orthodox Identity in the Late Nineteenth Century and Early Twentieth Century." (unpublished paper presented at Leiden University in 2004).

Kologlu, Orhan. *Osmanlı'dan Günümüze Türkiye'de Basın.* Istanbul: İletişim Yayınları, 1992.

Koptaş, Rober. A*rmenian Political Thinking in the Second Constitutional Period: the Case of Krikor Zohrab.* Master's thesis, Boğaziçi University, 2005.

Krikorian, Mesrob. *Armenians in the Service of the Ottoman Empire.* London: Routledge & Kegan Paul, 1977.

Maïla, Joseph. "The Arab Christians: From the Eastern Question to the Recent Political Situation of the Minorities." In *Christian Communities in the Arab Middle East: The Challenge of the Future*, edited by Andrea Pacini. Oxford: Clarendon, 1998.

Malek, Yusuf. *The British Betrayal of the Assyrians.* Chicago: Assyrian National Federation, 1934.

McCarthy, Justin. *Muslims and Minorities: the Population of Ottoman Anatolia.* New York: New York University Press, 1983.

Merguerian, Barbara. "The View from the United States Consulate." In *Armenian Tsopk/Kharpert*, edited by Richard G. Hovannisian. Mazda: Costa Mesa, California, 2002.

Mingana, Alphonse. "Garshūni or Karshūni?" *Journal of the Royal Asiatic Society* 1928: 891-893.

Murre-van den Berg, Heleen. "The Missionaries' Assistants: The Role of Assyrians in the Development of Written Urmia Aramaic." *Journal of the Assyrian Academic Society* 10, no. 2 (November, 1996): 3-17.

——. "The Patriarchs of the Church of the East from the Fifteenth to Eighteenth Centuries." *Hugoye: Journal of Syriac Studies* 2, no. 2 (July, 1999).

Naayem, Joseph. *Shall This Nation Die?* Translated by Viscount Bryce. New York: Chaldean Rescue, 1921.

Naby, Eden. "The Assyrian Diaspora: Cultural survival in the absence of state structure." In *Central Asia and the Caucasus: Transnationalism and diaspora*, edited by Touraj Atabaki and Sanjyot Mehendale. London: Routledge, 2005.

——. "The Assyrians of Iran: Reunification of a 'Millat,' 1906-1914." *International Journal of Middle Eastern Studies* 8, no. 2 (April, 1977): 237-249.

Nalbandian, Louise. *The Armenian Revolutionary Movement: the Development of Armenian Political Parties through the Nineteenth Century*. Berkeley: University of California Press, 1963.

Nazaryan, Alis. *Արիւնոտ Ժպիտ* [Bloody Smile]. Beirut: Mshak, 1962.

*Osmanlı Belgeleri'nde Diyarbakır Tarihi*. Translated by Ahmet Hezarfen and edited by Cemal Şener. Istanbul: Etik Yayınları, 2003.

Özcoşar, İbrahim. *Bir Yüzyıl Bir Sancak Bir Cemaat: 19. Yüzyılda Mardin Süryanileri*. Ankara: Beyan, 2008.

——. "Osmanlı Devleti'nde Millet Sistemi ve Süryani Kadimler." In *Süryaniler ve Süryanilik*, vol. 2, edited by Canan Seyfeli, Eyyüp Tanrıverdi and Ahmet Taşğın. Ankara: Orient Yayınları, 2005.

——. "Papalığın Müdahalesi ve Süryani Kiliselerinde Bölünme: Keldanî ve Süryani Katolik Patriklikleri." In *Süryaniler ve Süryanilik*, vol. 1, edited by Canan Seyfeli, Eyyüp Tanrıverdi and Ahmet Taşğın. Ankara: Orient Yayınları, 2005.

————. "Süryani Kiliselerinde Eğitim." In *Süryaniler ve Süry-anilik*, vol. 2, edited by Canan Seyfeli, Eyyüp Tanrıverdi and Ahmet Taşğın. Ankara: Orient Yayınları, 2005.

Pacini, Andrea, ed. *Christian Communities in the Arab Middle East: The Challenge of the Future*. Oxford: Clarendon, 1998.

Palak, Naûm Fâik. *Süryânî Millete Mahsûs İntibâh Neşîdeleri yâhûd Millî ve Vatanî Terennümler*. Paterson: Bethnahrin Press, 1917.

Parry, Oswald. *Six Months in a Syrian Monastery*. London: Horace Cox, 1895.

Perley, David Barsoum. "The Jacobites." In Yusuf Malek, *The British Betrayal of the Assyrians*. Chicago: Assyrian National Federation, 1934.

————. "Notes on the Article." *Nineveh* 5, no. 5 (1983).

Redhouse, James W. *A Turkish and English Lexicon*, 2nd edition. Constantinople: The American Mission, 1890.

Segal, Judah Benzion. *Edessa: The Blessed City*. Oxford: Clarendon Press, 1970.

Seyfeli, Canan. "Osmanlı Devlet Salnamelerinde Süryaniler (1847-1918)." In *Süryaniler ve Süryanilik*, vol. 1, edited by Canan Seyfeli, Eyyüp Tanrıverdi and Ahmet Taşğın. Ankara: Orient Yayınları, 2005.

————. "Osmanlı Devleti'nde Gayrimüslimlerin İdari Yapısı: Süryani Kadim Kilisesi Örneği." In *Süryaniler ve Süryanilik*, vol. 1, edited by Canan Seyfeli, Eyyüp Tanrıverdi and Ahmet Taşğın. Ankara: Orient Yayınları, 2005.

Şimşek, Mehmet. *Süryaniler ve Diyarbakır*, 2nd edition. Istanbul: Chiviyazıları, 2003.

————. "Şark Yıldızı Gazetesi." In *Süryaniler ve Süryanilik*, vol. 4, edited by Canan Seyfeli, Eyyüp Tanrıverdi and Ahmet Taşğın. Ankara: Orient Yayınları, 2005.

Sonyel, Salahi. *The Assyrians of Turkey: Victims of Major Power Policy*. Ankara: Turkish Historical Society Printing House, 2001.

Stepanyan, Hasmik A. *Ermeni harfli Türkçe kitaplar ve süreli yayınlar bibliyografyası (1727 – 1968)*. Istanbul: Turkuaz Yayınları, 2005.

Stone, Frank Andrews. "The Heritage of Euphrates (Armenia) College." In *Armenian Tsopk/Kharpert*, edited by Richard G. Hovannisian. Mazda: Costa Mesa, California, 2002.

Strauss, Johann. "Diglossie dans le domaine ottoman: évolution et péripéties d'une situation linguistique." *Revue des mondes musulmans et de la Méditerranée* no. 75-76 (1996): 221-255.

Sunguroğlu, İshak. *Harput Yollarında*. (İstanbul: Yeni Matbaa, 1958).

"Süryanice Ölüm Döşeğinde Yatan Bir Hastaya Benziyor." *Heto* 6, no. 10-11 (Ocak, 2004).

Taşğın, Ahmet. "Sezginin ve Bilgeliğin Sembolü: Öz Hikmet Dergisi." In *Süryaniler ve Süryanilik*, vol. 4, edited by Canan Seyfeli, Eyyüp Tanrıverdi and Ahmet Taşğın. Ankara: Orient Yayınları, 2005.

—————. "Süryani Kadim Ortodoks Kilisesinde Yenileşme Çabaları: Deyru'l-Zafaran Manastırında Patriklik Matbaası." In *Süryaniler ve Süryanilik*, vol. 4, edited by Canan Seyfeli, Eyyüp Tanrıverdi and Ahmet Taşğın. Ankara: Orient Yayınları, 2005.

—————. "Süryani Puşiciler." In *Süryaniler ve Süryanilik*, vol. 4, edited by Canan Seyfeli, Eyyüp Tanrıverdi and Ahmet Taşğın. Ankara: Orient Yayınları, 2005.

—————. "Süryanilerin Basın-Yayın Faaliyetlerine İlişkin Resmi Yazışmalar." In *Süryaniler ve Süryanilik*, vol. 4, edited by Canan Seyfeli, Eyyüp Tanrıverdi and Ahmet Taşğın. Ankara: Orient Yayınları, 2005.

Tepeyran, Ebubekir Hâzim. *Hatıralar*. İstanbul: Pera, 1998.

Trigona-Harany, Benjamin. "A Bibliography of *Süryânî* Periodicals in Ottoman Turkish." *Hugoye: Journal of Syriac Studies* 12, no. 2 (Summer, 2009).

Troupeau, Gérard. "Karshūnī." *Encyclopaedia of Islam*, new edition. Leiden, Brill, 1960.

Tunaya, Tarık Zafer. *Türkiye'de Siyasal Partiler*, vol. 1. İstanbul: İletişim Yayınları, 1998.

Tütengil, Cavit Orhan. *Diyarbakır Basın Tarihi Üzerine Notlar*. İstanbul: İstanbul Matbaası, 1954.

Üngör, Uğur Ü. *'A Reign of Terror': CUP Rule in Diyarbekir Province, 1913-1923*. Master's thesis, University of Amsterdam, 2005.

*Ünlü Asurlardan (Kildanilerden, Süryanilerden) Seçmeler II*. Edited by Kuroš Hërmëz Nazlu. Södertälje, Sweden: Nsibin Yayınevi, 1996.

Veremis, Thanos. "The Hellenic Kingdom and the Ottoman Greeks: The Experiment of the 'Society of Constantinople'." In *Ottoman Greeks in the Age of Nationalism*, edited by Dimitri Gondicas and Charles Issawi. Princeton: Darwin Press, 1999.

Wigram, William A. *An Introduction to the History of the Assyrian Church or the Church of the Sassanid Persian Empire, 100-640 A.D.* London: SPCK, 1910.

Yıldız, Efrem. "The Aramaic Language and its Classification." *Journal of the Assyrian Academic Society* 14, no. 1 (April, 2000): 23-44.

Yonan, Gabriele. *Journalismus bei den Assyrern: Ein Überblick von seinem Anfängen bis zur Gegenwart.* Berlin: Zentralverband der Assyrischen Vereinigungen, 1985 ["Asurlar'da Gazetecilik: Başlangıcından günümüze kadar bir bakış." Translated and serialised by Erol Sever. *Hujâdâ* 119, 120, 129, 130, 132, 133, 134-135, 136, 137, 138, 140, 143, 148, 149, 150, 151, 153, 154, 156, 157-158, 159 (April, 1988 – September, 1991)].

Zürcher, Jan Erik. *Turkey: A Modern History*, new edition. London: I. B. Taurus, 2004.

# INDEX

.